MOLLIE'S WAR

MOLLIE'S WAR

The Letters of a World War II WAC in Europe

Mollie Weinstein Schaffer
and Cyndee Schaffer

Contributing Editor, Jennifer G. Mathers

Introduction by Leisa D. Meyer

McFarland & Company, Inc., Publishers
Jefferson, North Carolina, and London

This work contains some letters from people with whom the family is no longer in touch. While we have made every reasonable effort to contact them or their descendants for permission, we could not find them.

LIBRARY OF CONGRESS CATALOGUING-IN-PUBLICATION DATA

Schaffer, Mollie Weinstein, 1916–
    Mollie's war : the letters of a World War II WAC in Europe / Mollie Weinstein Schaffer and Cyndee Schaffer ; contributing editor Jennifer G. Mathers ; introduction by Leisa D. Meyer.
        p.   cm.
    Includes bibliographical references and index.

ISBN 978-0-7864-4791-6
softcover : 50# alkaline paper ∞

    1. Schaffer, Mollie Weinstein, 1916– — Correspondence.
    2. United States. Army. Women's Army Corps — Biography.
    3. United States. Army — Women — Correspondence.
    4. Women soldiers — United States — Correspondence.
    5. World War, 1939–1945 — Personal narratives, American.
    6. World War, 1939–1945 — Participation, Female.
    7. World War, 1939–1945 — United States.
    I. Schaffer, Cyndee, 1949–   II. Mathers, Jennifer G., 1964–
III. Title.
    D769.39.S36   2010
    940.54'1273092 — dc22   2010022684

British Library cataloguing data are available

On the cover: Mollie Weinstein in front of the Eiffel Tower, November 1944 (author's collection).

Manufactured in the United States of America

McFarland & Company, Inc., Publishers
    Box 611, Jefferson, North Carolina 28640
    www.mcfarlandpub.com

Contents

To the memory of Rebecca Winston,
sister and aunt who saved Mollie's letters.
Without her, this book could not have been written.

Acknowledgments (Cyndee Schaffer)

The help and encouragement of many people have made this book possible. First and foremost, I want to thank my mother for her service to our country during the Second World War and for being so diligent in documenting it through her letters. I would also like to thank my late aunt, Rebecca Winston, for saving this collection of 350 letters, photos and newspaper articles. This is a project that took many years to complete. My late brother-in-law, Judd Silverman, helped me organize the letters in chronological order in 1999 but then I did not look at them again until 2007. Because of the prodding of two former colleagues, Lori Mueller and Fred Follansbee, I had the confidence to devote my time over the last two years to documenting and writing my mother's legacy to history. I would like thank Teri Embrey and Amanda Catanio of the Pritzker Military Library in Chicago for allowing me to use the facility and for their help in the research conducted for the book. I am especially grateful to my editor, Jennifer G. Mathers (Aberystwyth University), who edits *Minerva Journal of Women and War*. She has been amazing in her assistance in condensing these letters into a cohesive book, which would not have been possible without her hard work. The help and support that I received from Coleman Bricker, who served with my mother in France, and Catherine Levinson, the daughter of Mary Grace Loddo Kirby who served with my mother in Europe, was greatly appreciated.

Reviewing this book became a family project. My uncle, Jack Weinstein, reviewed the entire collection of letters. My son, Jordan Schwartz, reviewed the book as this project began and my sister, Roberta Schaffer, helped me in the final review as well as in translating all of the French passages. My brother, Joel Schaffer, and my daughter, Ariel Schwartz, helped in the overall review. Even my dog, Marshmallow, sat by my side and supported me through the long days of organizing, writing, rewriting and editing as well as selecting the images for the book. Most of all, I want to thank my husband, Douglas Schwartz, for his everlasting encouragement and support.

Abbreviations

AEF . . . . Allied Expeditionary Force

APO . . . . Army Post Office

AWOL. . . . . . absent without leave

CBI . . . . China-Burma-India

CO . . . . Commanding Officer

CQ . . . . Charge of Quarters

CZ. . . . . Communications Zone

DP . . . . Displaced Person

ETO . . . . European Theater of Operations

ETOUSA. . . . Headquarters European Theater of Operations U.S. Army

FFI. . . . . French Forces of the Interior

GI . . . . Government Issue (slang for the U.S. military or U.S. military personnel)

KP . . . . Kitchen Police

MCWR . . . . . Marine Corps Women's Reserve

MOT. . . . . . . Member of Our Tribe (Jewish)

MP. . . . . Military Police

OCS . . . . Officer Candidate School

OD . . . . olive drab

PE . . . . Pacific Electric (train)

PFC. . . . . Private First Class

PW . . . . Prisoner of War

PX . . . . Post Exchange (shop on the base for military personnel)

QM . . . . Quartermaster

SPAR . . . . Coast Guard Women's Reserve (Semper Paratus —
Always Ready)

SWPA . . . . . . Southwest Pacific Area

TD. . . . . Temporary Duty

UK. . . . . United Kingdom

USFET . . . . . United States Forces European Theater

USO . . . . United Service Organizations

VE . . . . Victory in Europe

WAAC. . . . . . Women's Army Auxiliary Corps

WAC . . . . Women's Army Corps, member of the WAC

WASP . . . . . . Women's Airforce Service Pilots

WAVES . . . . Women Accepted for Voluntary Emergency Service

Preface (Mollie Weinstein Schaffer)

I was enjoying the last days of summer at a cottage by Commerce Lake outside of Detroit, Michigan, with my sister and some friends. The rooms were filled with conversations and in the background a radio was tuned to a music station. Suddenly the music stopped. A voice came on the air: "Germany has invaded Poland." It was Friday, September 1, 1939.

The war in Europe seemed so distant from our shores until the Japanese attack on Pearl Harbor on December 7, 1941. Each day as I went to work as a medical transcriber at the Veterans Administration Hospital in Dearborn, Michigan, I would look at my coworkers with tears in my eyes, wondering how many of the men would enlist in the service and which of them would return and which would not. At that time I had no idea that in less than two years I, too, would join up.

As a shy young woman I did not seem a likely candidate for life in the Army. I decided to enlist after my first cousin, Jack Winokur, was killed early in the war in a flying accident in the South Pacific and two of my closest girl-friends, Ella Marcus and Helen Freidberg, joined the Women's Army Corps. I remember thinking that soon there would not be anyone my age left at home so I might as well join too! This turned out to be easier said than done, however. At first I was rejected for being underweight: at 5'4" I weighed less than 100 pounds.[1] I went home and fattened myself up with milk, honey and bananas.

This book tells the story of the everyday life of an enlisted woman between October 1943, when I was finally accepted into the WAC, and November 1945, when I was honorably discharged. This book is possible only because my sister Rebecca (Beck) saved most of my letters and the letters that had been sent to me by various friends (which I had mailed to her for safe-keeping). Somewhere in this host of letters, my sister reminded me that I once dreamed of writing a book. More than 60 years later, my sister is gone but some 350 letters remain. I am grateful to my daughter, Cyndee, for all her work in choosing and editing my letters which form the basis of this book. I am also grateful to my other daughter, Roberta, son Joel, granddaughter Ariel and grandson Jordan for their assistance in this project.

Most of the time during the war I could not disclose to my family exactly where I was stationed. Some of my experiences were harrowing: I survived the doodlebug bombs in England and I lived in tents in the mud in France after D-Day. Other times were very pleasant, such as attending the opera in Paris, seeing famous people and, most of all, meeting wonderful, lifelong friends, such as Mary Grace (Loddo) Kirby and Coleman Bricker.

When the Army sent me to England in April 1944 to be with ETOUSA (Headquarters European Theater of Operations U.S. Army) as a medical secretary in the Office of the Chief Surgeon, I was not aware that the Allies were assembling the largest military operation in history to launch against occupied France on the beaches of Normandy on June 6, 1944. The WACs[2] were there to release soldiers from office work so that they would be available for combat duty. My responsibilities included working in Medical Intelligence to determine the availability of hospital beds for the next military operation[3] and acting as a stenographer for a senior medical officer. Much of my work related to soldiers who had been injured and sent to military hospitals in the area, and involved drafting reports as well as taking dictation. Wartime military censorship prevented any detailed discussion of my job in my letters to family and friends.

I was among the first groups of WACs to land in Normandy after D-Day in the summer of 1944. I was also among the first groups of WACs to go into Germany after the end of the war. I was present for the re-dedication of the only standing synagogue in Frankfurt on Rosh Hashanah 1945. I never returned to Europe to see how England, France and Germany recovered from the war. All in all, being a WAC during World War II shaped the rest of my life. My experiences in the European Theater were enough to last a lifetime.

Introduction (Leisa D. Meyer)

In the current U.S. war in Iraq and the related conflict in Afghanistan, military public relations officers and media spokespeople talk about "our men and women" in the armed forces in their reports on military efforts. There is also frequent footage of male and female military personnel deploying from various ports and a general presumption that in America's military efforts women will be assigned to combat arenas as participants — whether in support roles or as carrier, fighter, or bomber pilots. While this seems unremarkable now, women's presence in the American military, and especially their service in combat theaters, has been the subject of vigorous debate since World War II.

I begin with this point because the roots of this shift in perception and perspective lie in the history of the servicewomen and female officers who served and were deployed overseas during World War II. During this conflict, over 300,000 women served in the nation's armed forces; 150,000 of these were members of the Women's Army Corps (WAC) and over 20,000 were, like Mollie Weinstein, deployed overseas to combat theaters.

In 1942, women's entrance into the Army was accepted by male Army leaders under the banner of expedience. Supporting the formation of a "women's corps" seemed a reasonable solution to the expected increase in the numbers of "women's jobs" involving tasks such as clerking, typing, stenography and communications, and enabled the Army to maintain control over this labor force and its employment.[1] Moreover, sponsoring the creation of such a corps allowed the Army, not civilian legislators, to dictate the terms of female military participation.

Women's entrance into the Army was also advocated by some who believed that women's rights and duties as citizens should not be limited. Other supporters of the WAC characterized the "female soldier" as a symbol of American women's patriotism, self-sacrifice and courage, a modern Molly Pitcher who, in response to a national emergency, left her home and family temporarily to lend a hand. Some, like Congresswoman Edith Nourse Rogers, saw the corps as a long-awaited symbol of recognition for all the women who had worked with the military in previous American war efforts. In fact, the initial bill to create a Women's Army Auxiliary Corps (WAAC) was authored by Rogers. In clarifying the importance of her proposed legislation to congressional colleagues, Rogers invoked her experience from the previous world war, explaining that because most women who served with the military during World War I were civilians, they were not eligible for the same benefits as the men in uniform whom they worked alongside. She held that women's service with the military must be recognized and that as "patriots" they must be entitled to similar rewards from the state for the "faithful" discharge of their duties.[2]

One of the biggest questions the new women's corps faced was whether women could perform the duties, maintain the discipline and endure the hardships and challenges of a military life. Thousands of young women responded to this question with a resounding yes! Many, like Mollie Weinstein, did their basic training at Daytona Beach, Florida, and endured the strict regimen entailed in such training — learning military protocol (how to march in step, how to salute, the forms of address for various officers and enlisted categories), how to keep their rack (bed), footlocker and uniforms spotless, their shoes and insignia shined and how to make all of these "new" tasks into habits so ingrained that they would require no thought in the coming months and years of service. These new recruits also discovered the "joys" of Kitchen Police duty (KP). Required of all enlisted personnel below the rank of corporal, KP consisted of domestic-service type duties, and predominantly involved cleaning up the "mess" or the kitchen area after each meal. KP was a duty assigned to both men and women and usually determined by roster rotation; enlisted men and women took turns performing these tasks when their names came up on the personnel roster. KP duty was mentioned frequently by Mollie Weinstein in her letters and would remain a common experience for enlisted female and male personnel. Some male officers, however, believed that women's entrance into the Army should mark an end to men's sentence in the Army kitchen. While this early push by some male officers to assign only WACs to KP duties was swiftly countered by both WAC and ranking male Army officials, the effort exemplified the tendency of some male Army officers throughout the war to determine WAC assignments not on the basis of their skills and training or specific job categories, but rather on presumptions about the types of jobs that they believed were most "fitting" for women.[3]

The opposition of "soldier" and "woman," battlefront and homefront, and the duties associated with each that underlay the attempt to assign WACs to permanent KP duty would become a central theme in the general discussion about the deployment of WACs overseas as well as in the more specific disputes about how women would be utilized once in combat theaters. It is important to remember, however, that despite public and congressional debates on the question of whether WACs should be sent overseas it had always been the intent of Army leaders to employ service women and female officers in support roles in combat theaters. It was the intention of Eisenhower, for instance, to take WAACs with him in his North African campaign. Unfortunately, the WAACs' initial auxiliary status created difficulties with such a move. As auxiliaries, not regular army, they would not be covered by military insurance policies if they were killed, and would have no official status as military prisoners if captured. Concerns with this issue of the corps' initial auxiliary status meant that only two units were sent overseas to join Eisenhower in North Africa, with the first WAAC unit arriving in Algiers in January 1943. Once the corps traded its auxiliary status for full military status in mid–1943 subsequent units were deployed in this theater throughout 1943 and into 1944 with the total number reaching 2000 in 1944.[4]

Although the WAC experience in the North African (later the North Africa and Mediterranean) Theater of Operations was a successful deployment, concerns about its appropriateness would continue in Congress throughout the war. There were several attempts to limit or prohibit Army women's overseas service because of the many dangers women might face in combat theaters. When such attempts failed, opponents to women's overseas service offered other bills aimed at withholding benefits to military women, such as higher pay in combat theaters, on the grounds that they were not combatants. These efforts were also defeated, in part because their passage might have called into question the status of male soldiers stationed in combat theaters but not operating as combatants.[5]

After the WAC gained regular military status, the War Department prioritized requests for WACs from overseas theaters over those from posts in the continental United States. One War Department official argued that such a prioritization was imperative because of the greater difficulties of operations overseas than in the continental U.S. and the subsequent need for the "best workers" for the jobs. Commanders in the European Theater of Operations (ETO) generally held that, as women, WACs had "superior skills" to men in jobs as typists, switchboard operators, clerks and stenographers for which there was a pressing need throughout the war.[6] The flipside to this affirmation of women's military service was that on several occasions male officers refused to employ women with more unconventional or, as several put it, "unfeminine" skills in the duties for which they had been trained. Unlike their civilian counterparts who were mobilized by the thousands into non-traditional jobs in war industries, WACs, though arguably entering the most "non-traditional" environment for women — military service — were employed predominantly in jobs defined as conventionally "feminine." This lack of flexibility in assigning WACs was remarked upon in the official Army summary of the employment of servicewomen in the ETO written after the war, which attributed the situation to "commanders considering the WACs more as women than as soldiers," and assigning them to jobs for which it would be possible for them to maintain a "semblance of femininity."[7]

Despite examples of the practice of highlighting distinctions between WACs and servicemen, Army leaders also concomitantly instituted policies that seemed to diminish such distinctions. In May 1943, for instance, the War Department policy on the use of female civilians overseas prohibited their employment in active combat areas but exempted members of the WAC, Army Nurse Corps and other female military organizations. Thus, a distinction was drawn between civilian women employees and female soldiers that allowed servicewomen and Army nurses to be utilized in active combat areas from which civilian women employees were restricted. This Army policy underlined the differential status of the two groups, female civilians viewed as women and protected accordingly, and WACs, employed as soldiers with many of the accompanying risks. Moreover, shortly after D-Day the question of whether or not WACs should accompany units forward into Normandy was a point of dispute among male commanders. Some male Army officers opposed such a move, arguing that WACs would be in danger of being killed or captured and that "concern over the safety and security of American women would impair the efficiency of the fighting men." Proponents of such a deployment responded that employing military women in Normandy was completely reasonable — that WACs were soldiers and should be utilized accordingly — and especially raised objections to the loss of productivity they feared would result in their units if WACs were prohibited from moving to forward areas.[8]

A similar scenario unfolded in the Southwest Pacific Area (SWPA). WACs were not employed in this theater until May 1944 as most Army offices and commands relied on Australian civilians for necessary clerical and office support. WACs were brought in because the Australian government felt it was too dangerous to send its civilian women outside of Australia and refused to allow them to be deployed along with U.S. troops. Most of the WACs who were stationed in this region moved from Australia to New Guinea and then on to the Philippines, often right behind male troops. In both cases it was deemed inefficient to indulge in employment policies that considered women's sex more important than their status as soldiers.[9]

The tensions between these two concepts, woman and soldier, were both embraced and challenged by female and male military personnel during World

War II. As Mollie Weinstein noted in one of her letters home — in preparing for a date while living in the mud and tents that characterized her Normandy experience, she put on "a few dashes of Cologne" to "make me feel I wasn't a soldier" (Chapter 6). At the same time, the WAC recruiting slogan of "release a man for combat," while offered by some young women as their reason for enlisting, was also one of the factors in some enlisted men's hostility toward WACs. For some young men, the presence of a woman in uniform signaled that an enlisted man had been released from his clerical job for deployment to a combat front and the increased dangers that inhered in such a move.

Once overseas, WACs like Mollie Weinstein had to adapt to new surroundings, cultures and the particular challenges of being American women in combat theaters where the ratio of male to female Americans was quite skewed. This resulted in both problems and opportunities for enlisted women and WAC officers. The greater opportunities for social interactions with military men led some WACs overseas to complain that they suffered from "burnout" in their attempts to keep up with the barrage of requests for dates from male soldiers. And WACs found themselves occasionally criticized for not being "more available" to enlisted men. In a letter to her sister Mollie Weinstein described meeting a young man who was a friend of a family she knew from Detroit. He did not like WACs because on one occasion he and his buddies had gone to a WAC facility looking for dates and had been rebuffed. Mollie notes in her letter that this was likely because these women had been overseas for awhile and already established social networks and connections in the area and had plans for the evening (Chapter 14). On the other hand, the greater numbers of men also created situations in which servicewomen could and did dictate the terms of the heterosocial engagements they decided to accept. Both in the United States and overseas some servicewomen made their acceptance of male offers conditional on men's ability to provide supplies for their barracks and food and clothing that were otherwise unavailable. "Every GI outfit vied with its neighbor in thinking up attractions to lure the WACs to parties," recalled one WAC. "Food was the most successful. But many a luxury was obtained by 'moonlight requisition' — a broom for our tent ... an air mattress, or GI comforter."[10] As with Mollie's friend Loddo, whose Navy boyfriend brought eggs and apples each time he visited (Chapter 9), such exchanges were based on the greater availability of such materials to male military personnel.

During World War II over 20,000 WACs served overseas, with the ETO and SWPA in that order housing the largest contingents of servicewomen and officers.[11] Their employment in combat areas was in part the result of the Army's integration of women into essential units in overseas theaters once they were an official part of the Army. During their deployment in these combat areas WACs sought shelter during the buzz bomb (V-1, V-2 rocket) attacks in Britain and from air raids in France.[12] In the Southwest Pacific, WACs encountered fairly harsh conditions in the forward areas in which they served. Difficulties were largely due to the necessity of carving space for quarters and offices out of the jungle. It rained continually and servicewomen found themselves mired knee-deep in mud and subject to constant air raids as well as occasional attacks from Japanese snipers. WACs also served with the 5th Army in Italy as part of an experimental unit to determine if it was possible to employ women with Army Ground Forces tactical units. They followed the 5th Army for the entire Italian campaign and lived in tents, wore enlisted men's wool shirts, trousers and combat boots. They averaged two weeks in each location and were generally twelve to thirty-five miles behind the front lines.[13]

The American women, like Mollie Weinstein, who served in combat theaters during World War II left a legacy for the servicewomen and female officers who make up 17 percent of the American military today. In her various works, Miriam Cooke, a scholar of gender and war, has argued the importance of women having a place in telling the war stories of a nation and a people. These are the stories that tend to become lost in the broader narrative of combat and male heroism that is so often the focus for our memories.[14] The experiences of military men during World War II of course must have a prominent place in our recollections. However, the military service of American women — as this book demonstrates — must also be a central part of this narrative. Women like Mollie Weinstein accepted the challenges of a world war and many emerged from this experience more certain of their own capabilities. As Mollie put it, she learned to adapt "easily" to changes, something she never would have realized about herself had she not been in service (Chapter 13).

When I was researching my book on the WAC and interviewing World War II and other era WAC veterans, many of them told me that the disbanding of the WAC as a separate entity in 1978 and the integration of women into regular army units was not good for women in the military. At the time I believed that they were mistaken and vigorously argued that such integration was necessary if women were ever going to gain greater parity in the military. In my hubris what I did not hear them saying and only later understood was that this integration would mean that future Army women would no longer learn of women's past experiences in the military. Prior to this integration, a central element of the WAC training regimen included presentations on the creation and role of the WAC during previous American wars. What they were trying to tell me was that this information and knowledge and history, including the role of WACs during World War II, histories like Mollie Weinstein's, would now be lost to young female soldiers. We must know, retell and remember the story of military women during World War II — a story that shows us the beginnings of military policies that understood WACs as female soldiers — "martial" women able to meet challenges and absolutely essential parts of the American military's operations overseas during the Second World War.

LEISA D. MEYER is an associate professor of history at William and Mary College and author of *Creating G.I. Jane: Sexuality and Power in the Women's Army Corps During World War II* (Columbia University Press, 1996).

1. Basic Training:
Daytona Beach, Florida
October–December 1943

Mollie Weinstein became an eyewitness to history in wartime Europe when she joined the Women's Army Corps on October 19, 1943, and was sent to Europe in April 1944. In the years before the Second World War, Mollie, like many Americans, seldom thought about foreign affairs or imagined that events that took place thousands of miles away would have a direct impact on her life. The bombing of Pearl Harbor on the morning of Sunday, December 7, 1941, changed that attitude. It also marked the beginning of a change in American attitudes towards the presence of women in the U.S. military. As Mollie discovered, the sight of a woman in uniform attracted attention and sometimes disapproval, but the contribution that women made to the work of the armed forces was essential to the American war effort. During the course of the war women were incorporated into the Army (Women's Army Corps, or WAC), Navy (Women Accepted for Voluntary Emergency Service, or WAVES), Marines (Marine Corps Women's Reserve, or MCWR) and Coast Guard (known as SPAR, derived from the Coast Guard motto "Semper Paratus — Always Ready").[1] Women also flew military planes on a variety of missions in the United States as part of the Women's Airforce Service Pilots (WASP) although they were regarded as civilians.

Mollie's decision to enlist in the WAC was the result of a combination of patriotic feelings and personal circumstances. She was deeply affected by the death of her first cousin, Jack Winokur, in a flying accident in the South Pacific while he was serving in the military and by the enlistment of two of her close friends, Ella Marcus and Helen Freidberg, into the WAC. Both of these events made her determined to do her part to help her country win the war and influenced her decision to respond to the U.S. War Department's campaigns to attract women to Army service.[2] It was nevertheless a very big decision for her to leave her close-knit family (her parents, Jewish immigrants from Russia, older sister Beck and younger brother Jackie), a worthwhile job and the familiar surroundings of her home in Detroit, Michigan, for the unknown. After an initial rejection by the Army for being underweight, Mollie was eventually accepted and received her orders to travel to the WAC training center at Daytona Beach, Florida, for basic training.

Mollie traveled south by train with other recruits from the Detroit area and immediately noticed that the WACs were treated much better than the civilians on the train. For example, the WACs always received their meals before the civilians were served. A constant theme in her letters to her family from the very beginning of her military service was the reassurance that she was well and that the food was good, although in fact the Army food was the source of some problems for her. Mollie grew up in a kosher Jewish household which observed the strict dietary rules dictated by the family's religious beliefs, but it was extremely difficult for those men and women who were serving in the U.S. armed forces during the Second World War to maintain a kosher diet. Mollie soon discovered that some foods which she had never previously eaten, such as those made from pork, became a staple once she joined the Army.[3]

From the very beginning of her Army enlistment, Mollie shared as many details of her new life with her family as she could so that they could understand the many adjustments she was making.

* * *

October 20, 1943

Dear Family,

We are traveling on a train in Pullman compartment sleepers—3 in a room —2 in lower, one in upper. Not too fancy but comfortable. Had my first G.I. meal—grapefruit juice, oatmeal, bacon (3 strips) and 2 eggs and toast, butter and milk—not bad. After we eat, the civilians can eat. Feel *ok*. I don't know when I'm dropping this off. I believe Tenn.

Love, Mollie

Sang some snapping W.A.C. songs already. Getting in the groove.

Mollie's family received confirmation by post card of Mollie's arrival in Daytona Beach, Florida.

Once she began basic training, Mollie was able to explain to her family the Army's rules and the new routines that she was learning. She found marching with the other WACs to be particularly thrilling.

```
                          HEADQUARTERS
                  RECEPTION AND STAGING BATTALION
            SECOND WOMEN'S ARMY CORPS TRAINING CENTER

                                          Daytona Beach, Florida
                                          22   October  194 3

   Mollie Weinstein                                   arrived safely at
Daytona Beach and is now assigned to the Reception and Staging Battalion.
She will be here approximately three days, during which time she will go
through what the Army calls processing. This includes issue of clothing,
testing, interviewing, and then a final classification. After this, she
will be assigned to a Company for basic training which will last for a
period of four or more weeks. As soon as she gets this assignment, she
will send you her permanent address. UNTIL THAT TIME, PLEASE REFRAIN
FROM SENDING MAIL TO HER.

                                          MARY K. MOYNAHAN,
                                          Capt., WAC,
                                          Commanding.
```

Postcard sent to Mollie's family announcing her arrival at the WAC training camp in Daytona Beach, October 22, 1943.

October 24, 1943

Dear Family,

We make our beds — army style, arrange our belongings in army order, sweep and mop our tent every day ... was placed on KP [Kitchen Police][4] duty next morning at 5:30 A.M. until noon. Wasn't too bad — just plenty of work. I was awakened at 5 A.M. by the guard and began duty on KP at 5:30 — hauled in milk crates — placed bottles on tables, scrubbed pans, eyed potatoes, that is took out the bad spots and cut up potatoes — about 3 bushels — with help of someone else. Thank goodness the army does have mechanical peelers. We sleep in barracks with a number of girls in each and of course have to keep it spotless and in order at all times. We're always on our toes and it does keep one alert. I'm on latrine duty tomorrow.... Honestly, I'm not homesick — but feel swell. I haven't time to think about anything except keeping up with the guy next to me.... Drilling, classes, movies in drilling, etc.; we have to take care of our barracks which includes lining up our clothes in precise order and leaving our lockers in perfect order at all times. We have to take care of our laundry, shoes, nails, hair, etc. — so you see we've been kept busy — and I understand this is the beginning. I enjoy it and have been eating just everything. I must eat about double. But probably work it off ... you cannot realize how much we are supposed to accomplish during our basic training ... we haven't time to worry about little things and consequently I feel swell.

Nov 1, 1943

Dear Beck,

It's quite a thrill to watch the WACS from Michigan marching in uniform. If you think we marched on that Tuesday in Detroit, you should see us now. We do right face, left face, present arms, order arms, right column, etc. Those are orders in marching that I cannot go into detail at this time to explain.... I'll admit it's a lot of hard work during basic but I do feel good.

Nov 3, 1943

Dear Jackie,

...They keep us too busy down here, we don't have time to do anything for ourselves.... (I don't know when I'll get a chance to finish this as we must "fall out.")

Here it is Nov. 5th 3:00 A.M. and I'm on "Fire Guard." That means for 2 hours I must sit in our Orderly Room and on the half hour go thru the various barracks, check to see everything is ok and then initial my name on a chart; also check up on the boiler rooms. I just went on my first round at 2:30 A.M. I have a flash light with me and as I go out of each barracks, I almost knock my shin against someone's footlocker as I try not to shine the light in the girls' eyes.

...Just went off duty 4 A.M.—everything in good condition.

November 5, 1943

Dear Beck,

I just seem to lose track of time out here.... But don't send me anything unless I ask for it, as when inspection comes, we have to hide all civilian property (clothes, etc.).

...I enjoy the army life out here but, I will say this, Beck, during our basic 6 weeks, it is difficult. We have to do everything "on the double." That means just as fast as possible because if you're not ready, when the command to "fall out" sounds, then you have to report your name. If you do that often, you get special fatigue duty—which isn't nice.

So far, I have gotten 2 gigs, one for having one of my shoe laces not laced up to the top under my bed. (If you can figure that out, you're a better man than I gunga din!)

And, another gig—when my shoes were not aligned properly under my bed. It seems someone moved my bed when I wasn't looking.... However, that isn't too bad—2 gigs in a week....

On November 11, 1943, the war in Europe had been raging for four years and the United States had been at war for almost two years. In this next letter, Mollie describes marching in a parade to mark the twenty-fifth anniversary of Armistice Day, the date which marked the end of the First World War.

Nov. 12, 1943

Dear Beck,

...Do tell Pa and Ma I'm just fine and although it's plenty hard. I enjoy it down here. I'm still doing justice to all the meals.

...Yesterday was Armistice Day and we marched in the parade in the city of Daytona Beach. It was beautiful and we all felt so proud — especially as we passed the reviewing stand with "eyes right." We marched to music down the Main Street with 9 abreast and the cool breezes of the Bay brushed our faces....

All of a sudden I was placed on Special detail with 2 other girls. We grabbed some brooms and some dusters and ran down to the Chapel which was our destination. You can imagine what our special detail was — cleaning up the Chapel — which is also used as a movie house. It wasn't too bad — just took about an hour. Then when we came back to the barracks, I was faced with a surprise. Our beds had been changed around. I now slept where my feet had been and under our G.I. clothes hanging from the closet. I put up a squawk and had my bed slightly re-aligned. Then, too, our footlockers were reassembled as to placing of our clothing. So there you have it. Nothing is ever very permanent in the army — as you can see from my little tale.

Nov. 16th

Dear Beck,

...I don't know what will happen to me after basic — so I'll just have to wait and see. I will be here anyway until Dec. 1st....

I must say the drilling is quite intensive & more than I expected. Physical training is another thing. Many of the girls gripe about it. They say "join the WACs & get killed in P. T." But it really isn't too bad. Just that you have to expend lots of energy....

As Mollie was completing her basic training, she did not know the type of job she would be assigned or where she might be sent, but she hoped that her assignment would have some connection to her job in civilian life, when she had been a medical transcriber at the local Veterans Administration hospital. As she and her fellow enlistees approached their graduation from basic training, their lives became less stressful. Antics and pranks abounded in their barracks while they waited to receive their first army assignment and be sent to another location. When those first assignments came through, the new WACs had to be ready to leave immediately — sometimes within the hour.

November 30, 1943

Dear Beck,

We had our exams yesterday & they weren't bad at all. We had a company party last night — just the girls & let me tell you it was really something. When we returned from our party, which was in the Recreation Hall — you should have seen our barracks. Several of the girls' beds had been stripped of all their sleeping materials — there were just springs on the bed!! Mattresses were hanging from the rafters as were blankets, comforters and sheets, etc. My bed was untouched. I thought "well, all is well." Then I got ready for bed and attempted to open my footlocker which contains all our underwear, pajamas, cosmetics (which I haven't used except on Sundays) and little odds and ends. I couldn't open the damn thing!! Someone had rearranged all the lockers and they were all jumbled up. The lights were out, too. We had a h_ _ _ of a time in the barracks when everyone got back. All of our Cadre members (instructors — Sgts and corporals) were besieged and drenched into the showers and some got very nice baths in the wash tubs — clothes and all. Well, we finally got to bed.

Then in the middle of the night our First Sgt just to get even with us gave us a fire drill. We all rushed out of the barracks pell mell — dragged out the fire extinguishers and stood at attention in our pajamas. It was the darnedest sight you could hope to see. There I was in the first squad with my pajamas rolled up to my knees. (The legs were slightly damp just before I got to bed because someone has squirted me in the latrine and I was too tired to look for pajamas in the night.) I gave one look at our Platoon Sgt. facing me and she had hers rolled up the same. It looked like a scene from one of those old comedies.

Mollie was happy that the grueling period of basic training was over and eager to begin her Army life, but until her assignment came through she was grouped in a "Casual Battalion"[5] with others who were awaiting assignments.

December 4, 1943

Dear Beck,

I still don't know anything about where, when or what. I'm still in Casual Battalion. We attend classes & drill, that is, when I'm not moving. We have moved about 7 times (from barracks to barracks) during the past week. Our

Michigan Co. has been split up — some have gone to Nebraska, Texas & Ohio. You get sort of a lump in your throat when you see the gals standing with their barracks bags all packed and ready to move. But such is the Army. You always meet some other girls that are just as nice.

Eventually her first assignment did arrive, and Mollie was very excited to be sent to Wilmington, California, located just outside Los Angeles, although she was not permitted to tell her family where she was going or go into detail about her job.

Dec. 8, 1943

Dear Beck,

...You understand we are not supposed to give our destination before we reach it. As you know, Beck, it is just the place I wanted to go. I don't know anything about the assignment other than I believe it is stenography....

Mollie made the long trip from Florida to California by train and described in her letters the excitement she felt at the changing scenery and at being able to eat oranges from many of the states where the train stopped along the way. When she finally arrived in Wilmington, she knew that her adventure had only just begun.

12-12-1943

Dear Becky,

...Another thing, Beck, the army is so temporary. I somehow have a feeling I won't remain at L.A. very long although I would very much like to.... Although the army life, especially basic training was hard, I have never regretted getting in. It's a great experience & something worth remembering.

2. First Assignment:
Wilmington, California
December 1943–March 1944

The morning after her arrival in Wilmington, California, Mollie had another memorable experience when she was whisked off to Hollywood and was selected to appear as an extra in a recruiting movie about the Women's Army Corps called *It's Your War, Too* on one of the final days of filming.[1]

* * *

December 17th 1943

Dear Beck:

...In as much as my job has not been assigned, I am free for a few days but have to be back each night. However, I've been so terribly busy, I don't know where to begin. We arrived at Wilmington at 12:30 A.M. Thursday morning and had to find our way out there from L.A. At 7 A.M. that same morning we were on our way to the Warner Brothers Studio in Hollywood. You didn't know you had a movie star for a sister, did you? That's Hollywood for you. They were just finishing up a WAC Recruiting picture and wanted a couple more scenes so the director saw me and my Pepsodent smile and picked me out. I'm in two scenes (if they haven't cut it out).

"Cookie," a make-up artist made me up. He works under Perce Westmore....[2] Later on "Cookie" fixed it up so I could have my hair cut by Howard Fleck.[3] And while I was waiting, Perce Westmore came up and sat next to me and asked me questions about the WAC life. While I was getting my hair cut, the rest of the kids got a chance to see Bette Davis work. Darn it, I was sorry to miss that....

We had not been assigned to work, however, our Lt. spoke with me today and said she thought perhaps I could get just what I wanted. But you can never

18

tell in the army. All our service records did not come up with us from Florida, therefore, the delay.

Los Angeles certainly is a big city and there's lots to do. We hope to get in tonight and inasmuch as bed check is 1 A.M., we ought to have a good time tonight. Wilmington is about 25 miles from L.A. and we go there on the P.E. [electric train — Pacific Electric] — the fare is only $0.50 round trip for service people....

From this point onwards, Mollie began to realize that, in spite of the hard work and uncertainties of life in the Army, being a WAC had its benefits. She was invariably stationed in areas where large numbers of servicemen were also located, and these soldiers, sailors and marines were eager for female company during their off-duty hours. As an attractive young woman in uniform who enjoyed socializing, Mollie was never short of dates and dance partners.

Sunday, 19 December 1943

Dear Beck:

...I would have telephoned but the weather has been pretty bad these last two days & inasmuch as it is very noisy in the day room where we make calls, I thought I'd send a wire. Sorry I didn't get around to it before but as usual I have been busy — not working but running around.

Last night I went into Long Beach with 2 other girls.... We had a 2 A.M. pass (until 2 A.M. Sunday). It was raining (California liquid sunshine) but we went anyway. We left our barracks about 7:45 P.M. & when we got there after 8 P.M., we ran for shelter under some apt. bldg. There were 3 sailors — invariably we run into the Navy. They were very nice fellows & immediately wanted to take us somewhere. However, we didn't care to go to any beer joints. So these fellows were so nice that they said seeing they didn't have any "cabbage" for nice spots that we ought to stay in at the Sky Room....[4] I immediately met a very nice Jewish fellow — air cadet. The other 2 girls couldn't seem to make connections as we split up and I spent the evening with Herby and I made an appointment to meet my gal friends at 12:30 midnight to go home. They went on their merry way.

I stayed at the Sky Room & danced. It was quite "swankee." The civilian girls wore very tricky evening gowns with stardust in their hair & ermine wraps draped about their milk-white shoulders. (Very Hollywoodish). However, I felt very good in my G.I. clothes. In fact, I like to see a WAC & soldier in preference to fancy gowns. But I suppose in the future, I'll grow tired of it. Later Herby & I left his friends & we went into a place something like Eastwood Park.[5] We stopped & had hamburgers & cokes. All in all I had a very delightful evening.... By the way, the civilians still stare at us WACS & there weren't many WACS in town last night — as I guess Herb was lucky to pick up a WAC & a Jewish one at that!

Mollie remained pleased with her decision to join the Army and energized by the challenge of life in the military. She was thrilled to be assigned to a job that she wanted and for which she was qualified.

22 December 1943

Dear Beck:

You have to fight for everything you want and then you don't know whether you will get it. You know how determined I am. Well today I went for my interview. They ask you what you want and naturally don't have it. Anyway, I told them I didn't want a job filing paper clips. I am assigned temporarily to Port Surgeon — to report Friday. There is a new Hospital open out here — which is 9 miles from Wilmington. Naturally, I wanted to get in there, but it seems that the civilians have all the top notch jobs but, of course, they will keep me in mind. However, with all its faults I don't mind being a W.A.C. I probably wouldn't give it up if I had a chance — perhaps it's just a challenge to me to see if I can make it — where the other gals have failed and continue to file paper clips.

At this point, Mollie was experiencing the time of her life. She enjoyed her job but was not required to do much work. She was never at a loss for dates and seemed to enjoy meeting so many "prospects." Many of the soldiers she met were Jewish, and it was important to her to develop connections with those who shared her religion and values. This is when Mollie first met Maurice Kaye, whom she dated while in California. He is frequently mentioned in her letters and she corresponded with him throughout the war.

December 25, 1943

Dear Beck,

...The Red Cross gave us each a couple of nice little packages — stuff we can actually use ... and a postal card to write them back "Thank you," which I shall do immediately....

Last night 2 of the gals and myself went into L.A. We went to the Zenda Ball Room.[6] It's a very nice place and we had a wonderful time. We met 3 nice air cadets. I started out with a fellow from Texas but somehow we interchanged partners and later in the evening I found out why. The guy [Maurice Kaye] I ended up with was Jewish and wanted to be with me. He's a very nice fellow and asked me to go out New Year's Eve. However, I want it to be a double date and he's to call me up during the week. His friend, who was with one of my girl friends, has to do tour duty all New Year's eve for receiving too many gigs. (A "gig" is a demerit and if you get a certain number of them, your superiors give you some kind of tough duty to perform, usually on a night when you are dying to go out.) By the way, the fellow I was with is a tall guy with sort of blondish hair. He looks more Irish than Jewish. He used to be an auto salesman. He used to go to Detroit and knows the section where we live. Hope I do hear from him but you can never tell — sometimes the guys get restricted and can't write out any mail but can only receive mail. I never take the guys address — I let them contact me first. By the way we had to "shake" so many fellows that it was really funny. We were the only WACs in L.A. as far as we could see and we sure had fun. All the boys saluted us as we walked down the street and we returned with the "non-com" salute, which is a salute in reverse — right palm outward over left eye....

Tell Ma and Pa not to worry about me. I'm not in an over-seas unit as they needed us WACs out here. But to tell the truth I haven't really done any honest-to-goodness work yet. I reported to work twice and the Lt. who's awfully cute let me take off for Xmas shopping — which I didn't do.

Mollie found that her work experience in civilian life exempted her from the lengthy training period in secretarial skills and administration which many other WACs had to go through following their basic training. Instead, she qualified for an accelerated course and was placed directly in a relevant job.

December 27, 1943

Dear Beck,

Just dropping you a line. My first day at the office. I wrote you already about the Xmas evening. Well, Xmas Day, I also went out with another guy — a Sgt. Knotts[7] from Virginia, about 6'4" with sort of blond, or very light brown, curly hair — Gary Cooper type. It was all quite unexpected. I met him on the streetcar from L.A. to Hollywood. My girl friend and I were mixed up with some sailors that we were trying to dodge and then we got on the streetcar and I happened to sit next to the Sgt. He was awfully nice and asked me about the WACs and also if I had been to Hollywood before, etc. and wanted to show me the town. He asked me if I had company that evening. I told him I was a bit tangled up with some sailors for the moment, but asked him if he had a friend for my gal friend. And, he did. We went to several of the nice bars and you know me, I didn't drink very much and he was very nice. I think he wanted to drink quite a bit more but didn't because I didn't. Please note the napkin from the Brown Derby.[8] I have one autographed by the kids I was with. By the way we didn't see any movie stars. I am sure Hollywood is nothing like it used to be. It is overflowing with service people. As usual, we were the only WACs around and the guys sure like to show us off. Our sailor friends ran into us in one of the bars and made some comment about the army getting all the breaks.

We wanted to go to the famous Canteen[9] in Hollywood but it was terribly crowded and furthermore I don't think service women are allowed. We tried to get into the Palladium, a very popular dance hall but it was much too crowded…. We went to a very nice place to eat and it was so crowded that two other soldiers sat down and ate at our table. One of the soldiers was from Detroit and immediately asked me what section of the city I lived in. I got a big kick out of that because you can tell they want to know if it is the Jewish section…. These fellows were real gentlemen. Instead of hiking to the P.E. (our train) we took a taxi for about eight blocks. We exchanged addresses and they want to come out to our post to have "chow" with us. (However, they stay at a Camp about 70 miles from L.A.) We are allowed to have guests. My friend, Sgt. Knotts wants to take me out again during the day time to see Hollywood and get a really good view of the place. So—time will tell. Anyhow, I am signed up to go to a dance tomorrow night with a bunch of gals from our post to an Army Post….

Well, I guess I had better get back to work. The Lt. here (very cute) is giving me the Army Regulation book to "swallow." I hope he doesn't expect me to memorize the darn thing. You see a lot of the kids were sent to Administrative School following our basic training for about 8 weeks to learn about Army Administration. But a number of us were given a "blitz" course for three days in basic to learn Military Correspondence and then we were sent right out into the field because of our previous background. Evidently they think we are readily adaptable. (I hope! I hope!)…

Mollie explained to her sister that she got the job she wanted but she could not go into any details about her work. Censorship of letters had not begun but the Army expected everyone to be discreet about their work. Therefore, in order to have something to say in her letters home, Mollie wrote about pleasant experiences and especially her social activities. Her California letters indicate that she and her fellow WACs could go out every night and easily get a date at any time.

31 Dec. 1943

Dear Beck:

Well, I guess I can tell you a little something about my surroundings, but, Beck, we can't talk too much as you know, the Army doesn't want their personnel to talk, shall we say, "loosely." In other words, the less said the better regarding our immediate surroundings and exact work. However, I am doing secretarial work, but at this moment, probably because of the holidays, am not too busy. This, I understand, is a temporary assignment. Today, I am working for the Colonel. He is a medical man. His secretary took the day off. (She is a civilian.) In fact, I am the only WAC at the Port Surgeon's Office. My work is not complicated. Taking a little shorthand, doing typing and some filing. Many things are going to be re-arranged in the office the beginning of the year as this office has not been in existence very long. I am temporarily assigned to the Administrative (Medical) Dept. and usually work for a Lt. (cute, he is). He is letting me off for New Year's Day and I guess I am very lucky. I have a date tonight with an Aviation Cadet [Maurice Kaye], whom I wrote to you about. He asked me for the date on Xmas eve and has phoned me several times during the week. He hopes to get tickets for the Rose Bowl Game tomorrow and wants to make it a weekend affair. I phoned Ida [Mollie's friend who had moved to California from Detroit] and will spend my sleeping hours there.... He is a

Mollie, right, and Dottie Dicks in Wilmington, winter 1943-44.

very nice fellow and dances swell. Has been in the army two years and is no dummy. He has also lived in Detroit. His name is Maurice, and he is Jewish.

...I guess I never did tell you what Wilmington was like. Well, we live in barracks as we did in basic training. However, we have more accommodations. In fact, we have two swell bathtubs and you should have seen me relax in a bubble bath the first opportunity I got. It was heavenly after not taking a bath for about 7 weeks. (Don't get me wrong, we take showers everyday — that is a must in the army.)

We WACS live together in several barracks with one mess hall and one recreation room. There are, of course, no men in our detachment. But the men have their own barracks, etc. not too far.

The town of Wilmington surrounds us. However I wish it were L.A. Wilmington is a dinky town with bars and a couple of theaters. Nothing much to say for it. However, when I am not busy at the barracks doing laundry that is washing and ironing and cleaning up my footlocker, etc. for inspection, I go to L.A. or Long Beach. We can usually get passes whenever we want them. However, once in a while we get restricted. I noticed on the bulletin board noontime when I went back to mess, "BARRACKS ARE IN UNTIDY CONDI-TION — Everyone restricted Monday, Jan. 3 and Tuesday Jan. 4 to clean up area." That means just what it says. Anyway, Beck, it's not too bad. That just gives us a chance to do a lot of fixing up on our clothing, etc. and arranging our closet and footlocker for the week. Otherwise, most of the girls run around from Monday night to and including Sunday. However, you know me. I know my limitations and if I go out and know I have to work the next day, I restrict myself for an evening. However, most of us get a chance to go out every night if we wanted to. In other words, there is quite a bit of social life — but you have to make connections. I certainly have gotten my share and don't complain at all....

We have had rain steadily for ever so long. However, today it was beauti-ful, I am just wearing my suit. Then when I get home (the barracks, about 4 blocks away) I will change into my New Year's attire, which happens to be my other WAC suit, which I pressed out myself. That's one thing I don't have to worry what I am going to wear. Anyway, this guy I am going with tonight likes uniforms— so I know he will want to show me off....

Although Mollie wrote to her sister very frequently and did provide many details of her social life, she did not reveal everything in her letters. For exam-ple, many years later she told a slightly different story than the one she relates in the letter below about New Year's Eve 1943. It was late at night by the time she and Maurice finished their date — too late to go back to her friend's house and Maurice suggested that they see what was available at the hotel. Mollie agreed as long as Maurice understood that there would be "no monkey business!" So rather than staying at the hotel with "another gal" as she tells her sister, she shared a room with Maurice, who told the hotel management that they were husband and wife. Mollie's family would have found this very shocking, even with the assurance that Maurice had been a perfect gentleman, and so she decided not to reveal this part of the story to avoid upsetting them.

3 January 1944

Dear Beck:

...I suppose you are anxious to hear about my New Year's date. Well it was with Maurice Kaye, the air cadet. We had a swell time New Year's eve. We went to a couple of famous bars, but don't have to worry about me, I'll never become a drunk. Then we attended a play at midnight. You'll just die at the title — "Two in a BED." But it's one of the L.A. plays that has been running for two years. It was rather risqué but cute. It was at the "Musart Theater." The actors were not from the screen, but they were rather good. You could just see the heroine had her eye out for a talent scout in the audience! By the time we got out of the theater and ate again, it was rather late so I stayed at the Hotel with another gal. I didn't want to disturb Ida.

The next day Kaye took me to breakfast, lunch and dinner. We didn't go to the Rose Bowl game as his pal, Joe, who was with us couldn't go because he had to get back to Santa Ana and we didn't feel like leaving him. Anyway I'm not so crazy about running umpteen miles to see football.... Kaye has been in the army for about two years and doesn't seem to accumulate gigs. You see he is very well adjusted to army life. He was in about a year and a half before he went into the air cadets.

Saturday evening I called Ida and Kaye and I went there. By the way Kaye is Jewish and when I introduced him to them, as soon as he walked out of the room, Ida said: "A shaygitz [Yiddish for non–Jewish young man]?" He certainly doesn't look Jewish, but he is. He looks Irish or Swedish. Kaye wanted me to be with him Sunday, but anyway he had to leave Sunday rather early so he could be in the parade at Santa Ana....

Kaye wanted me to go out with him next Saturday night but darn it I have KP [Kitchen Police] Sunday so I had to tell him I couldn't. Anyway he said he will phone me during the week. For KP — we have to wake up at 5:30 A.M. and work until 7:30 P.M. or so in that damn kitchen. But I guess it builds muscles....

Becky, you can tell those gals if they want dates — the army is the place for it. My god — I can't even keep up with them. However, maybe I just have the breaks. I have been rather fortunate in getting near L.A....

In this next letter, Mollie mentions her correspondence with Ruth Schaffer, a friend whom she met at a resort in South Haven, Michigan before she joined the Army. Mollie and Ruth kept in touch throughout the war and from time to time Ruth would send Mollie salamis all the way from her home town of Chicago.

Mollie and her fellow WACs were much in demand for socializing. Although at times Mollie complained that she did not want to go out so often and preferred to take it easy and stay in, she could usually be persuaded to go out nevertheless because everything was so interesting and exciting.

5 Jan 44

Dear Beck:

...I am okay and still at the same place. I just received a letter from Helen [Freidberg] ... she got to the place she wanted — Italy.... Well, tonight I have the opportunity of going to either of two dances — of course, all service men. But I am a bit too tired so will take it easy tonight — I think.

I have rec'd quite a bit of mail lately and it's a good thing I am able to squander a few minutes at typing out the answers. I also rec'd a letter from Ruth Schaffer which I have answered.

I can't take all of this gallivanting around so have to take it easy occasionally....

Tell Mom to let me know when the Passover holidays come out because I may as well get lined up for a furlough in case I am still around these here parts....

7 Jan 44

Dear Beck:

...Well here I go again revealing my latest escapade. Last night one of the girls convinced me to go with her to Long Beach, a nice town about seven miles from Wilmington where all the service people go. I told her I was not interested in going to a show or gallivanting around. So she said, "Okay, we'll just shop around a bit and get home about 10 P.M." I said, "Okay."

When we left, there were four of us gals.... When we got to the Pacific Electric train, which we take to go into Long Beach (a 25 minute ride) Barbara and I found room to get into the train and were pushed gently (?) ahead. Gertrude and Jean remained and waited for the next train and yelled out to us to wait for them at the station at Long Beach, which we promised to do.

When we got to Long Beach, we knew we would have a half-hour's wait for the other kids so we walked down the shopping district but practically everything was closed. We waited for the kids at the P.E. but they didn't show up. We thought we were perhaps too early. Then we decided to walk down to the *Pike*. It is something like Eastwood Park on a smaller scale. All the soldiers and sailors whistled as we walked by. However, before we realized it — the MARINES HAD LANDED. Two Marines were trying to convince us we should go dancing with them. They were very nice and we told them we had to meet our gal friends at the P.E. and in fact, they were waiting for us. Well the Marines insisted on walking with us to the P.E. We waited around and I guess we had missed the gals.... Well we went on our merry way with the boys.

We went to the Hilton Hotel, the Sky Room.... The Sky Room is like a dream. It is on the top floor and is practically all glassed in and looking out one can get a good view of the sky line. The dance floor is small but very smooth. The orchestra is small but good, and the singers are swell. Their tables are really darling. You can look through them and when you bend over, you can see your reflection in them.

...Before we knew it the evening had passed and here it was after 11 P.M. and we had to be back for bed check at 11:45 P.M. Well, the boys took us home in a taxi and we just made it.

Timmy, my friend, wanted me to go out with him Saturday night but I said I was busy. You see I have something else cooking — sort of a half promise with another guy, and if this other guy can make it, I just couldn't disappoint him. Can you imagine, Beck, being able to turn down dates? In fact, I had three dates lined up for Saturday when really I don't think I should go out at all as I have KP on Sunday. But anyway I'll let things work out for themselves. I sure am growing fickle....

---

11 Jan 44

Dear Beck:

Last night I was out with my Marine friend, the one I had met in Long Beach. He is a very nice guy and wants me to correspond with him. He is leaving the States very soon. Barbara and I went out on a double date last night and had loads of fun. It was mighty funny my finally breaking down to go out because after having KP on Sunday, they had nerve to make me do KP last night after supper when I returned from work because I had to relieve one of the girls who had been on duty so that she could hear the ARTICLES OF WAR read.[10] You see we have to hear the Articles of War every six months and since I have only been in three months I didn't have to attend the class.

By the way, Beck, it's getting so I can't keep track of all the guys. Can you imagine that? One thing the guys in the army aren't slow. They don't hem and haw around ... for months before they ask a gal out. I'm just wondering if I could stand civilian life right now. You know what I mean, the namby pamby way of guys that we know.

During this time Mollie began receiving letters from Sergeant Charles Knotts, whom she described meeting in her letter dated December 27th. His letter to Mollie below was postmarked from a different city, indicating that the Army had moved him already.

Saturday night

Dear Mollie,

I received your letter the other day and was really glad to hear from you and, in fact, surprised too. Yes, I do wish I could go into Long Beach tonight but as you see I am some hundred and fifty miles away. Too bad; I think, for I'd really like to meet you again.

So you are on KP tomorrow, are you? Well, I have to work tomorrow too, so that makes us even. We are really working. The only reason we are not working tonight is because they have no flashlight batteries. Well, Mollie, I hope that sometime soon we can meet again. I am looking forward to it, but until then I hope you can find time to write me a few lines now and then, soon. I'll call you up some time as soon as I am able to come down to L.A.

Goodnight

Charlie

In the next several letters, Mollie continues to give details of her busy social life and describes the camaraderie among the WACs but she also reveals a bit more about her working life. The fact that she was being recommended for promotion indicates that her work was highly regarded, although as she points out below, the Army did not seem to be approving many promotions at this time.

17 Jan 44

Dear Beck:

Was out with [Maurice] Kaye this weekend to Hollywood. We tried to get into several of the well known places but they were just jammed. Brown Derby was overflowing and anyway I had been there. Mike Lyman's was the same. We ended up at Sugar Hill, a very nice and cozy place. Had lots of fun. He sure is a swell dancer. Kaye calls me long distance a couple of times a week.

...My office has already put in a request for me to get a T/5 rating [promotion to corporal], which would mean no KP but I think all the stripes are frozen and it will be some time before I can get a rating. Any how I get along swell at the office.

Was out to Torrance Hospital Saturday with the Master Sgt. We were taken in a Govt. Car. I felt pretty important. I copied some hospital records for the Sgt. We passed San Pedro on the way to the Hospital and that sure is some tough town. I understand that most of the places there are "out-of-bounds" for the WACS. (Out-of-bounds means that we are not supposed to enter any place that is on such a list, which we have posted.)...

Although Mollie continued to see Maurice Kaye, Charles Knotts also wrote to her frequently. He always told her that she was the WAC behind him because he had joined the Army before she had. However, once she was sent overseas, he began to call her the WAC in front of him in their later correspondence.

1-23-44

Dear Mollie,

I received your letter yesterday and was very glad to hear from you again as a letter seems to help especially when a guy is in a place like we are in here.

We are up here at a landing strip 4 miles out of Paso Robles and it is a very small town with a hundred soldiers for every civilian so you can see when a fellow does get some time off he still has no place to go. I had planned on going to L.A. this weekend but found out we have to be back by eleven o'clock Sunday nite so I gave it up, several of the guys went to Frisco but I decided to stay in and take it easy like the WACs do.

We expect to return to Camp Haan before the 5th of Feb so could it be possible I could see you, tell me whether you think it possible or not I hope so anyway.... You really must be getting important riding in staff cars you probably won't recognize just a plain Sgt, or am I wrong?

I do hope you get your T/5 it makes one feel a little more important. I have been a Sgt since 1941. Maybe if the war keeps on someday I'll get a step or two higher but if it would stop now I'd be happy as would millions of others for lots of guys are growing pretty tired of it all, well here's one that is anyway the sooner the better for me.

I imagine I had better close for this time now be sure to answer soon and tell me if it could be possible to see you or do you think I am a little too much insistent? ... I hope you write soon.

Sincerely,
Charlie

P.S. There's a WAC behind me: I keep looking for that WAC you said was behind me.

---

29 January 1944

Dear Pop and Mom:

Just thought I'd drop you a little letter to let you know I am okay and enjoying myself out here.... I know Mom will be glad to hear this—as far as I am concerned there is no shortage of men out there. I have a date tonight with an air cadet (the fellow I have been seeing every weekend) and this noon when I went back for lunch, a Sgt. phoned me from Los Angeles twice. He had traveled 250 miles to see me but didn't let me know until he called — and I can't go out with him tonight because I have this other date. Imagine I have troubles because I got too many dates. Anyway this Sgt. is going to be transferred to a camp about 70 miles away from Los Angeles and will call me up during the week.

Yesterday I had KP We work in the kitchen from 6:30 A.M. to 7:45 P.M. I scrubbed pots and pans, mopped floors, washed dishes, scrubbed and set tables, scrubbed doors and just about everything. However, if we do our work pretty fast we get a chance to rest twice during the day for an hour at a time. Both times I went back to the barracks and laid down and really slept. In the evening I had looked forward to coming back to the barracks and scrubbing and cleaning up and making my bed with clean linens and the thought of all that work sort of tired me out more. But I was really lucky. The girl who sleeps next to me is really a "peach." When I got back to the barracks just before 8:00 last night everything was cleaned up for me and she had even ironed my dress shirt. She said: "Well, all you have to do is make yourself beautiful for your big date tomorrow night." ... Anyway, I did just what she said: — I washed my hair and even rinsed it in lemon; took a nice leisurely bath and did my nails. Today I feel bright as a penny and all ready to run around again....

---

31 January 1944

Dear Beck:

This morning we had a little Bond Rally[11] in back of our office — sort of our backyard. There was an army band and it sure was good. The Rally was for both civilian and army personnel at our Port. Charlie Winninger and Marjorie Rambeau — the movie stars— were speakers and were very good. We also heard a number of the WW II heroes speak and, Beck, if you would have heard them and seen how sincere they were, you sure would insist on everyone you know investing every cent in bonds—and I don't mean maybe. I wish I could buy more. But on my $30 or so which remains, per month, I wouldn't attempt it. So far, with the extra money I got from you and Pa and the $18 check from the govt., I have managed ok.

---

3 February 1944

Dear Beck:

...Heard from Kaye last night and he already has his orders but of course can't say where. He was pretty lucky not being restricted so I will see him this Saturday night. However, he hopes to be stationed nearby as his friend has a car and could drive in to L.A. weekends. Kaye told me he has tried to reach me for three nights on the phone but couldn't get the call through because the WACS had too many calls coming through and we have only two phones. Our barracks is the most popular and the girls get phone calls constantly. He said he missed two suppers trying to reach me in the evening. In fact, he said the switchboard operators at his end kept telling him they didn't think any girl was worth so much effort to reach. But I guess I was because he finally got in touch with me just before lights went out last night.

Last Monday night we drilled and our Commanding Officer took us through some of the quiet streets of Wilmington. I really wasn't too rusty and I think we all looked pretty good. Most of us kept our minds on marching — however, we heard plenty of whistling from onlookers....

In the letter below Mollie describes being asked to take a leading role in a Jewish Sabbath service although she was evidently not very interested in even attending. The Chaplain seemed determined to get Mollie and the other Jewish WACs to attend.

5th Feb. 44

Dear Beck,

Finally read your letter and Jackie's. I really miss not hearing from home as I sure like to know what's going on.... I will probably remain a private and come out of the damn war with no stripes— darn it. Did I tell you that my Lt.'s recommendation for Technician 5th grade was turned down for me because the Table of Organization (military personnel is based on that) was all filled up. Well on the Q.T. I heard that they have again put my name up for the rating. So time will tell. Anyway I am not worried because I am enjoying myself and have nothing to worry about. I understand that as soon as anyone has stripes they are always worried about losing them for some reason or other. All they can do to me is demote me — to you know what — a civilian.

Four of the kids left today for furloughs and they sure were all smiles. They tell me that one is anxious to get home but then after a few days, they are ready to come back to the barracks to live with the rest of the WACs.

...Last night I attended Sabbath services and I was literally forced into it. It seems the Chaplain tracked me down and naturally I had to attend. I had to say the Sabbath prayer in HEBREW and bless the candles. I got through it all right. Imagine the Chaplain picking me out to do that. Well, that's the way he got me to attend. However, it was very nice. Just two other WACs and two civilian girls were all the females there. The rest were the army. One of the Lt.s took me home and of course the other WACs. By the way, the Chaplain is from Detroit.

As the Sergeant entrusted Mollie with more responsibilities in the office, she enjoyed it and felt that she was really contributing to the war effort, although she still had not received her long-awaited promotion.

8 Feb 44

Dear Beck,

Just dashing off a letter to you to let you know I am okay. I've been very busy lately — in the office. In fact the Sgt. says I'll have to take over making a lot of reports he has made etc.; took care of the whole darn thing myself — and feel pretty important. (But when in the 'ell do I get my rating.)

I even worked last night. After supper I came back and worked with the Sgt. until about 7:30. Then we went to the Men's PX and I had a sundae and he had beer ... I was the only gal around. (I was supposed to have attended drill and company meeting last night but the Sgt. got me out of it, so I could help him at the office.) Then the Sgt. walked me home and when I got back I had to wash and iron my clothes that I had allowed to accumulate.

Met another Jewish fellow — Charlie from Jersey. He sure has the dough and wanted to take me out to some fancy places. I met him Sunday and he has already written to me. Got the letter today. However, I'm holding open the weekend for the Sgt. that I correspond with — the one from Camp Haan — that is, if he hasn't gone overseas yet.

In fact, I've even got the date of Feb. 16th in my calendar with the Sgt. here. (Beck, doesn't it all sound confusing. I really have to keep track of all my dates, etc.) Right now I am way behind on my correspondence — about 16 letters or so....

---

10 Feb 44

Dear Beck:

...Just talked with the Major here and he says by Saturday, I ought to know about getting a rating out here. They really are trying hard to get me a rating. I say nothing because I have learned to take things as they come. It's funny being in the army, I never look too far in the future nor too far back, in other words, just live today. Am I not learning fast? ... (Just got several compliments from one of the Staff Sgts here. Said I made a good looking soldier — wasn't five-by-five like some of the WACs, and by the way he's from Detroit!)

In February, Mollie finally saw *It's Your War, Too*, the recruiting movie that featured Mollie and other WACs. She was surprised to see that her two scenes had not been cut since the film was fairly short and she only arrived in time for the last day of filming.

---

11 Feb 44

Dear Beck,

...I am getting off early today 4 P.M. to see the picture we WACs made. Will write you later about it after I see it but right now I want to get this letter off to you.... Well, the Major here today put in a recommendation for the Technician 4th grade (comparable to a Sgt.) for me and I'm keeping my fingers crossed. You certainly can't say they aren't trying for me....

---

12 February 1944

Dear Beck:

Well, here's a follow-up on my yesterday's letter to you and since the Sgt. is away today, I can take a little time to write this to you.

All we WACS assembled in the Port Theater for the Premiere showing of "It's Your War Too," which is the title of the WAC Recruiting picture. It is quite short — runs about 20 minutes. Before the picture was shown our C.O. [Commanding Officer] made a little speech and said that many of the scenes were cut out, not because they were bad, but because of the continuity and because it was necessary to make it short. I naturally thought the brief scenes I was in were cut because I had come in on the last day and there were no retakes or "notting" on my *dramatic scenes*. I was watching the picture intently as it progressed (it's really just a group of scenes), and my gal friend sitting next to me said: "There you are!" It was funny that I had hardly recognized myself. It was the coverall scene. I don't look too hot, but it's not too bad. Then I saw myself in the conference scene. I'd better explain to you exactly where I am in the picture, or you might miss me.

In the scene where I am wearing coveralls, I am carrying a "walkie talkie" on my back and speaking through a phone (but you don't hear me). That scene follows one where the girls from the motor transport are shown sliding under cars for repairing, etc. In the conference scene, I am seated next to the man on the right, and that scene follows just when the narrator says something about the *Pentagon Bldg.* However, you can never tell when the picture is shown again other scenes may be cut out. But anyway it was quite a thrill to see it. It was shown over again and naturally I stayed to see it again....

When we all got through seeing the picture, we came back to the barracks, ate supper and got our clean linens. Then we all set to work — CLEANING AND SCRUBBING for Saturday's inspection. There are no temperamental stars in our barracks....

...The Major just sent me out on an errand as the Sgt. was away. I went out to one of the hospitals with a chauffeur in a staff car. Felt pretty important. The guard at the hospital gate saluted me — just to be cute.

Mollie continued to hope for an upgrade in her rating, but although this was slow in coming, her supervisors were pleased with her work and continued to give her more responsibilities. In these next several letters, Mollie indicates that not all the men she had been dating were really "her type" and that she had begun to pass some of them over to other WACs.

14 Feb 44

Dear Beck:

...Sgt. here has let me handle some of the reports — making them up myself — evidently thinks I'm competent — but where are the stripes? Guess I'll just give up and accept them when and if they come. I guess I wrote you and told you I was recommended for Tech/4th and was supposed to hear Saturday regarding them — but nary a word today. It's one of those things you don't say *notting* about, I've learned. So I let the matter drop. In fact I've never asked for anything; it has always been brought up by the Sgt., Lt. or Major. So — just be patient and maybe eventually you will have a Sgt. for a sister. Who knows — I sure don't.

Went to Hollywood yesterday to see the Drunkard.[12] Had lots of fun. We went in a bus or rather a govt truck — three WACS and about 12 guys. The performance was for service people only — they served beer and pretzels and it was most informal. I am sending you a program.... Jo (my gal friend) and I decided to go to the Hollywood Canteen — by ourselves. We left the boys we knew and started off to the Canteen — however, we didn't get more than a block away when a whole "platoon" of soldiers started tagging us. Of course, they wanted to take us out. Finally, when we got to the Canteen two of the boys stuck to us and insisted on going with us. After we waited in a line of service men about one block long—for about three minutes and I didn't see any other service women, I said that I thought they didn't let WACS and WAVES, etc. in—probably because the hostesses there didn't want any competition and sure enough we walked up to the desk and were told we couldn't go in but could go up on the balcony and watch from a pigeon hole—which we did…. Chased around Hollywood for a while with some sailors and then decided to go home early. By the time we got home it was 11 P.M. But we always do get a kick out of Hollywood as there are so few WACS around, we get all the attention.

---

17 February 1944

Dear Beck,

…Last night attended the dance with the Sgt. given for the WACs. Had a very nice time. Had only one glass of beer—scads and scads of olives—cheese sandwiches with crackers—nice gooey gorgeous entrancing chocolate cake (I sure would like to meet the cook). Danced only with Sgts there. Didn't even come in contact with the privates. Rushed home like mad to make the 11:45 bed check. Couldn't get a late pass because I had used one Sunday night and was saving one for Saturday night (we are only allowed two per week). I got in about 11:30 and dashed into the latrine—got washed, put my hair up and scooted up the stairs behind one of the gals who was ambling up slowly—and who should it be but the C. Q. (Charge of Quarters—the girls who check us in for bed check). She turned around and we both laughed. You see we are really supposed to be in bed.

Just turned over one of my Marine boyfriends to one of the girls in the barracks. Decided I couldn't take care of his dates and correspondence. He has written me several times and I just couldn't get around to answering and anyhoo he is not quite my type for me to carry on an extensive correspondence, etc. as I have to begin weeding out.—So I do hope she will take care of him and keep him happy.

Still no word regarding my stripes. So will just forget the whole thing.

The next letter is a reminder of the Army's high standards of order. Group punishments of the sort described below were (and continue to be) common in the armed forces to foster a sense of collective responsibility within the group.

19 February 1944

Dear Beck,

...Rather busy today at the office as the Colonel's Secretary is still off sick and I was on KP yesterday so there was plenty to do today. This Col. reminds me a lot of Mr. Burns [Beck's boss, a prominent Detroit attorney] — in his dictation, he is always striking out and changing his mind. However, I haven't been taking enough dictation around here to fill a thimble. Would like a lot more.

Our company had a bad inspection this Saturday so they are making it pretty tough on us. I was lucky and didn't get a gig. Yesterday I was on KP and when I came back after a strenuous day, I had to clean up not only my own area but the gal's next to me (the one that always helps me out) as she had la grippe. I guess that's why I am not raring to go anywhere that I have to exert myself. As a punishment for the entire company, we are having a formal inspection every day beginning this Monday.... They have also restricted us Friday evenings and everyone must be in bed by 11 P.M. and no late passes. It seems that just a few sloppy gals make it tough on the rest. We'll have to get after them....

Mollie was becoming concerned about her family and the effect that the U.S. federal food rationing program was having on them, especially on her brother, who was underweight. Rationing used a point system to set limits on the quantities of certain goods (including clothing and gasoline as well as some foods) that could be purchased by an individual, in order to ensure that civilians could get their fair share of items that were in short supply and were needed for the war effort.[13]

1 March 1944

Dear Jackie:

...I enjoy hearing from you so write me more often... How about the meat ration points? Are you getting enough? If not, get Dr. R to ask for more for you. You know, we have meat every day. Not only once a day but twice — for lunch and also supper.

...Must admit that it is pretty rugged on the boys. It was pretty tough for the girls but I understand the boys are treated more roughly than the girls. It certainly isn't any snap being in service, but now that I am out of basic training I am able to take it easier and enjoy myself out here.

...I know you must have read all my accounts of my running around. I certainly don't exaggerate a thing. In fact, I haven't related half of my episodes as I don't have time to write that much. So you can see as far as I am concerned I enjoy army life even though I gripe when we have to do KP and any other extra detail.

Judging from this next letter, Mollie did receive a slight promotion (to Private First Class) although that was far from the rank of corporal or even sergeant that she hoped to achieve. This letter also reveals the resentment some soldiers felt when they dated a woman who outranked them, even when the disparity in ranks was minor.

1 March 44

Dear Beck:

Am taking off, as usual, a few minutes during a busy day to write home so the family won't wonder what has happened to me.... Sunday, which was a gorgeous and sunshiny day, I spent with a Marine from Detroit. I had been out with him before and although I was supposed to go elsewhere with one of my gal friends, I went with Roy to Long Beach.... He wanted to buy me a little locket with an agate stone, but I told him I couldn't wear it anyway. The only thing I can wear is my dog tags. Anyway I didn't want him to spend his money on such foolish things ... and besides he is a private and makes less than I do—I am a PFC [Private First Class]. He kept making remarks about my being a PFC and him only being a private. I think it would have irked him even more so had I been given the Sgt.'s rating....

3. Preparing for Duty Overseas: Fort Oglethorpe, Georgia
March–April 1944

Mollie was granted a furlough and went home to Detroit to see her family and friends between the end of her assignment in California and the start of her next assignment at Fort Oglethorpe, Georgia, which was the staging area for WACs going overseas.[1] Mollie's friend Dottie Dicks, who was also in the WAC and also from Detroit, traveled with her to Fort Oglethorpe. Although the Army assigned them to different groups, they remained together as they traveled overseas. A few days after their arrival in England, they were separated, but they did see each other briefly later in the war, in Paris and then in Germany.

* * *

20 March 1944

Dear Family,

Well here I am at Ft. Oglethorpe. It sure is different from Wilmington but is somewhat like Daytona Beach in its setup. So many new faces—every once in a while we run into someone we knew back in Wilmington about a month ago. All the gals who have been here for a while seem to like it—so only time will tell. Any way every gal looks plenty healthy....

In the next few letters Mollie begins to give her family some hints about her next assignment (such as references to being seasick and looking forward to great experiences) even though she could not give them any details.

Mollie, middle, with her mother, left, and sister Beck, right, on furlough in Detroit before being sent overseas, March 1944.

21 March 1944
(First Day of Spring but you
wouldn't know it here)

Dear Family:

Just dropping you a line to let you know I'm ok. We haven't actually done any work as yet. Except as usual they start from the bottom of the alphabet and work up — and this morning I am on latrine duty already!!

Four of us from Wilmington sleep next to each other & we feel very much at home. It really is swell as they sure do split up the gals but we were lucky as we stuck close together.

Must admit that it looks as though we'll have lots of hard work — especially from the food they have been feeding us. Spinach for every meal except breakfast — so far. Milk at every meal ... was in bed by 8:30. No running around here. I'll probably get rid of the bags under my eyes— no doubt.... I'll probably have to send everything home that isn't G.I.... Even have to send my shoes home.

---

22 March 1944
9 P.M.

Dear Beck:

Well — we have been busier than a bee around here — we've even had night classes! Was weighed today. I weigh 110½ strip — that's not bad, eh? As usual —

passed the physical — oh well. I always wondered what it would be like to be seasick. We don't wear any make-up other than lipstick. We wear coveralls all the time. So you can see there's no glamour here. Life is rugged but healthful. (Spinach again today.)

I'll try to write when I have time but we really haven't begun all our classes so you see I'll be terribly busy. Please don't worry if I don't get a chance to write often. You write me anyway. Don't know how long I'll be here but it won't be too long. Thank goodness as I sure would like to get going. Have absolutely no idea where. There are so many rumors around here but they all add up to zero. In as much as everything is so damn restricted, I can't write about much.

You should see the 1st Sgts. do KP [Kitchen Police] around here. It really is amazing. You see a 1st Sgt. always runs a company but in our group they are just like everyone else. It really is amusing as KP is beneath them. I'm quite fortunate as yet as the KP roster was started from A — on — so they'll have to go some to W....

Really think I'm in for a great experience....

---

23 March 1944
9:30 A.M.

Dear Beck:

...Dottie went for typing test & so did the other gals I know. So here I am with a few other gals trying to hide somewhere in the barracks as the girls who aren't taking typing tests are liable to be yanked out the barracks to relieve the other gals on KP or some other goofy detail. About 5 minutes ago all the gals who were left dashed into the toilets as the front door of the barracks opened. There wasn't any place left for me to "hide" — so I busied myself with a bar of soap & washed my hands so many times that they are now chapped. It's really one of those episodes one reads about — so darn funny. When we felt the coast was clear, they still wanted to go out into the yard — but I was adamant. I decided to take it easy & lay down on my "little biddie bed" & write you regardless. I am tired of trying to escape — so if they catch me I'll do KP or what have you.

From this point it was becoming clearer to Mollie that the restrictions on what she was able to tell her family were increasing, in part because she was beginning to advance within the military and, of course, because she was on the verge of being deployed overseas. She does her best in these letters to prepare her family for the fact that she may not be able to write to them as frequently or as freely as she had previously. She reassures them that she is being well looked after and that her fellow WACs are sensible and competent — in other words, that they can be relied upon to help each other out during the dangerous times that are likely to be ahead of them.

24 March 1944

Dear Beck:

...We are busier than h--- here. It looks as though we're having truly a blitz course.

...Now I know why Ella's letters weren't interesting. There isn't much to write about & what is interesting, we cannot write. In fact, we are not permitted to take photographs on this area.

By the way, Beck, as soon as you are notified my A.P.O. [Army Post Office] number,[2] which the government will forward to you eventually, please go to the Dime store & buy one of those special boxes for packages overseas for 8 oz. You don't need a special request from me[3] for this.... I'm just telling you all about that because I have no idea where we are going. We may be sent somewhere we can get everything & then again somewhere we can get nothing. I hope this letter is not too confusing. If it is, please write me & I shall attempt to elucidate.

It is absolutely impossible to even get an idea where we are going as everything is said & done to confuse us & personally I think that's a good idea....

As usual, we're restricted Friday night for clean up & we are having a Major WAC inspect us tomorrow. So I guess I'd better get back to my mop & clean up. Will probably be in bed by 9:30 — had *spinach* again today.

---

25 March 1944

Dear Beck,

As soon as I have a minute to spare, I drop you a line as you notice. Eventually, I won't be able to write you, so want to write to you now as much as I can. No doubt our mail will be strictly censored very soon. Here I am sitting out on the steps with about 15 other gals writing. The sun is perfect and it is considerably warmer today than ever before here....

Had Saturday inspection this morning and we all passed with flying colors. I hid so many things in odd places. I do hope I can find them. I stuck a bag of pretzels under my helmet and a dust cloth in my rubbers!

One thing, Beck, please tell Mom and Pop not to worry because they sure take care of us down here. The girls are all very nice and not the dopey type. Every one of us seems to have a purpose.... Did I tell you — we even have classes on Sunday? Must admit I miss Wilmington and the good times there but I do believe we'll all have a far richer and greater experience where we are going — where ever that is????

...Dottie just remarked — three weeks ago tonight, we spent it in Long Beach, California, two weeks ago Detroit, last week Chicago and tonight Fort Oglethorpe, GA. Nothing boring about our army life!!!

Mollie used this next letter to follow the Army's advice to ensure that her affairs were in order in case she did not survive her deployment overseas to the war zone. The letter acted as a formal written and witnessed statement to notify her family of her wishes and various financial and legal arrangements.

27 March 1944

Dear Beck:

...I must get a lot of things straightened out regarding personal matters, as follows:

#1 — Just talked with our Lt & decided not to bother with a power of attorney or a will. My bonds are co-owners with you. My insurance is complete. My bank account is made out jointly with you. Therefore, when I was interviewed as everyone here is, it was really unnecessary for me to make anything out.

#2 — However, I did mention the fact that you had legally changed your name so everything in my records regarding you will be — Rebecca Weinstein (Winston). That's the way they put it down. You'll probably receive bonds in that name....

#3 — I increased my bonds to $18.75 per month — continued in our names as co-owners (I forgot, is that right?)....

#4 — Regarding my fur coat, should I still be gone next winter — do what you want regarding it — in other words if Ma wants to make it over, that's ok. If not, I suppose it will remain in style after the war....

#5 — Regarding my collection of coins, either Pa or Jackie can have same should I not show up after the war (sounds gruesome, doesn't it?). Anyhoooo, I want everything to be complete and in order.

#6 — I can't think of anything else. Except I want you to take care of anything else I may have forgotten.

Just to be formal about this, I may as well state I am in perfectly good health physically & mentally — after all the army just gave me a physical exam less than a week ago & pronounced me ok.

Witnesses: Margaret Sargo, Dorothy A. Dicks

Mollie continued to try to shield her parents as much as she could from the realities of being in the Army because she understood how much her parents worried about her. She also continued to drop little hints that she would soon be sent overseas — the reference to learning to pack a duffel bag suggests that she was being prepared to travel with just a few possessions. It was also routine for service personnel to be given medical and dental checkups before deployment to ensure that they were fit and healthy.

30th March

Dear Beck:

Just a line to let you know everything is okay. No, I didn't get KP yesterday. Thanks goodness. Instead I visited the dentist ... along with, of course, our classes during the day. We are learning to pack our duffel bag. It really is intricate.

Received a nice letter from Goldie,[4] wherein she gives me the impression that she knows I'm going somewhere outside of the U.S. I guess everyone back in Detroit can realize that. No one knows where it will be nor will we know until we are well on our way.

...Can't say much about the scenery around here as we've been too busy to admire same. However, away from the various barracks & G.I. buildings, there's a beautiful forest of trees. Then, of course, much of the terrain (is that right?) is "hilly."

We eat constantly here. After we finish our G.I. mess ...we go to the PX and not only buy cookies, candy bars, ice cream, etc. but eat them right then & there. It's amazing how much we gals put away. Ma sure would enjoy seeing me "fress" [Yiddish for overeating].

By the beginning of April, Mollie had started her journey to her first posting in Europe. In the months before D-Day, the Army's need for excellent typists and stenographers increased in the European Theater and Mollie's skills made her an ideal candidate to help meet that need.[5] Mollie was unable to say anything to her family about her destination or her route. At the staging areas for those bound for England, restrictions were very heavy. In fact, at one of the areas, there were signs on the mirrors stating, "If you talk, this woman may die."[6] At this point until VE (Victory in Europe) Day all of Mollie's letters were censored, with the initials of the censor indicated on the envelope.

Somewhere en route
April Fool's Day 1944

Hello Family:

Please 'xcuse this scribbling but it is the best I can do while riding on a train. We left Fort Oglethorpe not so long ago and are on our way to (?) & I don't know how long it will take. In fact, frankly speaking, I don't know where this train is taking us.... I sent my suitcase to the store C.O.D. with the key attached on outside.... Everything from now on has to be compact & consolidated. So if I write for you to send me anything — tins are best to have it packed in & small, too. Don't bother about anything unless I write....

The accommodations on the train are excellent & the food is good. The weather is perfect & scenery is grand.... Please note you are going to have trouble with me as I can't be too definite about anything.

It was important to Mollie to maintain ties to her old neighborhood.[7] In her letters she frequently asked about the Third Avenue gang, the group of friends she made when growing up on Third Avenue in Detroit. Many of the men from this group enlisted and Mollie was able to follow them and even meet some of them as her assignment took her to Europe.

2 April 1944
9:30 P.M.

Dear Beck:

Well here we are, for the time being anyway — and naturally, I can't tell you where we are. The accommodations here are swell & the food good. I've done my washing, taken a shower & washed my hair and am just about ready for bed. We have reveille at 6:15 A.M. & have to be completely dressed at that time so that means we have to be up pretty early.

Dottie & the other kids & I have been sort of split up but we are together for the time being anyway. It's too complicated to explain so I just won't bother. All the girls I am with are very nice & we get along well.

Please tell all the kids to write me as it is mighty lonesome to be waiting around when they are calling out mail & not get any. It's mighty funny but I expect to receive mail every mail call — so tell them all not to disappoint me.... Please write to me *now* about anything I may have omitted regarding my so called *will* & anything else you can think of. I just hope we won't have trouble receiving our mail out here. Certainly have no idea how long our set up will be here.

Please tell Mom & Pop not to worry at all in case you don't get mail from me so frequently — but I want you to write me anyway.

I'm feeling fine & don't have any regrets— although I do miss California very much & all my friends in Wilmington....

After Mollie left Fort Oglethorpe and the East Coast of the United States, it was at least two weeks before her family heard from her, and then it was from "somewhere in England." During the war, the families of service personnel learned that long periods of time without any correspondence from their loved ones usually meant that they were being sent overseas.[8] Mollie was not able to describe her voyage over to England and hardships it entailed until after the war ended in Europe and her letters were no longer being censored.

PART TWO : ENGLAND

4. "Somewhere in England": London
April–June 1944

In the months before D-Day, there was a dramatic increase in the Army's need for excellent typists and stenographers to serve in the European Theater. The WACs had demonstrated that they could do this type of work with great efficiency when they had been employed in other theaters of operations, and so the Army was anxious to identify as many WACs as possible, like Mollie, who had the relevant skills and could support the Army in these roles overseas.[1]

Mollie sailed to Europe on the SS *Île de France*, which was the first ocean liner to be entirely decorated in the Art Deco style.[2] She arrived in London in mid–April 1944 but she was not allowed to tell her family anything about her trip or her exact location, only that she was "somewhere in England." All of the letters that she wrote were now censored and the initials of the censor appeared on the envelopes or the V-mail,[3] although the mail that she received was not censored. The mail of service personnel was read by an officer based in the local area and/or by an officer at headquarters, in order to ensure that letters did not contain information that could help the enemy if the mail were intercepted.

While she was in England, Mollie began to form friendships that would last throughout the war and afterwards, as she continued to correspond with some of her wartime companions throughout the rest of their lives. The four women that she met and roomed with in England were her constant companions and roommates as they were transferred from one location to the next. Although they were rarely moved at the same time, they usually ended up together. Before joining the WAC, "Johnnie" (Goldie Johnson) was a secretary for an investment counselor in Louisville, Kentucky. She was older than the rest of Mollie's roommates. "Smitty" (Faye Lyne) was a draftsman from Georgia. She was always resourceful and she and Mollie spent a lot of

47

time together. "Loddo" (Mary Grace Loddo Kirby) was a stenographer from Pennsylvania. She was with Mollie on many of her escapades. "Bats" (Maria Battistella) was a statistician from Boston, Massachusetts. While in England Mollie also met "The Sarge," Alex Korody, who worked in her office and continued to move offices in Europe with Mollie as the Army transferred operations to different locations.

In her first letter to her family from England, Mollie described the welcome and the wonderful reception given to her and all the U.S. service personnel by the British people, who viewed the arrival of American troops in their country as marking the beginning of the end of the war and of all the hardships and sufferings they had endured.[4]

* * *

17 April 1944

Dear Becky,

Well here I am somewhere in England. Everything has been so darn interesting that I just don't know where to begin and, of course, just what I would like to tell you, I cannot. Censorship, you know!

Becky, I must tell you about the perfectly wonderful reception we received here. It was so unexpected that some of the girls actually wept. The fellows had a marvelous band and little floor show for us at our first dinner there. The food was superb. Roast chicken, mashed potatoes, carrots, beets, hot buttered biscuits and coffee and cake that crumbled like Sanders[5] birthday butter cream!...

Somewhere in England 4/23/44

Dear Beck:

...Dottie and I were finally separated. She received a very good and what I believe is a "choice" assignment. I must relate to you the episode concerning our last evening together. We had just gotten our good ole U.S.A. money exchanged for English shillings, florins, pences, pound notes, etc. (I had retained one American dollar bill and one penny for sentimental reasons.) We really didn't know from nothing except I had studied up a bit on American equivalents two minutes prior to our going out that evening. I decided to treat Dottie at a little tea room that is really G.I. insofar as the only people who frequent it are army. We have to stand in line to give our order to the waiter and carry it back to the little tables ourselves. I stood in front of Dottie with a florin coin (40¢), shilling (20¢), ½ pound note ($2). In other words I was prepared. Guess what our bill came to—total and final—sixpence. You could have knocked me over with a feather. I was taking Dottie out for five cents. Tea and cookies. Wanted crumpets or scones but they didn't have them....

Not long after she arrived, Mollie had the opportunity to get out of London and do some sightseeing. In this letter, she describes her visit to Warwick, about 90 miles from London on the banks of the River Avon. Warwick Castle is one of the largest and most complete surviving medieval castles in England and is the second castle that Mollie mentions in the letter.

Somewhere in England 4/24/44

Dear Jackie:

Well you finally broke down and wrote your wacky sister a letter. However, I must admit I have been a little late in answering. I was going to write Becky about my first sightseeing tour here, as I said in the letter I wrote Mom & Pop, but I decided I would give you a break.

Our tour took in the famous castles, one in ruins from Medieval wars and the other intact. At the second castle we had the opportunity of seeing a most interesting sight: — the peacocks with their tail feathers spread and strutting around. The most amazing thing is that they are so beautiful but their voices— "My Gawd." They sound like a couple of old crows. We also got a chance to see one of the most interesting spots in England. Am not able to divulge the name of the place.... The entire tour took a whole day. We had a very excellent lunch and the mayor of the village sat at our table opposite me. I learned many interesting facts. One — was that he, as a mayor of an English town, functioned differently from U.S.A. When they take office, they relinquish all their political life and act in a social capacity.... His wife, the Mayoress, took our addresses and the names of the people we wanted notified and in short order Mom and Pop will hear.

In the evening we had "tea" in another town. "Tea" consisted of cold cuts, salad, bread & butter, cake, coffee. The Mayor was unable to be there but his Mother was there. She was very nice and came up to the table I was seated at & asked me how I enjoyed British cooking. Only — she asked in broad British accent: "I suppose it is difficult to get used to English food & it is not as good as American." I assured her we enjoyed every bit of it. After all there wasn't a morsel of food left on our table. However, candidly speaking, I do like our G.I. food we have at our mess hall best of all.

After the tour that Mollie described in her letter, the Mayoress wrote to Mollie's parents to pass on her good wishes and express some of the gratitude that the local people felt at the support of the United States in the war. Although Mollie was not allowed to divulge the name of the town, the Mayoress was under no such restriction.

The Mayor's Parlour
Warwick
25-4-44

Dear Mr. & Mrs. Weinstein

Last week we had the pleasure of entertaining a contingent of the U.S.A. Army. They were a fine body of men, and were all most appreciative of being shown round the Castle and other historic buildings of our ancient town. At lunch I had the honour of sending a special greeting from the womenfolk of Warwick to all of you who are left at home, but by the request of your daughter who was well and enjoying her visit to our old town, I promised I would write to you personally and tell you that we will always do our best to make your people's stay in England as happy as possible.

That the day may soon come when you will all be reunited is the sincere wish of

A. Olivia Fonsell
Mayoress 1941/44

Mollie found that the social clubs provided by the American Red Cross in England offered servicemen and women overseas a range of services, such as American meals, a place to sleep, showers, barber shops, tailors, shoeshine parlors and recreation rooms. These clubs even provided a large map of the United States which showed the name and home address of all American soldiers who were using the club at that time. This allowed Mollie to pinpoint the locations of friends and family from Detroit who were also stationed in England.[6]

Somewhere in England
30 April 1944

Dear Beck:

...Here is what I want you to send me.[7] The sooner you send it out the better. You see it sometimes takes about six weeks for packages to get here.... Use your own judgment on some of the things if you can't get them; send reasonable facsimiles, which will be duly accepted and appreciated.... Here is a tip — when packing, use Kleenex as a stuffer. Kleenex is rather difficult to get around here but I imagine it is hard to get at home too.

As you can readily see by my typing, I am now settled in a job. Am still connected with Medics is all I can tell you.

Our living accommodations here are grand. So far we have charwomen do our cleaning and all we have to do is make our own beds. For Saturday's inspection we have to clean the windows as they don't do that.... We live in a very nice room — five of us girls together. We have heat, automatic of some kind. We have a lovely bathtub and HOT WATER.

All the girls from Calif. were split up but we do see each other, however, I find it easy to make friends in the army and the girls I live with are very nice.

Of course, Mom is interested in our food situation. I can tell you this: It's very good. In fact, this little incident I know you will find amusing. I happened to run into a Detroit girl that was inducted into the army the same time I was and we had basic training together. The first thing she said was — "You've put on weight, haven't you." And, I have! I do think my suit is a bit too snug. Can you imagine that, Beck??? We certainly have seen a lot of interesting things since we have come over and if I don't give you lots of details as I used to back in the States, you'll know the reason. Everything we say is so thoroughly censored, that it makes it impossible. But that is just as well.

...One thing I want to impress upon the family, Beck, is not to worry one bit about me. I am feeling fine and am certainly not undernourished.

I am going to try to get in contact with Benny [Ben Rosen — a friend from Detroit and the brother of Mollie's friend Ida who lived in California. Ben was also serving in the U.S. Army and was stationed in England] through the Red Cross and will try to do that soon. Tell his Mom and Dad.

...By the way, Beck, please tell me the date you receive this letter and also whether any part of it has been cut out.

Mollie had never traveled outside the United States before joining the Army and she was fascinated by everything she saw in England. She described her impressions of the most famous sights as well as of ordinary things. Based on her descriptions, it was apparent to her family that she was in London. At this time the preparations for the D-Day invasion (June 6, 1944) were under way, involving the assembly of the largest military operation in history to launch on the beaches of Normandy against occupied France, but due to the secrecy surrounding the preparations, Mollie was not aware that the invasion of France was imminent.

2 May 1944
Somewhere in England

Dear Beck,

Just thought I would bat out a few lines to let you know everything is just fine. Am just beginning to get around to seeing some of England and it really is fascinating. The architecture is simply superb and one cannot appreciate it by just looking at photographs. You cannot imagine how entirely different England is from America — not only in buildings, homes, people and even language. They call a flashlight, "torch," elevator, "lift," washcloth, "flannel," streetcar, "tram." Last night I went out with one of the G.I.s (soldier to you) who had been here for quite some time. This is what I saw: Westminster Abbey, House of Parliament, Big Ben (even heard it strike), Thames River, Piccadilly Circus (which is a street, I think), our mode of transportation was the subway (which is most interesting and confusing to me) and we also used the double-decker buses. I cannot tell you how impressed I was with everything. I just stood with my mouth open gazing at the sights. You may as well look them up in our Books of Knowledge [encyclopedia] as I am sure the descriptions there would be more articulate than my vocabulary could possibly be.

Although Mollie reassured her family that she was enjoying the food that the Army provided in the mess hall, she found that she missed the easy availability of ice cream and other treats that she was accustomed to in the United States. The food rationing program in Britain had begun in 1940 and was more extensive and stringent than the American version of rationing. Britain was not self-sufficient in food and relied on imported supplies which were transported by ship. Attacks by German U-boats (submarines) sank many of these ships, disrupting the food supply and creating shortages. Ration coupon books were issued to all citizens, and the coupons had to be used, in addition to money, when paying for any rationed item. Mollie's awareness of the food situation in England can be detected in her encouragement of her family to plant a Victory Garden. Millions of American households planted vegetables in their gardens as a way of helping the war effort.[8]

8 May 1944

Dear Jackie,

...I know you read the letters I send Becky so there is no sense in my repeating anything but I do say that England certainly has lots for one to see. Have you started the Victory Garden yet? I know that you said you hadn't but perhaps by the time you get this letter, you will have started it. I sure will miss those nice hard radishes but guess I won't mind skipping the lettuce with those little green bugs.

Food here is pretty good for our regular meals. However, we can't run over to the corner drug store as we used to and get candy, ice cream and gum. You see everything is rationed and furthermore they don't even have anything that resembles ice cream around here. So next time you have a sundae at Sanders—well just think of me.

---

8 May 1944
Somewhere in England

Dear Beck,

...Now for a little bit of what I have been doing. I have been working and enjoy my job very much. Every opportunity I get to go sightseeing, I take and, England is certainly the spot for sightseeing. Did I tell you that I saw Buckingham Palace?

...I am feeling swell Beck and certainly don't regret having made the change because I certainly will have lots to tell when I get back.

This next letter refers to Mollie's trip to the Royal Botanic Gardens at Kew, just a few miles southwest of London on the banks of the Thames River.

Somewhere in England
13 May 1944

Dear Beck:

Thursday—my day off—I had a most delightful day. My gal friend and I did a bit of sightseeing and inasmuch as she hadn't seen some of the places I had already been to, I took her around. We traveled by bus and subway. You would have laughed. We ran around just as though we knew the place. In fact, others asked us how to get to places. (Of course, we didn't know.) We asked plenty of questions and always got to our destinations. Among other points of interest, we took in Kew Gardens. It is a most exquisite spot. It is a park with gorgeous trees and flowers. We spent most of the day there and had tea in a little outdoor restaurant. Just too *Ducky* for words. We felt so cosmopolitan.

...when I got home there was a message for me at the Red Cross saying that a Sgt. Rosen called and for me to phone back—long distance—not too far from me. Am still trying to contact him....

Mail was the lifeline which connected Mollie to her home, but as she discovered, mail delivery to service personnel stationed overseas could be sporadic. Sometimes weeks would go by without a letter and then several letters would arrive in just one day.[9]

Somewhere in England
14 May

Dear Jackette,
        ...As you can see I am not getting my mail in the chronological order that you send it because those that were sent to Ft. Oglethorpe, etc. had to be re-routed. However, will probably receive mail in better order from now on.... You asked me if I have received any mail from our relatives. The answer is "Nary a one." (translated — not a one).

In this next letter, Mollie refers to the daily newspaper for the U.S. armed forces, *Stars and Stripes,* as well as *Yank*, an Army weekly magazine written by non-commissioned officers.[10] This letter also contains the first mention of Mollie's ambition to write a book someday based on her wartime experiences. Through her friendship with Alex Korody ("The Sarge") from her office, Mollie met a number of interesting people, including the family she describes below. The husband, Mirko Rot (sometimes spelled Roth), brought his wife Zuzana and son Georgie out of occupied Yugoslavia. He subsequently worked as a double agent for the Allies[11] and may have been involved with the Klatt network of German spies.[12] Mollie was completely unaware of his secret life.

Somewhere in England
20 May 1944

Dear Jackie:
        ...I sure do appreciate your writing me every week and your typing is certainly improving.... Regarding your wondering how they keep the fighting men informed of what is going on, I hope you received the Stars and Stripes paper I sent — I believe I sent it to Beckie. That is our newspaper and it comes out daily. I will send you more from time to time if I find envelopes for same. Perhaps I may send you a copy of the British edition of the "Yank," a magazine for the army that comes out weekly and is very interesting.
        ...You ask whether I listen to radio programs. No — we don't have one handy. However, last Sunday was the first time I heard radio since I began my overseas training. Went out last Sunday for dinner, etc., with a Staff Sgt. [Alex Korody] to some friends of his and that was the place we listened to the radio.

They are very interesting people and have been through a great deal in this war. They are a young couple with a darling boy of about four. They are natives of one of the small countries that was invaded by Hitler at the beginning of the war. They lost everything including their immediate families. And yet they have a wonderful sense of humor and are most charming. They speak umpteen languages — and so does my friend. I have heard some mighty interesting tales (in English though).

...Now for your letter of 6 May. Glad you liked my tour description. I think when I get through with the service that I will have to sit down in a nice quiet room and pen my memoirs — something like this: "G.I. Jane, Both Here and Abroad." How do you like that title?

Throughout her letters, Mollie described her sightseeing tours and in this next letter to her close friend Sarah Weinstein, she refers to a trip to Madame Tussaud's Wax Museum. Madame Tussaud began her career by making wax death masks of the aristocrats executed during the French Revolution and then left France for England, first touring the country with her wax impressions and later establishing a museum in London. A German bomb in 1940 destroyed part of the museum but the figure of Hitler was one of the few figures to survive without damage. In the 1950s a planetarium was built on the site of the bombed out part of the museum.[13]

London, England
22 May 1944

Dear Sarah:

Received both your letters. Good Friday one and V-mail of 11 May and as usual they are the newsiest letters I get. Thanks. As you can see by the heading — I am in London. (Now that we can state that fact, would you tell Beckie? She doesn't even know....)

I suppose you have heard from Beckie all about my sightseeing. Here is the latest. Yesterday I went to see Madame Tussaud's Famous Wax Works. It's amazing how life-like those figures are. In fact, as I walked in, I started to speak to the girl attendant to ask where we could purchase programs and was most chagrinned when I discovered it was a wax figure. I turned around to see if anyone had noticed my slight error. Then I walked cautiously about and decided not to speak to any of the attendants. You can imagine my further embarrassment when we were about half through with the exhibition and started to go on another floor. I edged up pretty close to a figure at the head of the stairs and stared at it quite frankly and then — he spoke to me. It was a male attendant and I understand he has been fooling the public for fifteen years.

I suppose you wonder how my social life is out here. Pretty good. Entertain both the army and the navy. However, I think I am partial to the army. Have been seeing a Staff Sgt [Alex Korody].... Most interesting fellow — speaks six languages. We speak English! Although I can't tell you anything about my job — other than it is medics and is now secretarial — it is most interesting.

By the way we have been issued overseas caps and wear that instead of our "Hobby" hats.[14] We also wear ETO (European Theater of Operations) ribbons over our left pocket of our jackets. It does make the uniform more interesting, don't you think?

We still have inspections on Saturday, KP [Kitchen Police] about every three weeks and occasional parades. Other than that our time after work is free. Thank goodness. You know there is so much to see out here that I attempt to utilize every free minute in sightseeing....

Mollie was concerned to learn about a series of strikes in her home city of Detroit, a major center of U.S. defense production. In the first three months of 1944, there were dozens of strikes each week and some became violent.[15] She was upset that the strikers' action could endanger the war effort and that some of the people back home appeared to be unconcerned about the war.

Somewhere in England
26 May 1944

Dear Beck:

Just thought I would take time off to dash a few lines to you telling about a most interesting evening I spent. It was a short time ago when I was in London and had the opportunity of seeing a wonderful performance put on by the Oxford Society Group (I believe that is their name.) It was a musical of the order of our "Pins and Needles."[16] This was called "Battle Together for Britain" and, Beck, it was excellent. It was given at the "House of Clive." If you can remember your history — Clive of India.[17] Anyway that group now owns his home and it was given there. A number of us WACs were present as were other service people. It was a most impressive evening what with our tea and get together with the performers after the show. They were just everyday people and I believe some of them were what we would call Grosse Pointe Society.[18] There were even photographers there. Everyone was most congenial and we sang some of our WAC songs for them. Then at the close of the evening we all sang "Auld Lang Syne" with our hands entwined — British and American. I shall never forget that nor the great hospitality of these English people.

After spending an evening like that and then reading in our "Stars and Stripes" about the strikes in Detroit — makes me so mad. (Am again bawling you out.) I can't understand it. Don't they know there's a war going on? By the way, here's something I read in one of their pamphlets and which I think is the truest statement yet: "If we sweat more on the production front, we shall bleed less on the battle front." I don't think the people ever stop to realize what each of their own selfish actions mean as a whole. So why in the H*** don't they quit that kindergarten stuff back in Detroit?

Well now that I have that off my chest, I can go back to my usual....

Somewhere in England
26 May 1944

Dear Beck:

...I can't complain as both you and Jackie have been writing pretty regularly to me.

...But just by chance I went there [Red Cross] and there was a message for me that Ben had telephoned long distance. That was the first inkling I had that Ben was still in the U.K. (United Kingdom). Then ever since that time we have been trying to get together — even to speak on the phone, which we were unable to do until this week. This whole episode has taken about a month. Can you feature that?

As D-Day was rapidly approaching, Mollie continued to be busy in the office but the degree of secrecy surrounding the preparations meant that she was not aware of the impending invasion.

Somewhere in England
4 June 1944

Dear Beck:

As you can see by the date line, I am working today. Just thought I would drop you a few lines to let you know I am just fine. Hope everyone at home is too....

Guess I had better get back to work....

5. Dodging the Doodlebugs: London
June–August 1944

Mollie continued to take advantage of opportunities to see the sights in England in her off-duty time, as this next letter indicates, and she was sometimes able to meet up with old friends from home who were also serving overseas. Word of Mollie's wartime adventures began to reach Danny Raskin, a reporter on the *Detroit Jewish News*. Raskin added to his regular column reports on the war in Europe based on her letters home; he designated Mollie as his overseas correspondent. Throughout the war, he used Mollie's experiences in the Army to give a human face to the conflict.

* * *

Somewhere in England
9 June 1944

Dear Beck:

Well, Ben[1] and I finally got together again and met at Oxford. We had a wonderful time. I had an overnight pass and stayed at the YMCA and Ben at the American Red Cross. My gal friend couldn't go at the last minute as she pulled "C.Q." [Charge of Quarters] so I went ahead anyway. Ben met me at the train Wednesday evening and we walked around Oxford for a while and he bumped into a very good army pal of his that he hadn't seen in over a year and a half. We decided to turn in early so we would have an early start Thursday morning. That we did the next morning, and we traveled some more — and he took me out to his Post and showed me where he worked and introduced me to all his G.I. friends. I had loads of fun. He took my picture in his studio. I don't know how it will turn out. If it is good, he will send it, otherwise I guess I just won't hear. Ben really has done some beautiful work and honestly, Beck, I feel darn proud of him. He certainly is well liked by everyone at his post, enlisted men and officers as well. We left his Post and got a ride into a small town and had lunch at a very nice hotel — quaint and interesting. There were many interesting pieces of furniture — some I would say were 18th century. The floor was oak inlay. The fire place was beautiful and had large silver platters and warming pans placed about it. They looked like relics of some old castle. He also took me to some interesting abbey (church) in that town. One of the rooms was piled high with stone that was probably parts of old Roman temples. Many of them were most intricately carved. Then Ben and I walked over to the bakery in town and he placed an order for his Post as they were having a party this coming week. It was a most interesting bakery shop and Ben and I walked right into the back where the baker was working. And, there he was up to his elbows in work — almost literally — but not quite.

Then we decided to go back to Oxford and we were most fortunate and got a ride in a station wagon with some British Officers. When we got back to Oxford Ben and I started on a little tour of our own. He took me to Balliol College and we went inside and through the grounds. Ben had his camera and took a couple of shots with me in them.... We walked about the streets and enjoyed it immensely — especially ME — you see WACs are quite a novelty in Oxford and all the GIs kept turning around and looking at us and made remarks about the Private 1st Class. We went into the American Red Cross and played ping pong and there again I was the only gal around — but I am getting used to that. We played three games and Ben won two. Must admit I was pretty stiff competition for him.

Ben and I went to a most interesting place for tea. It was one of those typically English clubs where people who are interested in the same thing get together and discuss not only that subject but other interesting subjects as well. One has to have a special introduction I believe to get into a place like that and of course Ben has been there before. The people who go there are interested in art, photography, etc. Ben and I sat and listened (while drinking tea and eating English pastry) to a couple of interesting people talk about their experiences in the war.... After we were through with tea, Ben took me upstairs where a man and a woman were in the process of making marionettes. He made the figures and she was cutting the clothes. I was so sorry that I could not remain there and see the finished products and perhaps later take in one of the performances.

Anyway Ben took me back to the station and went on the train with me but had to hop off pretty quickly as the train started a bit earlier than usual and so I waved goodbye. We did have such a grand time, Beck. Every time I think back I can just see Ben and me at a quiet moment either eating at the table or just walking and both look at each other at the same time and burst out laughing. It all seemed so utterly fantastic — both of us in England — and "G.I. Joe" and "G.I. Jane" seeing Oxford together.

And, here I am today, back at work — with a most pleasant feeling of having had one of the most enjoyable experiences of my army career. You must admit England certainly is fascinating.

...Sarah sent me a copy of that item that Danny [Raskin] placed in the Jewish News about me. Danny has written me and appointed me "Overseas Correspondent" for the "Listening Post," his column....

...PS Hope you are saving these letters as I know some day I would like to read them. You know we cannot keep a diary with us.

The D-Day invasion had started nearly a week before Mollie wrote these next letters but she still did not mention it to her family — the strict secrecy surrounding the landings in Normandy was maintained for some time after the invasion was underway in order to prevent any useful information from falling into the hands of the enemy. The WACs in England had worked around the clock on the preparations for D-Day although they were not aware of the scale or significance of the operations that were being planned.[2] Instead Mollie wrote about her social activities and frequently asked her family and friends back home to send her candy and gum. Sweets were a rarity in wartime England and Mollie enjoyed having some to give to the children that she encountered.

SOMEWHERE IN ENGLAND
12 June 1944

Dear Beck:

...Have been rather busy and don't have too much to write about. When I read over that sentence I know it sounds mighty odd — but it is true.

I still visit that refugee family [the Roth family] and was there a short time ago when on pass. They are always scolding me for bringing them my candy, gum and cigarette rations. By the way, they are Jewish. Also, the Staff Sgt [Alex Korody] that I see often, who speaks umpteen languages — of all things — is Jewish. He certainly doesn't look it and his name doesn't sound it — not even one bit. He didn't tell me he was, someone else did. It's a long story which I cannot go into now.

...busy as H_ **...

---

16 June

Dear Beck:

...I was out with my Staff Sgt. and had a very nice time. He is a most interesting person and I enjoy going out with him.

By the way, did I ever tell you that [Maurice] Kaye was transferred from Nevada to New Mexico? He is in the last stages of his training. Haven't heard from him in a little while—could be delay in mail or that he is busy with his examinations.

Have also been receiving nice letters from that Sgt. I met in California [Charles Knotts]. He now has an APO [Army Post Office] number and is on the East Coast. He says that I am no longer the WAC "in back of him" but ahead of him and he hopes to catch up with me sometime....

---

19 June 1944
Somewhere in England

Dear Beck:

I was rather amused today when one of the boys in the office gave me an orange. That is quite a rarity around here and one is really parting with something in giving you such an offering.

...Did you read how the children in the streets stop the American soldiers and say: "Any goom, Yanky" and of course, I am no exception. Not that I do give out all the gum, but it is fun giving it out to some of the little kids.

Did I ever tell you about the time I was in London on pass and stopped at Hyde Park (that famous park that has all those crack-pot soap box orators). It is most enjoyable to me and gives me a chance to see many types of people. One of the fellows I noted in particular was a dark complexioned soul with pitch black hair, long enough to make you feel that he should sell his violin. Anyway in the midst of his oration (I have forgotten what it was) he pulled out a comb from his pocket and calmly proceeded to come his hair.—Well with that—I guess I can quit....

---

19 June 1944
Somewhere in England

Dear Mom and Pop:

Just thought I would drop you a line on "Father's Day." I hope you received my cablegram.... I am feeling just fine.

Whenever I am on pass and have the time I go over to visit that Jewish family that I wrote Becky about. They are grand people and I enjoy myself there very much. They are a young couple with a son about five years old. The last time I was there, I telephoned before I came over and he talked to me on the phone. I laughed because he said to me:—"Don't bring me any candy, gum or no nottin." But I did anyway. His parents never know just what to do for me. His mother asks me every time if she can give me something that I don't get in the army. Last time I was there she made me hot chocolate with milk and of course that is a treat because the only milk we get is in our coffee or tea and then it is powdered. She was so happy to think she could give me something that I couldn't get in the army. But anyway — the army feeds us well and the calcium tablets I take make up for the milk.

This next letter contains Mollie's first mention of the D-Day invasion. Once the military operations were sufficiently advanced, the restrictions surrounding the events in France were relaxed and mail to the soldiers overseas began to flow more freely.

22 June 1944
Somewhere in England

Dear Jackie:

...Well, yesterday I hit the jackpot and received 10 letters all together. I imagine I will be getting mail more regularly now since the invasion is well on its way.

Did I tell you I graduated from a size ten suit to a size twelve? I just received my suit from alternations — just had to alter the skirt a bit — nothing to be done to the jacket. I know that Mom would be interested in that — I still weigh about 110 or 112.... Am glad that you enjoy the papers and magazines I send you and I shall continue to send them every once in a while. Of course, there is a lot I wish I could write you — but will have to wait until I get home.

Somewhere in England
26 June 1944

Dear Beck,

Yes, D Day was quite a day here and we all had a peculiar feeling — probably more so than the people back home because we were closer to it.

By the way, would you tell Mom to make some Korjeclach[3] (don't know how to spell it but you get the idea). I think the oatmeal kind are the best.... Pack them well — ask someone who knows about packing cookies for overseas. If they are not packed well, they crumble....

In case you didn't receive my last letter (I don't recall which one) I asked for some Sanders candy, chocolate and hard candies, and if it is not too difficult to procure — gum, too.

The date of the next letter is July 4th, Independence Day. In the Army it was just another working day although the WACs did have a special lunch in honor of the occasion.

Somewhere in England
4 July 1944

Dear Beck:

Just dropping you a few lines to let you know I am okay and feeling fine

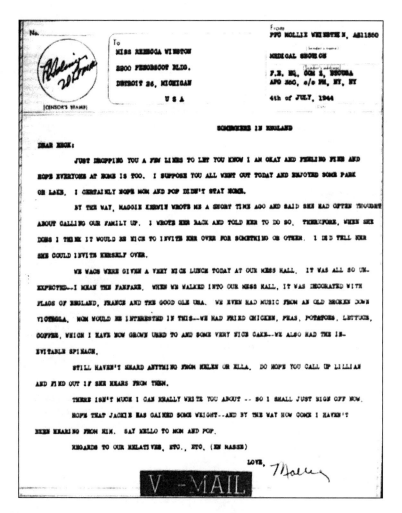

Mollie's letter to Beck dated July 4, 1944, written on V-mail. The initials of the censor are in the upper left hand corner.

and hope everyone at home is too. I suppose you all went out today and enjoyed some park or lake....

We WACs were given a very nice lunch today at our Mess Hall. It was all so unexpected — I mean the fanfare. When we walked into our Mess Hall it was decorated with flags of England, France and the good ole USA. We even had music from an old broken victrola. Mom would be interested in this— we had fried chicken, peas, potatoes, lettuce, coffee, which I have now grown used to and some very nice cake — we also had the inevitable spinach.

...There isn't much I can really write you about — so I shall just sign off now.

Somewhere in England
11 July 1944

Dear Beck:

...you know I was wearing my hat when I received the letter — and I really held on to my hat when I read that Pop finally retired.... I rather regret that it isn't possible for me to be home so we could all go out to South Haven for a few weeks as we had planned.... Please note APO number above. That is my up-to-date address.

Nothing much to say other than I am getting along fine and still enjoy my work.

---

15 July 1944
Somewhere in England

Dear Beck:

Yes, Beck, I was mighty lucky to get that pass after D-Day, and I did go the Thursday following D-Day. It seemed as though I was the only WAC traveling.... Yep, I was out with the Sgt. again. He's awfully nice.

By the way, in today's mail I received a letter from that Sgt. that I met out in Hollywood [Charles Knotts] and with whom I have been corresponding right along — well guess where he is— of course, in England. He says "somewhere in England." However, I know where it is but don't think he will be able to get a pass to see me as they have cut out passes for the time being for that distance....

Food features prominently in the next few letters. Mollie's experiences shed light on the way that the civilian population in England had to adapt to food rationing and the shortages or even complete absence of everyday foods, such as eggs, which most Americans would take for granted. The very high price that was being asked for a single, fresh peach reflects the rarity of any fruits or vegetables which were not native to England and would either have to be imported or grown in hothouses. The shortages, hardships and dangers which surrounded American soldiers stationed overseas made them value little treats from home such as familiar brands of candy.

> Somewhere in England
> 18 July 1944

Dear Beck:

Just dropping you a line to let you know that I am just fine and hope everyone home is too....

Last night I went out with my Sgt. friend and we had a delightful time. We were entertained by a friend of his, a British woman connected with the govt. We had dinner out in the garden. Of course, she apologized for the food, but it was really very good. The main course was some sort of roasted mushroom and egg (powdered — very difficult to have fresh eggs) affair. We sat out in the garden until quite late and ate cherries and cookies.

Wednesday night, which happens to be my birthday —'member?— we (Sgt. and I) are going to the cinema to see a play.

This is a little note by way of interest — one day I happened to be somewhere where they were featuring fresh fruit in the way of peaches— guess what the price was—(British money system) 7 and 6 — which is 7 shillings and 6 pence for ONE PEACH. (AMERICAN EQUIVALENT about $1.50) Tell that to Mom. I know she would be interested.

Am rather busy so guess I will get back to work....

> 22 July 1944
> Somewhere in England

Dear Beck:

...Had a very nice time on my birthday. By the way, I even received a box of candy from Sanders on my birthday. It was a two pound box. In it there was a card "Merry Xmas." It seems it came from that fellow from Detroit, the one whom I met when I used to wait for my ride in the morning. Anyway I haven't corresponded with him since January and at that time he said he had a box (5 lb) of candy being sent me, which I never received. Anyhoo, I noticed the postmark had May 29th on it. Can't quite figure out the situation.

The candy didn't look up to par as it had traveled to Wilmington, Calif. and then to Georgia, New York and on to England. However, one of the girls said she would sample it — really it was good—consequently there is none left. So— how about sending some candy, gum, etc....

In this letter Mollie is able to tell her family about her experiences with Doodlebugs. These were Hitler's "fantastic flying weapons" which were launched in the summer of 1944 after the D-Day invasion. Germany directed more than 10,000 jet- and rocket-propelled missiles against London and other population centers in England. They were called V-1 and V-2 missiles — *Vergeltung swaffen*— retaliation weapons. The jet powered V-1 missiles were noisy and slow so the British air defenses were able to shoot down many of them. The V-2 rocket, on the other hand, silent and traveling at high speeds, was more destructive. These missiles continued to plague England until the war was almost over and the Allies had captured or destroyed most of the launching sites.[4] Several Doodlebugs fell on British soil on June 13, 1944. Only one appeared to land in London but it damaged a bridge and demolished houses.[5]

26 July 1944
London, England

Dear Beck:

By the way, I wasn't going to write to say I was in London (that is where I am stationed) because I knew you would all worry — and if you promise not to say anything to Mom and Pop, I will reveal a few interesting items.

Restrictions on the Doodlebug situation as far as our mail is concerned have been lifted somewhat since Churchill's speech.[6] In fact, I could have written a few weeks ago about it but held off. But now I have gotten to a point where I feel a lot of those people back home, who sit back complacently, ought to know that there is a real war going on, and Beck, I see it every day. The air raid sirens are a frequent sound to us during the day as well as the night. And, it means the real thing over here — those damn buzz bombs come a floating round. They have been our unwelcome visitors both day and night since approximately one week after D-Day.

I am sure that many of the people I write to think because I write only of the pleasant things that there is nothing else that enters into our little lives. I don't believe that the people back home can grasp any part of the situation over here. For some unknown reason, I know it just doesn't penetrate.

However, the wonderful thing about it all is this one fact that will certainly defeat the other side and soon, too— we continue with our work. Work goes on as usual, which, of course, is something that the Axis are totally unprepared for.

I, of course, have many incidents to relate, which will have to wait until I see you, however, this one, through the courtesy of the censor, I know, you will find interesting. One night after a particularly busy day at the office, I was sleeping most soundly at our billets. It happened to be during the early days of those confounded "things." Well, anyway, their roar was terrific and yet I slept.

THE JEWISH NEWS   Friday, August 11, 1944

:IETY

iam Drive enter-
ome, in honor of
, The guests in-
Mrs. Jason Honi-
Mrs. Maurice Ja-

d are vacationing

do Ave. have re-

return this week-
ilis.

lotel are visiting

n Dr. and their
returned from a

ter, Bunnie, have

home in Grand
ifelson of Oak Dr.
of Cortland Ave.
ey will be guests

Chicago Blvd. are

returned from 21
v weeks furlough
of Birwood Ave.,
Tex,

', is visiting her
: Apt.
if Canterbury Dr.

ng Field, D. C., is
isses Solomons of
: Fairview, Mich.,

r of Calvert Ave.
n Atlantic City.
ater have left for
leyers who is sta-

iree small daugh-
inac Island.

Drive will be at
onor of the recent
n Emery.
id Arthur Lee, of
f., to make their

risit in New York

voix.

rd and Ralph, are

and Nancy, have
, Frankfort, Mich.

t Jews
l Medals
oic Feats

nan and Selling
oim Cited for
Under Fire

. Jewish members
Forces this week

Pvt. Ed Wishnetsky Serves in England

Pvt. Edward Wishnetsky, 24, assigned to the glider artillery, has been overseas for six months and is now stationed in England.

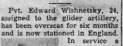

In service a year and a half, Pvt. Wishnetsky, who studied at New York University, was associated with his father, who is the largest distributor in the country of Manischewitz prod-

Pvt. Wishnetsky ucts.

He is the son of Mr. and Mrs. Morris Wishnetsky of the Bronx, N. Y. He was married in March, 1941, to Evelyn Sandra Hordes, daughter of Mr. and Mrs. William Hordes of 2308 Calvert Ave. They have a 7-year-old son, Richard Steven.

Pvt. Wishnetsky's younger brother, Theodore, entered active Army service three months ago.

Pvt. Wishnetsky's father is at present visiting in Mt. Clemens and Detroit.

Cpl. Milton London In Santa Fe, N. M.

In service for 14 months, Cpl. Milton Harold London, son of Mr. and Mrs. Julius London of 18105 Parkside Ave., is now stationed at Bruns General Hospital, Santa Fe, N. M., and is attached to the military personnel branch.

A graduate of Central High School and the **Cpl. London** 1936 class of the University of Michigan, where he majored in economics, Cpl. London was in the theater business here before entering active service.

He was married to the former Evelyn Morris on July 4, 1940. Mrs. London's mother, Mrs. Nathan Lerner, is at present visiting with Cpl. and Mrs. London in Santa Fe.

First Lt. Maurice Levin, son of Mr. and Mrs. Meyer Levin of 3342 Fullerton Ave., is home on a 15-day leave. He has been in active service for three years and is in the Signal Corps, attached to the air corps.

Robot Interrupts 'Permanent'

Pfc. Mollie Weinstein Writes Of Experience in London

Pfc. Mollie Weinstein is among the Detroiters in service who has watched the deadly robots go over London and has experienced the shocks that accompany these horrible weapons Pfc. Weinstein, daughter of Mr. and Mrs. Joseph Weinstein of 2254 W. Euclid, is assigned to the Office of the Chief Surgeon and is stationed **Pfc. Weinstein** in London. She writes to her sister, Rebecca:

"The air raid sirens are a frequent sound to us during the day as well as the night. And, it means the real thing over here—those damn buzz boms come afloating around. They have been our unwelcome visitors both day and night since approximately one week after D-Day."

Felt For "Dog Tags"

Stating that "I have gotten to a point where I feel a lot of people back home, who sit back complacently, ought to know that there is a real war going on," she recounts the following experience:

"One night, after a particularly busy day at the office, I was sleeping most soundly at our billets. It happened during the early days of those confounded 'things'. Their roar was terrific, yet I slept. I noticed a heavy feeling on my head and awoke drowsily to feel my bunk mate holding on to my hand and sitting on my bed; she had placed my helmet on my head and we both listened for the motor to shut off. Fortunately it didn't land where we expected it to. You can bet your boots we both felt to see if we were wearing our dog tags."

The Children's Evacuation

The women will be especially interested in this experience, also recorded by Pfc. Weinstein:

"Another time when I was getting a permanent in a particularly popular section for those Doodlebugs to land, the imminent danger signal went off for that particular vicinity. Those whistles started going off right in the middle of the hair cutting and I looked like 'madame Zulu' herself. The hair cutting stopped immediately. He (the hair cutter) took me to a particularly sheltered spot on the stairway of his shop and away from windows

away. Then Mr. ... took me back to the beauty chair and continued with the handiwork."

The Detroit servicewoman writes that the sight that gives her a peculiar feeling "and really penetrates is when I see the bus loads of children being evacuated from London, being separated from their families and friends. But the children are singing and hooting and they wave to us as they pass us."

Officers to Attend Mt. Sinai Hospital Group's Luncheon

Army and Navy officers, prominent officials and community leaders will be guests of the Sinai Hospital Association at the annual donor luncheon at the Book Cadillac Nov. 8, it was announced this week.

Through the efforts of Mt. Sinai, a reception room has been set up at Percy Jones Hospital in Battle Creek.

The Red Cross unit continues to function regularly.

A B-24 Liberator bomber has been named for Mt. Sinai Assn. as a result of the successful War Bond drives. The association also assisted the drive for a PBY4 Navy plane conducted by Detroit Women's Council of U. S. Navy League.

Members of the association serve at the Navy Recruiting Canteen headed by Commander Esther Gitlin.

The medical department of the Detroit Naval Armory was presented with a short wave diathermy machine by the Mt. Sinai Assn.

Reservations for the Nov. 8 luncheon are being taken by Mrs. Max Schubiner, TR. 1-6044; Mrs. Charles Gitlin, TO. 8-5466; Mrs. Jacob Harvith, UN. 3-0191.

Clipping from the *Detroit Jewish News* in which Mollie describes her experiences of dodging the Doodlebugs in London (courtesy *The Detroit Jewish News*).

I noticed a heavy feeling on my head and awoke drowsily to feel my bunk mate holding on to my hand and sitting on my bed; she had placed my helmet on my head and we both listened for the damn motor to shut off and fortunately it didn't land where we expected it to. You can bet your boots we both felt to see if we were wearing our dog tags. Another time when I was getting a permanent in a particularly popular section for those Doodlebugs to land, the imminent danger signal went off for that particular vicinity. (The imminent danger signal is usually a whistle that goes off in your particular vicinity and that means it is just about overhead. That is different from an air raid siren.) Well, those darn old whistles started going off right in the middle of his hair cutting and I looked just like a portrait of the old "Madame Zulu" herself. Naturally the hair cutting stopped immediately. He took me to a particularly sheltered spot on the stairway of his shop and away from any windows of any type. Of course, we did feel a jar when the damn thing hit not too far away. Then Mr._____ took me back to the beauty chair and continued with the handiwork. When he put me under the machine for the permanent, he told me if there was another imminent danger signal, that he would disentangle me from the contraption. But I was most rash—I said I would take a chance and go through—regardless. (I really don't think my hair is worth such a rash statement but I trusted to luck and the imminent danger signal did not go off while I was in the beauty shop.)

Another sight always gives me a peculiar feeling and really penetrates—when I see the bus loads of children being evacuated from London to safer places, having separated from their family and friends. However, during the early days of the buzz bombing, I happened to see and hear many bus loads of these children being evacuated. They were singing and hooting and waved to us as they passed us on the streets.

By the way, for obvious reasons, that family whom I used to see [the Roth family] has moved from London....

Well, Beck, I am enclosing in this envelope another letter addressed to Jackie [see letter below also dated July 26, 1944] and that is the letter Jackie can read to Mom and Pop.... Taking it all in all, it really is a great experience and certainly makes one appreciate the good old USA more than you can realize. I know you are anxious about me—but don't be because for some reason I am most calm about it. Even if I had the opportunity to go home right now, I don't believe I would take it—no—not until this war is really over.

...Beck, if I don't write too often don't worry but I am awfully busy and just don't get the opportunity to write. However, please keep writing to me anyway.

Mollie refers in the next letter to Ella Marcus, a friend who enlisted in the Army before Mollie did and was stationed in North Africa. Ella had been sent to one of the American Red Cross–staffed rest homes which were located in Great Britain for soldiers who had seen too much combat and were in need of a rest and change of scenery. These rest homes were located in large country estates.[7]

26 July 1944
Somewhere in England

Dear Jackette:

By the way, I received a very interesting letter from Ella and she is at a WAC Rest Camp taking it easy and enjoying herself. Of course, she would like to get home as she has been overseas so long. But she says she doesn't know if she will get the opportunity, however, other girls in her company have been going home by rotation. My latest sightseeing venture was Richmond and Hampton Court. We had a beautiful ride on the Thames River from Richmond to Hampton Court. We were able to go through Hampton Court, which is a palace, built in the reign of Henry VIII by the Archbishop of York in 1514. Anyway, I shan't go into detail about this as I am sending you a few folders on it. (I went there Sunday, 23 July.)

…Please excuse the briefness of this letter but I am rather busy.

In this letter, Mollie expresses frustration that some of her friends back home seemed to think that her life and the lives of the other WACs were carefree and full of fun instead of realizing that she was trying to spare her loved ones anxiety by writing only of cheery things. Many of the WACs felt this way and did their best to avoid including any distressing news in their letters home.[8]

SOMEWHERE IN ENGLAND (London)
29 July 1944

CONFIDENTIAL LETTER, BECK, and WHAT
I MEAN CONFIDENTIAL! MAYBE YOU OUGHT
TO BURN THIS WHEN YOU GET THROUGH.
CERTAINLY DON'T PASS IT AROUND!

Dear Beck:

Just received your letter of 19 June yesterday — so next time either send

V-mail or airmail as it certainly takes too long for regular mail. Somehow or other I really prefer airmail if you have time. In your letter you ask me to mark letters that are really personal as such, which I have done here. In your letter you speak about Minnie [a good friend of Beck and the sister of Mollie's former boyfriend, Aaron H.] saying I am lonesome and spreading rumors around. On the contrary, Beck, I thought she thought I was having a gay, old time in Merrie England. In fact, that is the reason I wrote my special letter, dated (I believe) 26 July, to you. However, maybe the mail hasn't been coming in chronological order, and somehow things get "screwed up." However, after I write to you an excerpt from Minnie's last letter (5 July) you will realize why I got so damn mad:

> So you're enjoying yourself. Well, why not make hay while the sun shines. There certainly is nothing here. Regarding Aaron writing, he told me he doesn't have anything to write if the girl isn't interested in him…. However, he sends his best regards to you and hopes you are making the most of everything.

Furthermore, you know me, I wouldn't under any circumstances write anyone in Detroit and say I was lonesome. As I once made a pact with you, if you will remember way back, I said that only you would get a true picture of anything.

…I shouldn't be taking off this time to write you because I am busy but I just had to get it all off my chest. Now, Beck, definitely do not show this letter to Sarah and the rest of the gang. I know there will be a temptation on your part to do so—but it will just involve things. Don't you think? You will agree with me that this is a really confidential letter—eh what?

…Will have to admit we are still dodging "Doodlebugs" over here—but we can take it.

…If you think Mom and Pop can take it—you might release a little information to them—but frankly speaking you know how excited Pop gets—so maybe you had better let the subject alone.

The newspaper clippings that Mollie refers to in the letter below were from Danny Raskin's column in the *Detroit Jewish News*, which devoted a considerable amount of space at this time to reports of Mollie's exploits overseas.

1 August 1944
London, England

Dear Beck:

Received your letter of 17 July with the two newspaper clippings. Sure enjoyed your letter. Had lots of news in it. Don't know if you picked me out but that sure is me. I showed the picture to the girl who was in front of me and she was positively thrilled. We all look so kooky in that photo. Raskin sure is giving me plenty of space in his column. (Please excuse all the "sures" in this paragraph as I just noted I am giving that word "free play" and I am in a rush trying to get this off to you.) Very busy.... Will keep the clippings a few days and then send them on to you.

...As for the Xmas package — I will think of a few things and write you what I want. However, at all times candy is welcome — just as a start. In fact, I would like a box of candy every month if you can possibly make it.

...I have a camera that I borrowed and am trying to get film — I believe 620 for it. I have a sailor friend — very nice boy I met when I first came over — he is supposed to try to get some. Next time you send me a package if you can get film, send me a couple of rolls. I don't believe it makes any difference what size either 620 or 120 because I can scout around to see if one of the kids has a camera. However, the one I borrowed belongs to an English gal and I won't be able to keep it more than a week or so.

...Yes, we are still dodging "Doodlebugs." Am still seeing the Sarge.

This next letter is from Mollie's sister, and it reveals some of the effects of the war on American civilians back home. Although Mollie sought to protect her family from distressing news, the fact that she revealed confidential details to her sister put Beck in a difficult situation and there were clearly some times when Beck felt that she had to share some of the information she received from Mollie with the rest of the family. In this letter Beck also refers to an argument with her good friend, Minnie, about Mollie's personal life and her motivations for joining the WAC. Minnie's assumption that Mollie enlisted in order to find a man was one made by many Americans about the women who served in uniform during the war.[9] Beck also reveals that their father, who had recently retired, had taken a job as a riveter in a local factory in order to support the war effort. The factory's willingness to hire a man of retirement age indicates the extent of the labor shortage during the war.

Detroit, Michigan
August 4, 1944

Dear Mollie:

Ma and Pa know about your letter of the 26th. I felt it would be better that they should as they keep inquiring. Also I had shown your letter to Dena, the girl at the Jewish News and she asked permission to show it to Mr. Slomovitz, the editor. He begged me to allow him to use some of it. He said it was so interesting and after all you can't be an ostrich about such things. I will try to send you the clipping. By the way, any clippings that you have and want to send on, perhaps you had better do so and I will save them.

Your confidential letter of the 29th arrived yesterday morning, in 5 days. That certainly is remarkable. I am glad you told me about the straight mail. I just did that sort of experiment and wanted to know how long it takes.

...Prior to receiving your confidential letter, I seem to have had it out with Minnie. Nothing serious and we are still the best of friends.... Somehow or other our conversation always turns on you and I showed her some of your letters and the dandy picture that Ben had sent of you. Then she started saying something about Aaron. I guess that was after I had casually mentioned the fact that you had not been hearing from him, etc. "Well" she said, "Mollie is not interested. Aaron is not a kid and he wants to get married. He liked Mollie a lot but she did not seem interested".... Then she said something about your probably finding someone over there, again inferring that that was your whole scheme....

Ma and Pa are getting along fine except that Pa has had nothing much to do and walks around from "shmunya to bunya" [a Yiddish phrase meaning wandering from place to place with no purpose] (do you get it?) but today he went out and got himself a job, of all things, riveting. I think it is a DeSoto plant, but he has to go to school first and learn!!!

You know, Mollie, even though your letters previous to the July 26th were merely of social activities, I felt all along that you were in or very near London, because of the frequent times you spoke of having been there on pass. The papers at this time, of course, are filled with the numerous and constant robot bombings and the fact that they seem to be more frequent than less. We naturally are concerned and would appreciate hearing from you as often as possible.

...Lots of love and instead of saying "Keep 'Em Flying," I guess I had better say "Keep Dodging 'Em."

Dodging the Doodlebugs was a normal part of Mollie's everyday existence by this time. Like most of those living in England, Mollie became so accustomed to the attacks that she would ignore the warnings and continue going about her daily activities.

LONDON, ENGLAND
11 August 1944

Dear Beck:

This paragraph you can leave out for Mom and Pop. Anyhoo, this morning while slapping on my make-up, we had a couple or three of those Doodle-bugs glide over our billets or close enough to feel a vibration, which I can assure you was most uncomfortable — but did I stop my make-up — no! Anyway, we did hear two of them land. In other words, if the people back in the States think this war is already over, I do think they are a bit mistaken.

During the week Mirko Roth (Zuzana's husband) came into London. The Sarge, Mirko and I went out to dinner and then walked over to Hyde Park and took in the fresh air, along with the hot air (listening to the soap box orators of Hyde Park). They still don't have a very definite address, however, I will write you as soon as I get something more definite and tell you what to send them.... Zuza (*Zuzana*) wrote me a very nice letter several weeks ago and I have actually been so busy that I haven't gotten around to answering it but must today or tomorrow.

...Don't want you to worry now — or else I won't write you of the interest-ing (?) things — so will sign off now....

This was Mollie's last letter from England but she gave no inkling that she was about to leave for her next assignment, as the movements of service person-nel were kept secret. Mollie's next letter to her family was dated August 19, 1944, and was written when she was living in the tents and the mud in Nor-mandy.

PART THREE : FRANCE

6. Camping in the Fields of Northern France: Normandy
August–September 1944

In August 1944, after four months in London, Mollie moved with the ETO (European Theater of Operations) Forward Echelon to Normandy, just as the fighting resulting from the D-Day landings in June was subsiding. The Allies chose Normandy for their invasion of occupied France because of its 35 mile beach front and because of its location near good roads which provided ready access to the interior of France.[1] Although many troops were lost on both sides in the fierce battles, by the time that Mollie arrived the Allies were making great strides in claiming the area and the German armies in the region were on the brink of total destruction. Field Marshal Gunther von Kluge, who had assumed command of the German forces in France, realized that his forces were fighting a losing battle and committed suicide on August 18, 1944, leaving behind a written plea to Hitler to bring an end to the war.[2]

The first WACs to land in Normandy started arriving in boats on July 14, 1944, and were assigned to Forward Echelon, Communications Zone. They camped out in an apple orchard and slept in shelters or tents on Army cots, living in the mud and the cold.[3] Mollie enjoyed these experiences and did not seem to mind the primitive conditions that she and the other WACs had to endure, which included taking "baths" in their helmets[4] as there were no bathing or shower facilities available. Although her living conditions were less than ideal, Mollie always wanted to look her best, especially when going out on a date during her off-duty hours. Make-up in particular acted as a psychological boost and Mollie frequently referred to using cosmetics in the letters she wrote while in Normandy. Along with many of her fellow WACs, Mollie felt it was important to look feminine even when working in what was essentially a man's world.[5]

It was in Normandy that Mollie first started using her high school French, often acting as an interpreter when she and her friends wanted to speak to the local people. French and Americans alike often encouraged Mollie to use her French and told her that they enjoyed hearing her speak the language.

Some of Mollie's friends from London moved with her to France and their camaraderie continued as they faced new challenges. Familiar faces in Normandy included Smitty, Johnnie and Bats, three of Mollie's roommates in London, and the Sarge, Alex Korody, who continued to work with her in the office.

* * *

Somewhere in France
19 August, 1944

Dear Beck:

Comment allez-vous? Oui, c'est vrai que nous sommes en France. Je suis tres heureise ici. [How are you? Yes, it's true we're in France. I am very happy here.[6]]

It's so different over here from what I have been used to that you cannot imagine. I am over here with the same group that I was with in London. There's so much to tell you that I just don't know where to begin — so I shall begin in the middle — as usual!

If I give you a description of my first date here, you will certainly be amused at our life here. My girl friend (the one who is a draftsman) and I were asked out for a date to drink cider. That's about all there is to do out here. These boys are a couple of Sergeants that I know very well from London. After work we had mess. It's such a cute set-up. We eat in mess kits and stand in a line about a mile long. Boys and girls together. Everything is in tents. However, most of us get our food and then eat it in the grass in a large open field. So we ate with our friends. Then we stood in the line to wash our mess kits.

Then we made our appointment definite with the boys—"we'll meet you in front of the Chateau." Smitty (my girl friend) and I dashed back to get dressed — as follows: a quick wash in cold water with our helmets used as a wash basin. We brushed out leggings and shoes. (We wear the clothes that you saw me pictured in). Use a clothes brush to get some of the sand, etc. out of our clothes. Put our make-up on with a mirror propped up on a tree. Put on the liner of our helmets (boys and girls wear that instead of overseas caps). Grabbed our canteen cups (we are not permitted to use the French drinking cups). Use some of my "stinkem" [perfume]—"tweed" [brand of perfume popular in the 1940s]—this time and dashed off to meet our friends in front of the Chateau.

We had a wonderful time, Beck. We each had only one canteen cup of cider. But you know me — that's sufficient. I was the only one in the group who could speak (?) French (?) and you should have heard me carry on a conversation. The boys sure got a kick out of it. They want to drag me around everywhere.

Yep, Beck, we live in tents—with hot and cold—air. Am in a tent with four very swell girls. It's amazing but all of us enjoy it out here very much. It's a bit rugged but certainly far more healthful than London. And, as you know London had many aspects which we didn't care about and besides I really have seen everything there. I do hope to keep in contact with the Roth family and have written Zuzana (Mrs. Roth). Am acquiring a bit of a tan being in the open constantly and my city pallor has dwindled.

Now to answer your letter of 1 August written on legal sized scratch paper. Yes, Beck, I sure will have lots to tell you when I get back about the doodlebugs, etc.—No, I don't care if Mr. Slomovitz [editor of the *Detroit Jewish News*] wants to use that letter—because it sure is true and not one bit exaggerated! Do Mom and Pop know that I was in London? Did you tell them all? I just wonder. You can now tell them because I'm away from it all now....

This next letter is one that Mollie received from John McNeil Burns, a prominent attorney in Detroit and her sister's employer. Mr. Burns had a son, Jack, whom he mentions in the letter, who was also serving in the armed forces at this time. This letter demonstrates the way that the experiences of the men and women who were serving overseas during the war were shared within their home communities, not only among family but also among friends, neighbors and work colleagues.

To PFC Mollie Weinstein, a Grand Girl Overseas
Dear Mollie:

If you are surprised to receive a letter from me, it is because you do not realize how much better I feel I know you than I ever did when you were home. You see, Mollie, I get your sister to read to me at least parts of almost every letter you write. So I know a lot about your experiences, your reactions to what you are doing and what you think, more than you would imagine. I find myself asking your sister if she has heard from you. The other night when I left the office I saw a red jacket hanging on the clothes tree. I told Rebecca that it looked like Mollie, and she said it was. So you see, in lots of ways I know you better than you think I do.

It was nice of you to send me a card. Now I hear you have sent one to Jack. As you know, he is still in this country. As long as he is doing necessary work here, I am glad he has not been shipped out yet.... He is so disappointed not to be in a combat plane that I am glad he has something really interesting to work at. I am sure that he will be glad to hear from you.

Your sister, your family and your friends are interested in hearing about all of the little things you do as well as the big ones. They are proud of you and know that you are a grand girl, Mollie, and so is your sister. At times I have had quite a job persuading her that someone has to stay here to do the essential work. I am almost afraid that if you had not advised her to stick to her law that she too would have been in the service. She has been with me so long and has always taken such an interest in the things that we do every day that she has come to be more and more like an associate rather than an employee. She introduced me one day a while ago as the man she works for, and I told her to say as the man she works with. I am proud of her work and her marks in school. I think that you both have one thing in common, and that is that it never enters your mind to do other than the best that can be done whatever you tackle.

I do hope, Mollie, that you can keep some sort of a diary. When you think of the things that have happened to you in the past year that never happened before and never will again, it is really quite thrilling. Can you tell us any more about your work? The Nazis seem to be getting hell right now and we are all hoping as hard as we can that the Doodlebug factories are blown sky high and the fiends that operate them go along with them.

You really write clever letters, Mollie. Observation and expression seem to come to you naturally. Good luck and good-bye.

Sincerely yours,
John McNeil Burns
August 20, 1944

In the next several letters, Mollie explained to her sister in more detail about her everyday life "somewhere in France." Even living in such rugged conditions, Mollie always wanted to appear at her best and was eager to secure a steady supply of perfume and nail polish, even though she only had a few changes of clothes to wear. She also continued to enjoy a busy social life and was obviously much in demand as a date for the male soldiers nearby.

Somewhere in France
21 August 1944

Dear Beck:

Really wish I had time to detail our present existence to you. One of these days I shall. Life is really rugged out here, but I enjoy every bit of it. We eat, sleep, and work in the open. I even wear long underwear!! Can you feature that? Yesterday I wore arctic boots. When it rains, it's very muddy so we sure are glad to have those "dainty gun boats." (We work seven days a week — with one-half day off sometimes to do our washing so that it will dry in the sunshine — when it shines.)

Yesterday, wearing those charming "habiliments" including galoshes with mud draped all over (glamorous wouldn't you say), I turned down four dates. Had to re-arrange my duffel bag, my bed, etc. for inspection today. We live out of our duffel bags — which is pretty tough if you know what a duffel bag is like. Every time I want some article of clothing, it's at the very bottom!

If anyone thinks this is a soft life, they are NUTS. However, Beck, frankly I am enjoying every bit of it. (as above mentioned).

---

22 August 1944

Dear Beck:

Last night the mud was so deep, etc. etc. that we didn't even go out to mess. We have a little stove and we built a nice little fire and cooked up some K rations and C rations[7] and had a nice supper. One of the girls had gotten four fresh eggs and we really had a treat. Back in England we would have fresh eggs about once every two weeks but I believe it will be much easier for us to get fresh eggs here. Especially since I speak French, all the kids want me to go out with them to trade cigarettes, etc. with the French people for eggs. I will no doubt be inveigled to go out bartering one of these fine evenings.

This noon my gal friend and I were most fortunate. Instead of trudging thru the mud we got a ride back to work in an ambulance.

This, Beck, is really overseas living — especially when I think of taking a bath out of our helmets

Mollie, right, and Bats in Valagnes, Normandy, August 1944.

and bracing up a mirror against a tree to put on our make-up and comb our hair.

How about some candy, gum, etc. I do hope you can mail me that Parfum (L'Orle), and one bottle only of Revlon Windsor and remover (goodness knows when I shall use it but I do like to have it in case I feel in the mood to do my nails fancy even in these primitive surroundings.)...

Beck, I haven't rec'd any mail in the longest time. Just don't get any because of my moving around. Please make all my excuses but get them all to write me because eventually I will receive the mail.

SOMEWHERE IN FRANCE
25 August 1944

Dear Beck:

Still here, Beck, however, please note the address above. We are stuck out in the woods and as yet I have not received any mail here and I believe even my mail to you must be going out slower but do have patience and write to me.

I really am enjoying this open air life, Beck, strange to say. You remember how I never liked to go out to camp — well this reminds me a lot of it, but yet I like it.

Our office had beautiful trees and ivy surrounding it. We have only to step out a few yards and we can pick blackberries that have ripened in the sun (when it does shine) — these bushes are used as hedges surrounding the offices.

You should have seen me get ready to go out on my date last night. You would have really laughed. First I took a cold shower (am used to that by now — we are having hot water installed within a couple of days). I got all dressed in my goofy combat clothes and put on a fresh pair — never-been-worn leggings, which made me feel dressed up. I hung my mirror out on the limb of a tree and put on the "war paint." Fixed my hair, with my bobby pins hanging out of my mouth and a comb in one hand and brush in the other. Put on a few dashes of Cologne to make me feel I wasn't a soldier; put on my helmet liner; grabbed my flashlight; canteen and cup and off I went for my date at 8 P.M. — which consisted of a hike (busman's holiday)[8]; a chat under the apple tree; picked up some cider for the gals at my tent; threw in a few French words with the natives and was back ready for bed by 10 P.M. So — Beck, with a healthful life like that, I really ought to be in the pink of condition, n'est ce pas [isn't it so]?

I know you are anxious to know what I want for Xmas. With my limited baggage space, I don't want a lot of junk. Candy, dried fruit, nuts and gum are most welcome. We cannot buy a thing around here. In fact, one of the boys was telling me after having gone into a large town around these parts, that candy, the Xmas hard candy variety that we can buy back in the states for about 30 cents lb. was $1.75 for ½ lb. So—as I said above sweets are most welcome and I like to pass them around to my pals too....

Mollie continued to find her French language skills very useful. Her ability to speak to the local people not only helped Mollie and her friends navigate the countryside and find places they were looking for, it also enabled her to learn more about the conditions which the French had to endure during the German occupation.

26 Aug 44

Dear Beck:

I had this letter kicking around my pocket and decided to add a little more. Last night Smitty (my gal friend, the draftsman) and I went out with a couple of Sgts. We stopped at a very nice farmhouse and the man who lived there gave us cider and wouldn't let the boys pay for anything. He gave us fresh figs and kept giving us more, not giving any to the boys—of course we gave them out to the boys, too. The old Frenchman kept saying: "Les filles Americaine sont tres jolies." [The American girls are very pretty.] Smitty and I kept laughing. We translated it to the boys. Then the Frenchman said: (to make the boys feel good) "Les soldats sont jolis." [The soldiers are pretty.] That really made us laugh. I learned a lot from that Frenchman—They hadn't had soap in 2 years; no sugar for months, and many other things, I learned.

Mollie and her friends used their off-duty hours to explore the local area and found it easy to entertain themselves with very simple activities.

27 Aug 44

Every time we went to a party in the old apple orchard. One of the boys had a victrola and we had apples fresh off the tree and someone had some cookies and peanuts. Lots of fun.

Still 27 Aug 44

We are working today but will get off around 4:30—maybe take in a swim if we find a place. Recd that swell box of Sanders 2 lbs chocolates. Thanks. Keep sending candy. Can always use it.... Still don't receive any mail.

Mail was the link to family and friends back home for all the servicemen and women overseas, and Mollie was no exception. As the war continued it was difficult for the postal directory unit to keep up with the volume of mail going in both directions and with the movement of the troops. It was estimated that the total of U. S. service personnel was about 7 million—but only the War Department knew the exact numbers. At one point the postal unit knew that they had at least 7,500 Robert Smiths.[9] As Mollie remarks in the next few letters, the mail would come in spurts and sometimes answers would cross in the mail.

28 August 1944
Somewhere in France

Dear Beck:

Certainly wonderful to receive mail. These last few days have been receiving about six letters a day. Received four letters of August 4, 11, and 19 and Jackie's screwy letter of the 9th. Received Jackie's letter last night and read it by flashlight. I went into hysterics over it. (I hope Jackie won't mind my answering his letter by incorporating in this one to you. You see at this moment I am busy not only in the office but other mail, too. I know there is a lot more mail that I haven't received because the letters that I did receive seemed to be from those that hadn't written for some time and then the letters trailed me forever so long.)

I will answer your letters chronologically.—4 Aug. ... Thank Sarah again for that candy. I will probably be receiving it soon—as everything comes along in bunches around here—mail and packages. I received a letter from Sid [Cohen—a friend from Detroit] telling me that he was in England and wanting me to look him up—but I guess I won't get a chance to and probably won't see him until the end of the war. I will write him soon. I sure get a kick out of Pa working as a riveter. That probably has been his secret passion all along and being an inspector too—what do you know....

Beck, I received one box Sanders chocolate from Mom & Pop. **Thanks. Received another box chocolate who was that from.... By the way, I really could use some Kleenex if you can get some.

Jackie's letter.... Above mentioned I did enjoy it a lot and hope he finds time to write me some more... Am glad that he got into Law School. Who's the gal in South Haven?

...Have I answered everything so far? Hope so. Let me know if not. Don't bother about sending me underwear...And when we wash it and hang it out on the line—better it should be khaki and not pink as it camouflages better in army color. (Ha! And I'm not kidding)...

Here's my usual request for candy, dried fruit, nuts, etc., in other words we can't get anything other than our three meals a day around here and four candy bars a week — no ice cream sodas, no cookies, no nuttin'.

By the way — yesterday afternoon we were out — my friend Smitty and two Sgts (You know who?) were looking for a place to swim. We met a number of French people who were ambling down the highway.[10] My friend asked directions of the men and I talked (?) with the French women. The children looked sort of hungry — I couldn't resist so I passed around the Sanders candy — was saving it for our picnic but decided to let the French people in on it. I know they all enjoyed the candy. The woman was holding a baby in her arms and it didn't look more than 6 months old — I almost fell over when the woman said it was 20 months old. My friend passed out cigarettes to the men and I think everyone was happy. We couldn't find a spot for swimming but did find a beautiful spot for wading and after eating our K-rations, we took off our shoes and socks and waded in the creek. There were cows and goats in the background but they didn't bother us — other than getting Smitty excited to the point where she threatened to milk the cows. She and my friend, the Sgt. decided to give it up when they walked close to one of the cows, helmet in hand and "she" (the cow) gave them a dirty look....

---

1 September 1944
Somewhere in France

Dear Beck:

Please note slight change in my address. In fact, you had better note my address in each letter as I go along. First of all, I want you to know I am feeling fine and although this life is a bit rugged with only the bare essentials at hand, am enjoying it. I am very busy at the office, however, will try to write you every spare moment that I have.

I am attaching a check, which was from the month of July and which I knew I wouldn't need — so I didn't bother to cash it. I have quite a bit of francs on hand, approximately $12.00 and we certainly have no place to spend it and I will be paid again very shortly.

Also, I am enclosing some French money, invasion money, as we call it, three 2 franc notes. A franc, by the way, is worth 2¢ — so each of these attached papers is worth 4¢. Keep these as souvenirs. I have a number of English coins that I will keep with me as souvenirs. Haven't come across any French coins as yet — but no doubt will soon.

By the way — last night Smitty (my gal friend) and I attended a USO [United Service Organizations] show. My friend the Sarge was there too. It was an outdoor show in the green fields in front of the Chateau and we all sat out

on the grass on our raincoats or what-have-you. There certainly weren't any
well known actors but the fellows were rather good. One of the boys sang
"Desert Song" and "Water Boy." He was excellent. There was a master of ceremonies, too, with the usual run of jokes…During the entire performance,
which was about two hours, a few stray sheep, dogs, and I think one lone cow
lurked in the background. A few times I thought we might have an animal
show instead — but the menagerie kept their place. Thank goodness! After all
you know I am a city gal!

　　By the way — I wish you would send a nice box of candy out to that family
I used to visit. Send it to his office address as follows….

Mirko Rot

Jugoslav Office

Kingston House

London, SW7, England

Please spell the last name that way as I believe that is the way he is addressed in
the office. You might send his wife, Zuzana, a couple pairs of silk hose….

　　…Au revoir for now and write. The mail is very slow getting here. Don't
get it too often. But keep on writing and do make my excuses if the people
back home don't hear from me because how can I write them when I don't get
their mail and also don't have time anyhoo.

　　One of the challenges of being stationed overseas in wartime was the
problem of finding suitable gifts and cards to send to family members to mark
special occasions. As Mollie explains in the next letter, the extensive rationing
in England meant that she had not been able to buy a birthday card in any
of the shops there to send to her brother, while in Normandy, of course, she
was not near any shops at all.

　　　　　　　　　　　　　　　　(Somewhere in France — Your Birthday 1944)

Dear Jackette:

　　"HAPPY BIRTHDAY!" When I was in London, I looked all over for an
appropriate card but nary a one — so I sent that little gift [a notebook] on to
you without a card but with an inscription in my own "iddie biddie" handwriting. Wouldn't you know that I would choose something goofy like that
for you but that was all I could find that didn't require coupons and also
was something in the way of a souvenir of "Merrie England." Hope you like
it.

---

3 Sept. 44

Well, Jackie, you would be amazed at our Saturday night dates around here. We went to the cinema (our tent show) and saw "Ladies Courageous." Wasn't bad, except the wind kept whistling through the leaks in the tent and the picture stopped about 3 or 4 times while they changed reels or else it broke down. (We were dressed in our usual *habiliments*—combat clothes, leggings, helmets, etc.) When we got out of the cinema, it was still early, shortly after 9 P.M. Of course, there is no ice cream parlor to go to around here so instead Smitty and I and the boys decided upon some fresh apples. But where to get them??? We have come to the point where we are not above going into someone's orchard to pick (steal???) apples—so we did. We picked a nice orchard and my friend and I sent Smitty (who's a real tomboy when it comes to climbing apple trees) and her friend as a sort of reconnaissance and the coast was clear so we went in. It was a lovely orchard and we made a good haul. In our mad scramble to get hold of a couple of luscious looking apples, I turned around to find Smitty missing. We were really hysterical with laughter when we discovered her in a prone position—she had fallen into a fox hole! We rescued her and then sneaked out of the orchard. We found an old horse trough and sat on the edge of it, each of us with knife in hand, peeling green apples and eating them. We, of course, reminisced of other Saturday evenings we had spent in the states. It was great fun anyway.

Today, back at the office working.

PS—Wonder how long it takes for you to get my letters—let me know re: dates. I haven't received a "stitch" of mail since I last wrote Becky telling her I had received some.—We really are out in the "sticks."

This was Mollie's last letter from Normandy. Although she was on the verge of another move, this time to Paris, she was not able to give her family any information that might disclose her current or future location. Mollie had seen a great deal of destruction and human suffering during the month that she spent in Normandy and was glad to be moving with the troops to Paris, which had recently been liberated from German occupation.

7. After the Liberation: Paris
September–October 1944

Mollie entered Paris in September 1944, just a few weeks after it was liberated from Nazi occupation on August 25th. After the basic living conditions in Normandy, Mollie and her fellow WACs were able to enjoy relative comfort and even occasional luxuries in Paris, where they were housed in a hotel[1] and were relieved of some of the tedious chores of Army life, such as KP (Kitchen Police). During the nearly ten months she spent in Paris, Mollie took advantage of the opportunities to see the sights of the city as well as to experience some of its nightlife. Although all public entertainment had ceased by August 17, 1944, as the German occupation of Paris ended,[2] once Paris was liberated, entertainment slowly returned to the city and Mollie discovered a love of opera. She was fascinated by the glamour and sophistication of Paris and the Parisians, and seemed to feel very much at home in the French capital. The city had not been destroyed during the German occupation (1940–1944). In 1940, Paris had been declared an "open city," which meant that it should not be attacked by either side, in the hope of protecting the city and its people from harm. As a result of this status, retreating French troops bypassed Paris and the German troops occupied it without facing any opposition and without firing on the city. The Germans intended to keep Paris alive because it was an ideal place to entertain occupation troops and soldiers on leave from other war zones. Maintaining a semblance of normal life in the city was also an attempt by Germany to pretend to the world that life under the Nazis could be good. However as the Allied liberation of Paris began, General Dietrich von Choltlitz, who was appointed to oversee the evacuation of the German troops from Paris, received orders to destroy the city if necessary. Fortunately he felt there was no military justification to do so and Paris was spared.[3]

But while most of the buildings and monuments of the city were still standing, the war had taken its toll on the people and the resources of France. Food, fuel, clothing and other basic items were in very short supply and rationing continued for some time. Those who had money could pay the very high prices charged in shops which Mollie referred to in her letters, as well

as the even higher black market prices. Many ordinary French people, however, suffered greatly in the months following the Liberation and their lives
were made even more difficult by the hard winter of 1944-45, when snow and
ice disrupted the transport of goods, exacerbating shortages and putting the
health of an already-undernourished population under further strain.[4] Mollie's
letters repeatedly refer to the conditions that the civilian population had to
endure and the hardships of the U.S. military personnel such as the frequent
lack of heating and hot water. However, for the most part, those in the American armed forces were protected from the worst of the local conditions, especially the food shortages. The Army provided food for its men and women
in uniform, who ate all their meals in mess halls.

As Mollie indicates at the end of the next letter, it was written on the
Jewish New Year and it was the first time that she had been away from home
on such a religious holiday. Although she was missing her home and her
family, in her letters Mollie tended to concentrate on cheerful matters and on
relating interesting and amusing anecdotes. Her ability to speak French continued to be of use as she was often called upon to translate for her friends
and work colleagues and even for complete strangers, as the first letters that
she wrote from Paris demonstrate.

* * *

PARIS — FRANCE
16 Sept. 1944

Dear Beck:

I wrote you a V-mail yesterday rather hurriedly and I couldn't say very
much in it, but today we are permitted to say PARIS. Yep, I am in Paris. It is a
lovely city and they really have welcomed us with open arms. If I said that
London was fascinating to me — Paris is even more so. The women's dresses
here, Beck, are really a dream. Tight waist and full skirted dresses, luscious
shades, beautiful lines, stunning suits and gorgeous chapeaux [hats] — what I
mean gorgeous! You know that I have been around, Beck, and I haven't seen
anything to compare with it — not even Hollywood. Perhaps I am waxing too
enthusiastic about it because I had been away from civilian clothes for a while
amusing (?) myself with the mud in France. But every day that I am here I find
myself more convinced that it is the fashion center — could be that I am
wrong — haven't been to New York. However, I must tell you one thing that
amuses me no end — that is seeing these beautifully dressed women riding
bicycles down the streets…. There are no buses running and no streetcars.
They do have a subway, which just started running again this week.

Continuing with stuff that is nearest and dearest to our hearts— their hairdos are also something out of this world. Am still working 7 days a week but eventually will probably get some time off and indulge in some beauty care — whee — after tent life, etc., etc., that we have gone through this is really heaven. Oh — by the way, don't bother to send me any cologne as you know Paris is the center for perfumes, cologne etc.... Really, Beck, there is so much perfume around here that sometimes I think that these French gals bathe in it. Many a time we have been strolling down the "main drag" — des Champs Ely-sees, and we have been almost knocked out of this world by the numerous scents that are wafted about as some French gals pass us by. My friend Smitty and I bought some "Le Numero Cinq" de Molyneus. It is a very small bottle and we paid 157 francs for it, which amounts to $3.14. I imagine it would be at least double that in the States. When I get a little more settled around here and PAID, and find that I can package this kind of stuff off to you, I may send you something. I am really not in need of money — it's just that we haven't been paid in a while and will be soon, though.

So many interesting incidents have occurred to me that I cannot relate all of them — but will a few. Yesterday, my friend Smitty and I were walking to our Hotel (wonderful accommodations) to eat and some little boy about five years old dashed up to me and grabbed my hand and pumped it up and down. He kept saying "How do you do? How do you do? How do you do? I am American too!" He was so cute. His daddy and little sister came up to me and his dad told me the little boy was born in USA. He spoke a little English and told me that he had lived in N.Y. for a short time and had been called back to France for their army, etc., etc.

I know that you wonder how I am getting along with the French language. Am doing wonderfully well. In fact, yesterday I acted as an interpreter. Last night a number of us went to the Arc de Triomphe. We wanted to go up into it and see the view of Paris but the gendarme [French military policeman] there said that we could not at that time as it was closed for the public — perhaps later he said. All that in French and he could not speak one word of English. Then we walked away. We didn't get very far when I heard a shuffling of feet and turned around — there was the gendarme making a "bee-line" for me with an Air Corps Captain in his tow. The Captain asked me if I could speak French and I said a little. He asked me to ask the gendarme several questions and I translated the answers. It was great fun and I understood everything. They were trying to determine whether our pilots had flown any planes under the Arc, which was against regulations. Anyway, the answer was no.

...am still seeing the same people connected with the office and it is won-derful being with all of my army friends. No, I am not working in a hospital — sorry, I cannot tell you much about my work other than the fact that it is medical, very interesting and we are very busy. You mentioned something about hose and in my V-mail yesterday I asked you to send me some — so please do. I haven't priced hose here but I imagine they are about $8.00 a pair and then I don't know if you need coupons for them. Anyway I certainly wouldn't be interested — they aren't worth more than our $1 hose. Also, I told you to send Suzanna[5] the two pair 8½. You can send them to her husband's business address. Be sure they are packaged well.

I suppose you wonder why I am always writing for stuff to eat. I imagine you have read in the papers about the food situation being so bad for the French. Well — there is nothing to buy in the way of food around here for the Americans— at this time, everything is rationed. Of course, you know, candy is impossible to get. We haven't even been able to get it at the PX — I think we are rationed to two bars a week — when they have it.— So send candy, etc. Anything in the way of food is more appreciated — and besides that — I have some nice pals that I like to share my packages with. Will admit the army does feed us rather well but the portions don't compare with what we have been used to. However, they will probably improve as time goes on and supplies come through more readily.

Have lots more to write but don't have time — in fact am finishing this 17 Sept.— HAPPY NEW YEAR to YOU, MOM, POP, and JACKIE....

As some elements of censorship began to be relaxed, Mollie was able to describe the places she had traveled through on her way to Paris and the extent of the damage caused by the Allied bombing before, during and after D-Day, which was targeted primarily at transportation links.[6] Towns in Normandy such as Caen, Saint-Lo, Valognes, Carentan and Montbourg ceased to exist.

In several of the letters she wrote to her family from Paris, including the next few reproduced here, Mollie used stationery that she found among the supplies that were left behind by the fleeing Germans. By using these symbols of the occupation, Mollie felt that she was demonstrating the extent of the Allied defeat of the German Army and emphasizing the freedom of the city of Paris and its citizens.

den 19 Sept. 1944

Dear Beck:

I know you will be greatly surprised to see this stationery and I don't blame you. You can really see that we have taken over in Paris, n'est-ce-pas [isn't it so]?

...I am so terribly busy at the office and yet feel that I must write home at least.

...By the way I don't think I shall bother to buy very much in Paris. This noon we walked down the main street, like Woodward Avenue [in Detroit], des Champs Elysees, and we were looking in the windows. One thing really struck me — in fact stunned me — a little pink slip — priced somewhere in the neighborhood of $56.00 and I am not kidding. I certainly wouldn't pay more than $3.95 for it!! Prices for clothing are way out of line.

...When you write Ruth Schaffer, please say hello for me. I haven't heard from her in ages...By the way, Sunday, in the vicinity of Notre Dame I saw an old man pushing a baby buggy. He was wearing a beret and honestly, Beck, he looked just like Uncle Osher. It made me feel a bit homesick. But you know me — not for long. Life is too interesting around here.

Another thing of interest that we can now state that we couldn't just a short time ago was the places that we went through on our way from our previous station and also places that we visited while we were in France. Yes, Beck, I have seen St. Lo. You cannot imagine the destruction there. There is nothing left. Have also seen Caen, Valognes and many places surrounding those cities. When one gets a view of some large city with only bricks piled as debris and a few stray walls that were stubborn enough to withstand the terrific pounding, one can then realize what this invasion must have cost in lives. (Can't go into detail now — wish I had time.)...

---

den 21 Sept. 1944

Dear Beck:

...Yep, we are finally in Paris and you can see that the Americans took over the situation. Can you imagine — ME — with the "handle" that I've got [that is, her Jewish name] using Hitler's stationery?...

First of all — Paris is really wonderful and I love it. I was rather glad to get away from London and the "Doodlebugs" and also the mud of Normandy. (Yes we were there for a while living in tents and undergoing quite a rugged existence. I did enjoy it because it gave me a chance to really live in the open and was so entirely different from anything I had ever experienced — for instance, taking a bath out of our helmets. However, I am glad that we won't have to live there in the winter — what a relief.)

I have had so many interesting experiences that I just don't know where to start. But here goes: —

Sunday (work day), my friend Smitty (another WAC — a draftsman) and I took off some time in the morning to go to church. She wanted me to accompany her to hear Bishop Spellman[7] and I wanted to hear him too. He was speaking at Notre Dame. There was no means of transportation to Notre Dame, however, had we been smart we would have waited around for G.I. transportation in trucks. But no — we wanted to see if we could get there our-

Reichsgesellschaft
für Landbewirtschaftung m. b. H.
(Reichsland)

Generalverwalter für die öffentl. Landbewirtschaftung in den eingegliederten Ostgebieten

HAUPTGESCHÄFTSSTELLE PARIS

Bankkonto : Reichskreditkasse Paris — Drahtanschrift : Reichslandbau Paris — Fernsprecher :

Aktenzeichen :	Postanschrift :
(bei Antwort anzugeben)	Paris,

den 21 Sept. 44

Dear *Beck*:

The censoring above was done by myself at the request of the officer who is censoring this letter. Yep, we are finally in Paris and you can see that the Americans took over the situation. Can you imagine--ME--with the "handle" that I've got using Hitler's stationery?

I am really terrifically busy but have just a few tiny minutes at the end of the day to rap off this epistle to you--regret very much having to make this a carbon copy, but it is the best I can do and I know you won't let a carbon copy letter stand in the way of our friendship. Right? I know there are a number of things that are of general interest so I shall start right off.

First of all--Paris is really wonderful and I love it. I was rather glad to get away from London and the "Doodlebugs" and also the mud of Normandy. (Yes we were there for a while living in tents and undergoing quite a rugged existence. I did enjoy it because it gave me a chance to really live in the open and was so entirely different from anything I had ever experienced--for instance, taking a bath out of our helmets. However, I am glad that we won't have to live there in the winter--what a relief.)

I have had so many interesting experiences that I just don't know where to start. But here goes:--

Sunday (work day), my friend Smitty (another WAC--a draftsman) and I took off some time in the morning to go to church. She wanted me to accompany her to hear Bishop Spellman and I wanted to hear him too. He was speaking at Notre Dame.

There was no means of transportation to Notre Dame, however, had we been smart we would have waited around for G.I. transportation in trucks. But no--we wanted to see if we could get there ourselves. We got to the Arc de Triomphe and a short distance from there, there are a number of horse and buggy taxis. We thought that was fine and I (speaking French (?) asked if they would take us to Notre Dame. The taxi driver replied that it was too far for the horse but that we could walk! Smitty and I looked at each other and began laughing. We went back to the Arc de Triomphe and happened to see a Red Cross Sight Seeing Tour in progress with a nice bus attached to it. We waited until the lecturer (a true Frenchman) came up to the bus and asked him if they were going any where near Notre Dame. He said yes and that

Mollie's letter to Beck dated September 21, 1944, written on stationery printed for the Nazi occupation of Paris.

selves. We got to the Arc de Triomphe and a short distance from there, there were a number of those horse and buggy taxis. We thought that was fine and I (speaking French [?]) asked if they would take us to Notre Dame. The taxi driver replied that it was too far for the horse but we could walk! Smitty and I looked at each other and began laughing. We went back to the Arc de Triomphe and happened to see a Red Cross Sight Seeing Tour in progress with a nice bus attached to it. We waited until the lecturer (a true Frenchman) came up to the bus and asked him if they were going anywhere near Notre Dame. He said yes and that they would be there in about one-half hour. We both managed to look helpless and he said we could go along. The wind-up of the whole thing was that we took a tour instead of going to church as we had changed our time schedule one hour's difference from the French time so that we missed Bishop Spellman. Anyway, the tour was excellent. We saw a number of places that I have read about — Tomb of the Emperor Napoleon, Louvre Palace, Notre Dame, Eiffel Tower, Palace of the Invalides. Then they took us back to the origination point of the tour, Hotel de Paris, which is the American Red Cross. We, of course, decided to pay for the full tour and so the Frenchman accepted our money and we felt better.

We still had the problem of getting back to our office as the Hotel de Paris is quite a little way off and we were a bit tired. It was around lunch time and all the horses attached to the little taxis were being fed; they had their heads buried deep in the feed bag. Every taxi driver we approached pointed to his horse. What a situation! We, too, had to get back to eat at our hotel. Finally we found a horse — and a man — to take us back. What a relief. It was great fun riding in the little taxi — trotting down the streets of Paris. Everyone waved to us and we waved back. We finally got back to the hotel, ate and went to work. But we did have a very nice day and an unexpected tour of Paris.

Paris is really wonderful and I do hope someday we will all get the opportunity to visit in peace time and buy scads and scads of beautiful French clothes and see the wonderful places here brilliant with lights — in the soft evenings.

PARIS, FRANCE
25 Sept 44

Dear Beck:

Just dropping you a few lines to let you know I am just fine — and busier than h — .

Saturday night Smitty, another WAC and myself met some very nice French boys at a G. I. show. They understood my French very well — anyway they are coming over to our Recreation Room at our Hotel and they want to learn English and will teach us French. One of the fellows insisted he would have to bring a hammer with him to teach one of the girls (Loddo— another one of my pals, who can't seem to twist her tongue for those French words) and really pound that into her. They didn't think I would need such drastic lessons. They didn't speak a word of English and I was the only link. What a spot to be in — I had to translate everything my friends wanted to say. Many a time I would be actually stuck for a word — without a dictionary at hand. Anyway they seemed to understand me without difficulty. — Maybe someday I will have a few minutes to write out the episode of how we met those fellows. Very cute!

This next letter was written on the day before Yom Kippur, the Day of Atonement and one of the most important Jewish holidays. It is a day set aside for fasting, praying and attending services and seeking to atone for the sins of the past year. It is clear from the letter that Mollie had given considerable thought to the way that she would spend the day and wanted to explain to her parents that she planned to work in order to continue making a contribution to the war effort. During the war those Jewish soldiers who were serving overseas observed this Holy day in a variety of ways. Some attended services and fasted for the day just as they would have done at home, whereas others used it as a time to be connected to their families by writing to them as though they were all gathered together.[8]

> PARIS
> 26 September 44

Dear Mom and Pop:

This is the eve of Yom Kippur and I somehow felt that you would want to know how I am spending Yom Kippur. I am spending it just like any other day in the army — work day. I really could have gotten time off — but I felt that I would rather work. It's the first time you know for me, but I feel right about it. I also decided not to fast — which is also unusual for me — but there is no sense in attempting to work on an empty stomach. — So there you are, and I feel right about the whole thing.

Even this moment at the office I feel just as if I were home — there is a soft reflection of a light against my window with the grayness of a September day — and it's almost as if I were home and Mom had lit the candles on the living room table. I don't think I will go to the synagogue as it would make me homesick — and I don't want that to happen.

…If the war news continues as it has in the past, it won't be too long before we shall all be home. — Though I can't make any predictions, — as to dates. Wish I could.

I am feeling fine and enjoy being in Paris. It is a beautiful city and I can just see you both walking down the streets of Paris taking in all the beautiful sights. It would be wonderful to be here in peace time. Maybe someday —

I know you are wondering how our living accommodations are here. They are wonderful — hotel rooms — the best we have ever had. The food is very good and plenty of it. (Mom, I know, is always worried about that.) One thing makes me very happy — no KP. We even have French maids!

I shall close now and here's wishing you a HAPPY NEW YEAR. Hoping to be home for the next one....

Mollie kept herself informed about what was going on back home and was concerned about the infantile paralysis (polio) outbreak, especially since several friends were affected by it and were kept under quarantine with the disease. Polio claimed hundreds of thousands of lives in the United States from 1942 to 1955, until the widespread use of the Salk vaccine for Polio prevention was implemented. During this time, Detroit reported approximately 2,500 cases annually.[9]

PARIS
29 September 1944

Dear Jackie:

...certainly was glad to hear from you. Have been getting very little mail lately — because of my numerous changes of addresses, and haven't received any of the packages that Becky speaks of....

I note what you say about poor Eddie, Calvin and Gloria being quarantined. If they are quarantined like that, are they allowed to pass around their comic books? I can imagine the racket they must make with Gloria trying to run everything. I just heard about the infantile paralysis epidemic in Detroit... One of the boys in our office received a Detroit Times of 2 Sept. and honestly one would think from reading that — that the war was over. But Jackie, it isn't — I can tell you that.

...Right now the food we are getting is excellent and plenty of it. Did I tell you we eat at our Hotel where we live? It's very nice. Sometimes in the evenings, the boys from Special Services come over and we have dinner music! Not bad! EH?

We still don't have hot water at our Hotel. (Imagine a Hotel like the Statler[10] not having hot water — ever!) Anyway, we take our baths at the office.

I don't believe I have ever gone into detail in my letters to Becky on our accommodations here. They really are wonderful Jackie. Very large room, beautiful mirror, lots of closet space, three beds and two cots, adjoining bathroom with two wash basins. There are five of us in the room and we were friends in London, and we pal around together — so what more could we ask! — Well, there is one thing — HOT WATER. I must tell you about Napoleon's Josephine. She is also there with us. She sits on the mantel piece with

Sgt. Smitty's helmet at a rakish angle and wears a Detroit brand of lipstick. (Cut-ups, aren't we?)

Today, we finally tracked down a French tailor. I had to get a size 14 uniform cut down a bit to fit me — what with the added few pounds I gained and the extra clothing I wear, etc., etc. — (NO I DON'T LOOK LIKE AN AMAZON, JACKIE!) anyway I had my uniform fitted. He didn't speak a word of English. For a moment I thought he was going to give me a fit — something like we see in the movies. You know, where they hold the front of your suit up while you look at the back and vice versa. However, I do think it will come out well — I hope! Extra padding in shoulders and a seam here and there — you know.

My French is coming along very well, and I enjoy it no end. In fact, today I happened to pick up a French paper and was amazed at how much I could actually understand. It just dawned upon me that I am adding new words to my vocabulary every day. However, I still can't understand a word when two excited Frenchmen get into an argument....

After the success of the Allied landings in Normandy and the liberation of Paris, many Americans believed that victory was just "around the corner," expecting the war to end quickly and their loved ones who were serving in the armed forces to return home soon. By this time U.S. involvement in the war had been going on for almost three years and enthusiasm for the war was waning. Mollie, however, was very realistic in her assessment of the progress and likely duration of the war, and in many of her letters home she warned her family not to expect a speedy end to the fighting. Both President Franklin Roosevelt and British Prime Minister Winston Churchill demanded unconditional surrender by the Axis powers, which meant that the Allies would need to achieve decisive victories in order to convince the political leaders of Germany, Italy and Japan that there was no alternative to accepting defeat on Allied terms. In the autumn of 1944 the forces under General Eisenhower's command had forced German and Italian troops out of North Africa, had taken Sicily and were fighting their way through Italy, with the enemy armies being pushed back and sustaining heavy losses. In the South Pacific General MacArthur's troops were closing in on the Japanese forces, fighting from island to island.[11]

PARIS, FRANCE
4 October 44

Dear Beck:

Haven't heard from you in the longest time. In fact, again, I am not receiving mail. I suppose you will be hearing that complaint from me right along — so you and Jackie, at least, had better write me — and I don't mean maybe. However, have been hearing that a lot of our mail is being held up for want of transportation. So — please make excuses to anyone who says I am not answering their mail — I am not receiving it — is the answer.

I wrote Jackie (on a postal card) that I had been over to the Louvre Palace but was not able to get in to see the paintings, etc. as it was closed. It is open only on Tuesdays for a few hours. Hope someday to get around to seeing it. We expect to go this Saturday on an American Red Cross tour to see Versailles....

Last night we were entertained by some top-notch vaudeville actors — ballroom dancing, acrobatics, swing pianist, tap dancing, singing, etc., etc. — it was 2½ hours. Really high-class entertainment. Now I know why we never got a chance to see that in the states — it was all over here. However, it is really needed over here as there isn't too much in the way of good entertainment for the service people. — On our way over to the show, we happened to meet some boys who had been over in France since D-Day and had seen some real action. It was funny the way we met. We were walking down a crowded street and they bumped into Smitty and myself. As soon as they saw we were American girls, they just wouldn't let us go. We shook hands and when they found out Smitty was from Ga., they yelled "REBEL" and when they discovered I was from Mich., they screamed "YANKEE" but Smitty threw in an adjective, she said it was "damn YANKEE." Anyway, we all laughed. In fifteen minutes I believe we heard their lives' histories. When they heard that we had gone through the mud of Valognes, living in tents, etc., they kept saying "We know what you girls have been through." etc. blah, blah. Then we said goodbye and good luck. Then they said the same to us with a slight addition that made us feel so good — "You don't know how wonderful it is to talk to real American girls. Sure want to go back to the States soon."

Which leads me to this thought, Beck, I know that everybody expects us to be home soon — but don't kid yourself — we won't be home for Xmas. In fact, it will still be quite a long, long time. I may be wrong; maybe I am pessimistic. I hope so!...

Am busy now, Beck, so will get back to work. But do write me even if it is only a few lines.

Paris, den 10 October 1944[12]

Dear Beck:

Just thought I'd drop you a short note on this classy German stationery. Not bad, eh? Within the last few days rec'd your 3 letters.... I almost fell over when I read the paragraph about Ella[13] being back home. I am so anxious to hear from her. Do hope she will write me soon — after all, her letters from the States to me won't be censored — so I'd really get some interesting mail from her. I was all set to send her a card of Eiffel Tower but I guess I'll have to send her another card with new address. Please give her my love & tell her to write.

...I went to a piano recital ... given at a Countess's home. As you know, Beck, I am not musically inclined in the least but I did want to attend such an affair. It was small. Rather good pianist but I couldn't help staring at the different woman's hats. I guess I enjoyed that more than the music!

...I got a kick out of Mom's wanting me to send you a hat. I guess by now you realize that buying clothes here is out of the question — completely. One day I looked around for a sweater — one that I could wear in civilian life — Well the prices are way out of line. The only thing that was half-way decent was 1745 francs — translated $34.95. It ain't worth it! ... By the way, I shall be sending home some perfume very soon. Trying to get hold of Chanel 5 but so far could get Chanel "gardenia." I guess all the G.I.'s cleaned out Chanel 5.

I note what you say about my dropping Mr. Slomovitz [editor of the *Detroit Jewish News*] a line — I shall. I know you will be interested in this. Today I received Danny Raskin's letter dated 19 July. I shall answer it shortly... I enjoyed the clippings you sent. That's true about using "K" ration (not "A" ration) for hair rinses.[14] That's what I've been using right along!

...Yep, Beck, still enjoy Paris — wouldn't miss it for the world.

Almost forgot to tell you about the French chemist I met. He was so amazed to hear me speak French. He said something that would make my old French teachers so proud. He said I was one of the few Americans that spoke French without an English accent. He said he had spoken to an American officer (Colonel) who perhaps had a greater vocabulary in French — but spoke it with a distinct English accent which made it difficult to understand. By the way, this chemist spoke only French!

Must sign off now to take a hot bath. We get hot water (if we are lucky) once a week. Have discontinued taking baths at the office — reason — no HOT WATER there either.

...I am feeling fine, Beck. *No* complaints whatsoever.

In the next letter, Minnie H. described an evening that Mollie's friends in Detroit had spent together to welcome home Ella Marcus (mentioned in Mollie's letter dated October 10, 1944) who had recently returned from serving with the WAC in North Africa.

October 12, 1944

Dear Mollie,

So nice to hear from you and that you are in best of health. Your letter was quite a treat after not receiving one for such a long time. However, I heard quite a bit about you, when I last visited your home which was a few days ago. As you probably know by now, Ella has returned to the States and with due respect to your family spent an afternoon there, and of course in the evening the *girls* (nothing else) came and talked and talked. She looks very nice but I could see that she was happy to be back again and partake of some of that good U.S. food. She has lost considerable weight but being thin does her justice, and then you again on the other hand now weigh 120 lbs. Seems as though the Army does things to you that you yourself wish. Of course, we all took a gander at your last letter to Sarah which she brought with her and it seemed so strange to read a letter from you, and Ella being there at the same time. It seemed so short a time that you were reading her mail to us.

...so Mollie with loads of love and best wishes and regards, I remain
Minnie

When Mollie was transferred to Paris she continued to date the Sarge (Alex Korody) and in October 1944 she acquired a new boyfriend, Coleman Bricker. Coleman was from California and his family was acquainted with one of Mollie's cousins who lived there, Jean Black, who encouraged him to get in touch with Mollie when they discovered that Coleman and Mollie were both stationed in Europe. Coleman became one of Mollie's constant companions throughout the war and their first meeting marked the beginning of a lengthy and complicated romantic situation for Mollie, as she was simultaneously dating two gentlemen. Although both the Sarge and Coleman Bricker were Jewish, they were from very different backgrounds. The Sarge was several years older than Mollie. He was born in what later became Yugoslavia and his family had escaped to Switzerland when their home was threatened by the Axis powers early in the war, so his outlook on life was decidedly European. Coleman Bricker, by contrast, was a much younger man from a less affluent background who had had to give up some of his own personal ambitions in order to help support his family.

Like many of her fellow Americans serving in France, Mollie would sometimes collect small objects left over from the Nazi occupation and send them home to her family. Mollie enclosed a yellow Star of David in one of the next letters reproduced below. From June 1942 the Nazis required that all Jews living in the occupied areas of France wear a yellow Star of David on their outer clothes to denote that they were Jewish. Some French people who were not Jews wore yellow stars as a gesture of sympathy with their Jewish fellow citizens and as a sign of defiance to the anti–Semitic policies of the Nazis. Any non–Jews caught wearing the Star of David were promptly arrested.[15]

Paris
16 October 1944

Dear Beck:

Haven't heard from you in a long time — in fact, haven't been receiving any mail. Pretty soon, I think I shall stop writing and you all won't hear from me until I get home — maybe in 1946!!

I really didn't mean all that stuff above but I can't waste this paper — so just ignore it!...

Please open the little long Lelong perfume box. It contains 3 bottles. Distribute as follows: Goldie Weinstein, Sarah Cohen & Raye Sternberg. The Je Reviens & Molgneux 5, I would like you to keep for me. However, if you really want to, you can use them but let me know so perhaps I could get some more. You know how perfume evaporates & goodness knows when I shall get back home.

The only thing I am keeping back here with me is Chanel Gardenia. I want you to know it was quite a struggle to get that Chanel 5 — in fact, any Chanel product. I had been hunting around for it ever since I got here. I even went out to the Chanel factory. Couldn't get it. Finally the Major here got it for me & that was all he could get: 2 Chanel 5's, 2 Gardenia & one Chanel 22 (I sent that to Jean Black as she was pretty nice to me in sending me that very nice box with a darling little bottle of Avon perfume when I was in the Forward Echelon & couldn't probably get hold of anything like that.)

By the way, the Sgt. here just learned that his home in Yugoslavia has been liberated & would like to get some staple foods to have when he is able to get to his home ... make it up in a couple of packages. He said he would reimburse you for it. Mail to me.

...Haven't done much gallivanting around as I've been too busy.

PARIS, FRANCE
23 October 1944

Dear Beck:

Just today received your airmail letter (on new stationery — I like it)... So you see that letter was a bit late in getting to me.... In that letter you also tell me about Ella being in Italy, and, of course, by now I understand she is home. Imagine how people's lives must get involved by not receiving certain letters. I have no idea of what mail I have not been getting. I have never received any of the packages you speak about. However, did receive a few days ago those two very nice pairs of hose. Thanks a lot. I note what you say about maybe having to "chisel" $5 out of my fund. Gosh, that's perfectly all right. I'm leaving it all up to you and use your judgment on whatever you want to withdraw.

...Today received Sarah's very nice long letter. Yours and hers are the only letters I've received in about 10 days. Gets rather disgusting at times, but of course everyone is griping about not receiving mail so I am not any different than the other guy.... I have conveyed your regards to the Sarge. He said thanks.

By the way, have been going out with a fellow from L.A. Jean Black sent my address to his mother and she sent it on to him. He received it when he was stationed in a small town in England and traced the APO [Army Post Office] number and of all things—he is now stationed here. His name is Sgt. Coleman Bricker. Nice fellow. Saturday night we went out to a very nice night club, four couples. Had champagne. Not bad! Last night, we went to the GI show—saw a movie with Jean Arthur[16] called "Impatient Years" and there was also a vaudeville. Really giving us G.I.'s good entertainment.... Coleman wants me to see if I can take off the same day during the week that he is going to so that he can show me Paris as he has been around and knows where all the important places are.

...By the way, I still see my French friends once a week and learn French. However, didn't see them last week on account of my cold. You would have laughed your head off if you had heard me talking with my French friend on the phone, explaining my cold in a darn nasal voice—but maybe it helps French pronunciation—you know that language!

...So long for now and let's hear from you soon—Jackie, too. Don't have to write a long letter—just a line so I know everyone is okay at home....

PS Please note the Jewish Star enclosed. Those emblems that the Jewish people in Paris had to wear during Germany's occupation. Not only the people of Paris, of course, but the Jews in all occupied countries had to wear them.

8. From Visiting Refugees to Sophisticated Nightlife: Paris
October–December 1944

As Mollie settled into life in Paris, she found that her family remained very curious about the job she was doing in the Army, but she was still not permitted to give them any details. The article she refers to in the next letter was published in several popular magazines and described the Medical Intelligence Division, which she worked for. It was established by the Army's Surgeon General to provide medical- and health-related information about the areas which the Army was preparing to move into so that the medical services would be prepared for the conditions they would find when the troops arrived.[1]

Mrs. Weissenburg, mentioned at the beginning of the next letter, lived in Detroit and knew about Mollie through Danny Raskin's column in the *Detroit Jewish News*. She was able to find Mollie's family from the information in the newspaper and rang their doorbell one day to ask whether Mollie might be willing to help her make contact with some members of her family who were in Europe. Mrs. Weissenburg's family, originally from Germany, had fled the country in the 1930s when Hitler's National Socialist Party came to power and began to persecute Jews. Some members of the family, such as Mrs. Weissenburg, had escaped to the United States, while others sought refuge in Poland and France. Beck wrote to Mollie, explaining the situation and asking Mollie to try to find Mrs. Weissenburg's sister, who was believed to be in Paris. Mollie did indeed find the sister, Sally Fish, and her young son, Victor, and visited them on several occasions.

* * *

PARIS, FRANCE
24 October 1944

Dear Beck:
    ...Regarding that address you want me to look up, that Mrs. Weissen-

burg's sister, there is no need to be secretive about it. When I get the opportunity and time, I shall try to look her up. You can tell Mrs. W. that, and I surely will make the effort.

You ask me what Medical Intelligence is. Of course, I cannot go into detail on the subject to you but it is all the information of a medical character pertaining to a country that we (Allies) would be interested in. That's putting it very briefly and into a nut-shell. (Just asked my Colonel if it would pass censorship. He said okay and even gave me a suggestion. Medical Intelligence is explained in Colliers magazine of 19 October 1942; also in Reader's Digest, during the early months of 1943 (can't recall the exact issue). That ought to help you out, n'est ce pas [isn't it so]?...

In this next letter Mollie describes some of her experiences of French culture. She attended the opera in the first week that it reopened after the Liberation of Paris. She also enjoyed going to see French films and unlike many of the Americans stationed in Paris during the war, Mollie was able to understand enough French to follow the dialogue.

29 October 1944

Dear Beck:

Just a line to let you know I am okay. Haven't heard from you in quite some time. I believe I wrote you that I received the two pair of hose that you sent me. They are really beautiful. I wore them last night.

Went out with Coleman [Bricker] last night and saw a French movie. Really they are a scream. I don't think they have any censorship on them. The way those dames prance around in black underwear! Whee! However, the movie we saw last night was not as risqué as one we saw earlier in the week. Erich von Stroheim[2] seems to be in all the movies. He speaks very good French but somehow even I can tell that it is a foreign language to him by the way he speaks it. The first all French movie I saw was "Gibralter" (including the bedroom scenes); the one I saw last night was "Tempete." I was going to relate my impression of the "Tempete" to you but maybe I had better forego it. As far as "Gibralter" goes, we, of course, would laugh and during one of those touching clinches, one of the G.I.'s would yell "Break it up!" The French audience wouldn't understand but would laugh and say "Les Americains!" However, there are very few G.I.'s who go to the all French movies because our special services give us our own movies in a very nice theater, gratis. But I enjoy struggling through a French movie and besides I think it adds a few words to my vocabulary — but not much — I'll agree.

Coleman has tickets for the Opera next Friday and I do hope I can make it; it starts at 6 P.M. which is rather early. And, inasmuch as France is nothing like America where you can go out and grab a sandwich, I will have to try to make mess, which starts at 5:30 and make the Opera too! Did I ever tell you that you cannot go out to eat because they just don't have it. Well, it's true. Our food in our mess is excellent and we just never miss a meal. It is served in the dining room of our hotel; French cooks and French waitresses. No KP [Kitchen Police] for us.

Haven't had a chance to look up that family (Mrs. Weissenburg's sister, Sally Fish and her son) but shall the first opportunity I get. I shall wait until I have a day off because I don't care to go around visiting neighborhoods in the evenings.[3]

---

den 2 November 1944
PARIS, FRANCE

Dear Beck:

Regarding the weather here — it's no military secret that it is very cold and rains quite a bit. Almost like the weather we have in Detroit. However, we don't have any heat here, which makes it rather uncomfortable. I believe I also told you that we have hot water only one day a week. But other than that Paris is grand.

...Last night Coleman took me to his hotel as they were having a movie in their lobby. It was very funny as the movie hadn't begun and as we walked in, everyone applauded. I blushed and asked Coleman if the applause was for us and he nodded and said "Yes." You see I was the only gal there! It was a very good story — "Conflict" with Humphrey Bogart. Coleman and I had planned something else but inasmuch as yesterday was a holiday, "All Saints Day,"[4] everything was closed excepting G.I. movies. But we did enjoy it.

I guess I told you that I am going to the Opera tomorrow night with him to see, I believe, "Damnation of Faust" — whatever that is. But it should be very good. Anyway, I shall be able to see the women's hats there!

Yes, I still see the Sarge [Alex Korody].

...Am going to try to get in touch with that Fish family within the next couple of days and will let you know about it....

Mollie and Coleman Bricker managed to find Mrs. Weissenburg's sister, Sally Fish. Mrs. Fish and her family had been in hiding during the Nazi occupation of France in an attempt to avoid the harsh treatment which Jews, and especially foreign-born Jews, were subject to, such as being arrested, beaten or sent to concentration camps.[5] Although Mrs. Fish and her son survived to return to Paris after the Liberation, Mr. Fish was not so fortunate. He disappeared during the war, and Mollie never discovered his fate.

PARIS, FRANCE
4 NOVEMBER 44

Dear Beck:

Just dashing you off a letter. Really don't have time but I have so much to tell you that I'll just have to get it off to you as best I can. First of all I am feeling fine and hope everyone at home is okay. I just had the afternoon off yesterday and accomplished so much that I hardly know where to begin. But here goes:—After lunch Coleman met me at my hotel and we went searching for Mrs. Sally Fish. We had absolutely no trouble finding the place. Coleman has a wonderful sense of direction. He doesn't speak French but can find any place in Paris. (You guessed it. He used to be a Boy Scout!) As we stood in front of her address, we weren't quite sure that was the place. There were stores on the ground floor and then a doorway leading into a courtyard. It was a very old and dreary looking place. An old Frenchwoman saw us looking around and asked us who we were looking for. I said "Mrs. Sally Fish—does she live here?" She said "Yes—second floor." We crossed the courtyard and walked into the old building. They were uneven stone steps and the hallway gave me an eerie feeling. I turned around to Coleman and said I was sure glad that he was with me. You see it's not too good an idea going traipsing around Paris to places you don't know. Anyway, we got to the second floor and there were three doors. Coleman said "Try this one." I knocked on the door and a short woman with blond hair answered. I said "Are you Mrs. Fish?" She said she was. I said—"You have a sister in America, Mrs. Weissenburg, who gave me your address—which was sent to me from America by my sister." Mrs. Fish asked us to come in and was so happy to see us. She asked us to sit down. Her apartment was most bare. She has absolutely nothing. Only one blanket for covering on her bed. Victor, her little son, who is just darling was scooting around the room with his scooter and he had a few broken toys strewn around the room. He is four years old—reminds me a lot of Georgie [Rot] in England. I immediately gave him a couple of Nestle's candy bars that I had saved from my rations and also some little candy Charms that I had received.... Victor was so cute—he said: "C'est tres gentile de vous" [It is very nice of you]. And I said: "Il n'y a pas de quoi" [You're welcome]. You know candy is a rarity for the French people. As he sucked one of the Charms, he kept telling his mother—"Il y a du sucre" [There is sugar]. He was so happy. I guess they hardly ever get anything with sugar in it.

Anyway, Mrs. Fish asked us what language did we want to speak. She did not speak any English at all. So I spoke French and Coleman spoke German and we got along just fine. She spoke French, German and Yiddish. With the three languages working at all times, this is the story I got from her.

She has just returned to Paris. Has been here only two weeks. Eight months ago her husband was taken away by the Germans. They had been hiding successfully until then — but he happened to go out on the street one day and they picked him up. She has tried to contact him through the Red Cross but they know nothing. She has had to buy herself free (herself and child) twice. Once she had to pay a ransom of 10,000 francs. These stories are unbelievable, sad, but true. She, of course, has no way of knowing what has happened to her husband. She also does not know how the rest of the family is — I believe two sisters (or maybe three, can't recall) fled to Poland. Has no word about them. Also, no word regarding brother.

I told Mrs. Fish I would write you and would let her sister know. I asked her if there was anything I should ask her sister to send her. But she kept saying they are both well (she and the child). Of course, she needs just everything. Food, clothing, etc. Now, I don't know what the status is for civilians sending packages to people here in Paris. But anyway, this is what her sister can do. Send a package to me — with anything in the way of staple food or anything, clothing, etc. I will see that she gets the package. However, I have no way of knowing if I will still be here by the time the package arrives, but I could forward it on to her. Be sure that the package is wrapped well. I will attach another sheet to this letter and write it as though it is a request for myself but will ask Mrs. Weissenburg to send me stuff — but it will be for her sister — get it?

I gave Mrs. Fish her sister's address and as I understand it if Mrs. Fish writes in French or English, it can be posted and go through as civilian mail to the States. Mrs. Fish said she would have one of her friends write the letter in French to her sister. She cannot write in French herself.

Now, Coleman and I had a camera along — and I know Mrs. Weissenburg will be very happy. We asked them to get dressed and took some pictures of them. I do hope they come out well. I took one picture of myself with her and the boy. As soon as they are developed, I shall send them to you and you can give them to Mrs. Weissenburg.

Mrs. Fish wanted to know how long we were going to be in Paris, etc., etc. But that is something no one really knows. However, I told her that I would be back again and asked her when would be the best time to call — she said that her time is always free. Evidently, as of yet she is not doing anything in the way of work. However, I am sorry I neglected to ask her what her plans were for the future. But she seemed so happy to see us and rather confused by everything — however, I shall try to find out more when I see her again. I couldn't give her a definite time when I would call again because I don't know exactly what day I will have off — but I shall go again very soon and bring her something in the way of food. (Beck, you can't imagine the scarcity of food here. We, being in the army, are most fortunate and can't complain in the least.) We shook hands and said goodbye and I promised to come again. (Must make it in the early part of the day with a friend. Don't care to go around alone.)

It was only about 3 P.M. when Coleman and I left and we did a little sight-seeing — not much. We did a little shopping. He bought me a lovely hankie that has "Mollie" on it. He threatened to buy one for me some time ago when he had seen it in a window. It is a large beautiful red silk with *Mollie* in white. I didn't want him to buy it, but he insisted. The darn thing cost 200 francs ($4).

We had to rush back early as we went to early chow 4 P.M. so that we could make it to the Opera. Beck, it was gorgeous. The opera house is magnificent. The Opera *Damnation of Faust* superb. What more can I say? I guess I was the only WAC there again but there were plenty of G.I.'s.

We got back to my hotel about 9:30 and we had a dance in our lobby. But we ran into my pals "Loddo," "Bats," and "Smitty." They were going out (with their friends) to a café for a little drink and were coming back and asked Coleman and me to go along. We all ordered white wine — only one drink — and drank to speedy victory. Went back to our hotel and danced a bit and everything broke up at 11 P.M. What do you say, Beck, quite a day, n'est ce pas?...

PARIS, FRANCE
9 Nov. 1944

Dear Beck:

It's been swell hearing from you so often.... I do hope the Rot family[6] receives that package you sent out. Haven't heard from them in quite some time. Am sending Zuzana some "Quelque Fleurs" perfume by Houbigant....

You really do read my mind, Beck, don't you? I've been thinking I'd like one of those sleeveless V neck sweaters. Many of the girls have them. Would like one in beige or that olive drab shade. I'm sure the Red Cross won't be furnishing them to us....

Sorry to say, have never received Mom's cookies (Korjeclach — spelling?). If you can dig up nice relish (to spread on bread or crackers), send that — always talking about food, aren't I?

...Can't buy soap outside of our PX and we are rationed one bar soap

Mollie and Coleman Bricker outside the Paris Opera House, November 1944.

every 2 weeks— which doesn't go very far considering we do our "own wash-ing," etc. If you come across Kleenex, that would be wonderful. (I suppose that is pretty much extinct back in the USA too!)

Rec'd a letter today from our cousin Sammy. He's in Southern France. I answered it right away as I know how much the boys like to receive mail. Used some pretty stationery from one of my bunk mates— a lavender pink & I put "Tabu" perfume on it. I bet the guys will hang over his shoulder when he reads it!

By the way, have been seeing a quite a few movies with Coleman lately. I think he gets a kick out of my going with him to his cinema — my being the only girl there. Am going to a dance at his hotel tomorrow night....

Mollie witnessed a historic moment as she watched the parade down the Champs-Élysées on Armistice Day, November 11, 1944. Winston Churchill and Charles DeGaulle welcomed the Allied troops in a newly liberated Paris to mark the anniversary of the signing of the Armistice Treaty in Versailles in 1918 which ended the First World War.[7] The minute's silence at 11 A.M. referred to in the next letter is a tradition still observed in Europe, to pause at the eleventh hour of the eleventh day of the eleventh month in order to remember in silence those who have lost their lives in war.

PARIS, FRANCE
12 Nov. 1944

Dear Beck:

Must tell you about the Armistice Day Parade here in Paris. I still recall the ones we used to go to— you, Jackie & myself— but this was really the "cat's meow." It started about 6 A.M.— maybe not actually but there were gendarmes (or draculas as we call them with their all-enveloping capes) & G.I.'s, too, directing crowds that early, lining up the streets near the Arc de Triomphe, along with the great numbers of people who probably ran back to get sand-wiches & hustled back to regain choice spots from where they would have an advantageous view of the celebration. And, Beck, I think the parading or cele-brating was still going on this morning.

Florence (another WAC) & myself left the office at 10:30 A.M. & we made a "bee line" for Champs Elysees (one of the main streets in Paris that runs into the Arc de Triomphe). Honestly the people were packed like sardines (trite but true). Florence & I were standing on tip toes but couldn't see very much. All of a sudden I felt my feet leave the ground & I had a most wonderful view of marching soldiers. I turned around as I felt myself being put gently back to earth — it was the captain! I thanked him & both Florence & I laughed. We walked farther on & we decided to stand back near the buildings away from the crowds along the streets. We did have a better view. We saw Churchill go by in a car but weren't quite sure. However, when we heard the people shouting "Vive Churchill," that confirmed it. Besides I had said to Florence "I know we have a long range view of the parade, but no one but Churchill's cheeks are puffed out like that!"

The one minute's silence at 11 A.M. brought to mind the folks back home — wonder when we'll be coming home. I know, Beck, it won't be too soon.

The streets were so crowded, we couldn't get over to see the Arc de Triomphe where the Tomb of the Unknown soldier is located but from the distance (only about three blocks) we could see displayed on the Arc de Triomphe the immense, magnificent Tricolour (flag) which had been used in previous ceremonies — but had been hidden these 4 yrs of occupation.

Today, at noon, we braved the crowds & went to see the flower-covered tomb. We didn't have time to stand in the queue to pass around to see all the flowers. Smitty, Loddo & I walked along the sidelines & saluted the tomb where the Unknown Soldier rests & the eternal flame flickers. We did get a good view. The flowers were beautifully arranged in oblong fashion about 3 yds wide & half block long. It was a most touching sight. ** I hope we don't have to fight this war over again in 20 years!

It's getting late now so I shall have to close — I know it's abrupt....

Paris, France
17 Nov. 44

Dear Beck:

Too bad that you haven't been receiving my letters. I do (after thought) try to write at least once a week. There's no need to worry if you don't hear too frequently as the mail situation isn't too good. I am not receiving much mail and haven't received as yet any of the packages — not even Mom's cookies from July. So please make my excuses to everyone if they complain that I'm not acknowledging their mail. Can't answer if I don't receive it.

...Yes, Bricker — (I call him "goldbricker") is a very nice fellow. He took me to the Folies Bergère Wednesday night and it really was something!!!!! Am enclosing a program. By the way, Bricker sure gets around. We went to the Opera the first week it opened — and now to the Folies the first week that opened, too. I don't know how he does it — but he gets the tickets whereas many officers have difficulty in securing them.

...By the way, I think Kaye[8] is on his way overseas — (but where?). He's a

Lt. now with a combat crew, which is pretty tough. He says he hopes he is sent to "my theater" but you know the army — he'll probably be sent to the S. Pacific.

...By the way, you would have laughed at me today and would have gotten a big kick out of my situation. Loddo, my bunk mate, who works on the floor above me, rushed down this morning for me to come into her office to act as an interpreter. It seems that the First Lt. in her office was having a little difficulty explaining to two Frenchmen what he wanted done with two telephones. It seems he wanted one phone to be left in its place and the new phone to be installed. The Frenchmen wanted to pull out the old phone and install the new one in another place. I couldn't think of the word "remove" — but the Lt. was pretty cute — he said "removeeee" (trying to help me out) so I looked at the Frenchmen and in the course of my conversation threw in the word "remove" with a questioning look on my "pan"[face] — I said it very French-like but it didn't work. I guess there is no such word in the French dictionnaire. Anyhow, I finally got them to understand the problem. It's very silly but I often "fake" words and it's surprising how many times it does work....

Shall close now as I must get to bed — am feeling OK....

Paris, France
20 November 1944

Dear Beck:

I just sent you yesterday an airmail with 18 snapshots and a program of "Folies Bergère." (However, it may be dated 18 November but I sent it yesterday.) I meant to send off this V-mail at the same time but just didn't get to it. Anyway, please let me know the date you receive this V-mail as compared to the airmail I mention above. I may have to write you V-mails inasmuch as you don't seem to be receiving mine. Frankly, I don't like V-mail.

...You should see the smiles on everyone's face. They have just begun to give us heat in the offices. It is really wonderful. We still don't have heat at our hotel but do have hot water practically every day now. Things are surely looking brighter....

PARIS, FRANCE
28 November 1944

Dear Beck:

Your letter ... arrived in such good time, received it today, that I think I shall send this "par avion" [airmail] instead of writing a V-mail and besides I think I shall enclose a couple of snapshots, which, by the way, aren't too hot.

By the way, the last time I saw Mrs. Fish and Victor, they looked much better.

Regarding the money situation — it's true I am not flush with do-re-mi. In fact, am in the red at this point. However, payday is in two days— so all is well. I was all set to give Mrs. Fish some money as you suggested but today received from Mrs. Weissenburg an American Express money order for $25. I will have to cash it into francs and get it over to Sally the next time I have the opportunity, which I think will be soon — probably Coleman will go with me.

By the way, when I saw Sally the last time I gave her my red cotton robe — remember? I had a G.I. one issued just before I left London for Normandy. I gave her one of the jars of Nescafe you sent me quite some time ago— real coffee is impossible for civilians to procure — other than on the black market. I also gave her a few other things.

With further regard to your letter of 17th wherein you tell me you are trying to get the Sarge's package[9] together — please accumulate a good selection of stuff for it — staple things and pack it nicely. If you can think of other things to pack in it, do so. I am going to tell the Major this is a *personal* letter and see if he will sign it without reading too closely. I suppose you have gathered by now that the Sarge works in the office with me — the one that was in London and Normandy. Have you got the story straight now — I hope so. (When I speak of the "Sarge," it refers to Alex.)

PARIS, FRANCE
1 December 1944

Dear Jackette:

…Well, you can tell Mom that I finally received her cookies today. I see by the wrapping that it was dated 9 Aug. You should have seen the can — it sure looked like it got here by way of the South Pacific. However, we delved into the can; most of the cookies were broken up, but they tasted good anyway. We will probably make tea or coffee tonight and have the "korjeclach" or shall I say "crumb-korjeclach" with it. You know we have a little hot-plate at our hotel and have an evening snack about 10 P.M. or so. Tell Mom "thanks." Too bad she can't send me some "kreplach"[10] but will probably be stuffed with food like that when I get home. I guess you gather by now that it won't be this Xmas. Hope it will be next Xmas at least — .

I still think Paris is pretty wonderful and am trying to get around to see all the interesting places. It sure is a thrill to see those places in actuality. You know I pass the Arc de Triomphe every day and I can still remember somewhere having seen it in one of our books back home — was it the "Books of Knowledge" [encyclopedia]?

Mollie and the Sarge (Alex Korody) in front of their office in Paris, December 1944.

Last night I went to the Opera again. Saw "La Boheme." It was really wonderful. Jack, I guess I might turn out to be a high-brow yet. I enjoy the Operas so much, would rather go there than to any kind of a movie. If the Operas come to Detroit, I hope Mom and Pop get a chance to go and you, too.

I don't believe I ever told Beck that Coleman has been just dying to take me to a place where they have potato chips. Well, we finally went to that place — a little café. We had a glass of beer and when Coleman asked for the potato chips — they said "fini." So darn it — we didn't get any. And, after he gave them such a build-up. Well — the payoff is this — the next time he got ready to take me there, the fellows told him the place had been closed up — so it looks like I'll have to wait till I get back to the States. By the way, here's a thought — next time Beck sends me something how about some potato chips — could she pack them somehow so they wouldn't get broken up?

"Fraid I'll have to get back to work — will say "au revoir" and give my love to Mom, Pop and Beck. MERRY XMAS & HAPPY NEW YEAR.

Mollie continued to visit Sally Fish and her son Victor when time permitted and tried to help them as much as possible, for example by getting them extra money and goods that were in short supply. Mollie also seemed to be the main means of communications between Mrs. Weissenburg in Detroit and her sister in Paris, especially as Mrs. Weissenburg could not read or write French or German and Mrs. Fish could not read or write English.

PARIS, FRANCE
2 Dec. 44

Dear Beck:

Just a brief note as I am busier than ----. Thousand pardons, please ... received your airmail of 20 Nov. today wherein you tell me you are writing between classes and that you will send me soap — maybe you have sent some in one of your packages but haven't received it yet. Could still use some anyway. Include soap that I can use for washing clothes, like Ivory. Also in this letter you tell me about Mrs. Weissenburg coming over to the house to tell you about the 25 dollars. I have written her acknowledging same. I have already cashed it and hope to see Sally tomorrow. By the way, I am sending you the "Stars and Stripes" which explains the money situation here. We certainly aren't getting a very good exchange on our money.[11] At the Finance Office I received 1239 francs for the 25 dollar check. A franc is worth only 2 cents. But you don't even get 25 dollars there. Then when you go out to buy anything — nothing is worth the price they ask and GET. For instance, one of the boys here was telling me he paid 600 francs for one meal, which is simply terrible, don't you think? Of course the price of clothes is way out of line, too. By the way, did Mrs. W. include silk hose for Sally? If not, it would be a good idea to send that. You can use this letter as a request (tell Mrs. W.)

...Oh, I forgot to tell you this. I included a request for Sally in my letter that I wrote Mrs. W. Sally didn't ask me but I know she can use that stuff. You can also tell Mrs. W. that I had someone translate her (Mrs. W.'s) letter into German and will let Sally read it. I know it will be a great thrill for her....

If Mom gets around to it how about some strudel — but you will have to do better on packing. You will have to wrap the pieces individually and stuff paper around it sort of like a buffer — or something. Anyway, Mom could include that in one of my other packages you have already as requests — but don't include in a package with soap. Because you know how soap odors tend to make food smell the same. (When Mom has time & you do, too — for cooking & packing.)...

While she was in Paris Mollie continued her correspondence with Charles Knotts, a soldier she had met in California who was by this time stationed in Belgium. Charles was a combat soldier and wrote the next letter just days before the Germans launched the surprise offensive that was known as the Battle of the Bulge.[12] The postscript demonstrates that Charles had noticed that Mollie was moving up in the ranks and was now a corporal.

Somewhere in Belgium
Dec — 3 — 1944
Sunday Nite

Dear Mollie,

I received your letter yesterday and was very glad to hear from you again. I see our mail delivery has speeded up a bit, that's a help anyway.

Well here I am standing by waiting for I wish I could tell you what but impossible at the moment, so during my spare moments I am trying to drop you a few lines using my knee for a writing pad so please excuse writing!

I am getting along O.K. except the weather isn't just what it should be at times but considering everything it isn't too bad.

Yes I do wish I could have visited Paris. Surely it would have proved better than London at least for our chance of seeing each other but maybe someday we will eventually catch up with each other, I hope!

...Say why don't you come on up? You probably will be in Germany the next time I hear from you because you are always keeping ahead of me.

How's prices on things in Paris? They are really sky high here. This stationery cost about 80 francs. Everything is awfully high. Well Mollie I must close for now I just found I have some work to do. Will write more later — so good-nite. Write soon.

    Love,

    Charles

    PS Congratulations Corporal

    Mollie spent much of her free time with Coleman Bricker. As this next letter demonstrates, Coleman had also been asked to get in touch with a refugee family with connections to someone back home (in California, where Coleman was from). But they also enjoyed the entertainment of Paris as Coleman always seemed to be able to obtain tickets for performances and social events of all kinds.

PARIS, FRANCE

5 December 44

Dear Beck:

    Just a quickie as I am quite busy today but thought I would come back early from lunch to dash this off to you....

    Went to the circus with Bricker Saturday night. It really was good. Isn't like our circuses out in the field, etc. Instead it was in a little theater — but must admit — it smelled like the circus atmosphere. Am enclosing a program.

    Sunday, both Bricker and I had errands to do. He had to see a refugee family for someone back in L.A. and I had to go over to see Sally. Well, we were fortunate in getting over to see his friend; they were home. However, Sally was not so I couldn't leave the money but will have to go again. Bricker's friends live in a rather poor section of the city — tenement set-up I would say. I understand the homes, or I should say, apartments are rented to families with three children or more. Oh, by the way, we had our choice of 5 languages to speak with that family — French, German, Russian, Polish and Yiddish. I stuck to French and Bricker to German. You would think they would talk Yiddish when they realized we could understand it although not speak it — but no, they insist on talking French or German but, I don't care as it gives me more experience; and Bricker, too, with his German. By the way, Bricker, too, had to deliver money to them. The eldest boy in the family is in the French Army (FFI),[13] the other son was sick in bed (wearing a cast or something — strained back) and there are two daughters— they were at the cinema. The father had been taken by the Nazis three years ago and they have been unable to contact him — and of course don't know whether he is alive or not. The mother was very nice. Bricker brought some candy over and gave her 500 francs. It was rather amusing — as soon as we heard her putter away in the kitchen, we got up to leave as we know food is difficult for them to secure. But she insisted on feeding us apples and even peeled them for us. We each ate an apple. It did taste good. You see we seldom get fresh fruit.

PARIS, FRANCE
13 December 44

Dear Beck:

Last night received two of your rather old letters: 11 Nov. and 12 Nov....

You asked me about Coleman. Yep, I think he has a cute name and he is a swell fellow and I like very much to go out with him — but am not serious with him at this point. Comprenez-vous [Do you understand]? In fact, will probably see him all day tomorrow — which is my day off. Will attempt to go over to see Sally and get the money situation settled. Then in the evening — what again????— going to the Opera. Am enclosing a program of one of the Operas I saw last week — or rather two as it was a double feature.... I note you ask how my weight is. Haven't gotten weighed for some time but it is probably the same as I know I couldn't have lost any as my clothes fit the same. By the way, it is a good thing that I never got those suits altered when I was home as I turned both of them in — one in London and the other here as they were too small. Am now a size 12.

...Did I tell you we have French cooks who do most of the cooking and I imagine occasionally a WAC cook will throw in her two cents, which always causes us to remark: "That tastes just like a WAC cooked it." But on the whole our WAC cooks aren't bad, but of course, the French cooks have more experience. Did I tell you we don't have KP anymore; that we have French waitresses in our hotel?

In fact, Beck, have I outlined our routine to you — don't think I have. We don't have reveille any more, nor any of those stiff inspections in parade formation, etc. We must be at work at 8:30 A.M. We get up at 7:30 and can make it easily. We walk to work. It's only about 6 blocks and a very enjoyable walk. We go home for lunch, too. We have bedcheck at 12 A.M. now. Saturday inspection (our personal inspection) consists of our WAC officer inspecting us as we walk in to have breakfast at any time from 7:00 to 8:00. Everything is most casual and we certainly wouldn't act any different if we were civilians. Our rooms are inspected too but we have maids that tidy up our rooms. We have only to make up our bed and arrange our drawers and closets neatly. Pleasant existence, wouldn't you say? Anyway, I am enjoying it to the utmost because one can never tell in the army — tomorrow one may be living an entirely different life.

I received a package from one of the branches of B'nai B'rith[14] organization in L.A. and among other things received a cute little cardboard checker board....

P.S. Am feeling fine!

PARIS, FRANCE
21 December 44

Dear Beck:

Tuesday night, Bricker and I went to the Allied Club,[15] which is in a beautiful Hotel — gorgeous dance floor. We went dancing. (Did you know that cafes and night clubs here in Paris do not have dancing any more. Some new ruling. Don't think it will last long though.) However, all G.I. places permit dancing, such as Red Cross, etc. They also have "real, live cokes." It's quite a treat. Can you beat that — making a fuss over a silly coca cola?

Anyway, when Bricker left me to get the cokes, I was sitting near the dance floor waiting for him. I heard a fellow's voice behind me say: "Corporal?" I turned around and the fellow said to me: "Would you please say — 'Glad to see you.'" I smiled back, flashing my uppers, and said: "Sure — Glad to see you!" He said: "Gosh, that sounds good — just like back home." He asked me for a dance very politely and I said: "Surely." — Then Bricker came back — the music didn't start again — the fellow got up and walked over to me and said: "Thanks anyway."

So the moral of the story is — there are plenty of American boys who still think the American girl is tops — You can tell that to Sarah W. to build her morale, and I am not kidding.

Must sign off at this point.

It was at this time that Mollie invited Charles Knotts to visit her in Paris but he was not able to accept the invitation — the Battle of Bulge was under way and as a combat soldier, Charles was needed with his unit.

Dec — 28 — 1944
Belgium

Dear Mollie,

I received your letter yesterday and was very glad to hear from you again, from the way you write you seem to like Paris very much, I do hope it will be possible for me to visit there sometime maybe I'll be lucky I hope!

Yes Mollie I received the invitation and I thank you very much for your efforts even though it was impossible for me to be there. I appreciate it very much and not for one minute did I stop thinking of you and how nice it would have been if we could have spent some time together again. No, it doesn't complicate things in any way at all. I only hope it turns out to be that way, that's my wish for the New Year, have any suggestions?

Well, Mollie I must close for tonite so thinking of you very much I bid you good-nite.

Love,

Charles

In this next letter, which Mollie referred to as "Portrait of Four WACs," she provided a detailed description of the close friends she made in the Army. They were together in London, Normandy and now Paris, and although they were never transferred at the same time, somehow they always ended up together. The close friendships that Mollie formed with her fellow WACs were typical of the experiences of many women serving in the Army during the Second World War, who found a special camaraderie there. The pressures, demands and exhilaration of war, together with the knowledge that they were serving their country in uniform, brought an intensity to everyday life which helped to forge strong bonds between the WACs far more quickly than would be the case in civilian life.[16]

PARIS, FRANCE

29 Dec 44

Dear Beck:

...That is odd my not telling you about the girls I pal around with and with whom I live. Completely slipped my mind I do believe. I think by now you have received pictures of all the gals: "Johnnie," "Smitty," "Loddo," and "Bats."

Johnnie is the one I know best of all, that is, because we were together in the Forward Echelon and "sweated-out" the London doodlebugs together. The one picture that I've sent home of her certainly doesn't do her justice. She is just about your build, nice-looking with a shock of gray hair over her left temple. I would swear if I didn't know her as well as I do that she dyed those hairs just to give herself that "Isn't she young to have gray hair?" look about herself. I think we really became fast friends the night I made her bed. You see in London every Thursday we had to strip our beds in the morning and change linens in the evening. Well, Johnnie had the day off and left early that morning. I really didn't know her but realized that she would be coming in late in the eve-

Mollie with Loddo, center, and Smitty, right, in the Luxembourg Gardens, Paris, December 1944.

ning and tired—she bunked next to me—so I went ahead and made up her bed. Of course, that night when she walked in the room it was completely dark and instead of having to struggle to make her bed, it was already made. She was a pretty good investment, Beck, when I recall all the things she has done for me since then.

For instance, the time when our billets in London spouted nothing but cold water for a whole week. She had the day off and I had to work. But what did Johnnie do—traveled practically across London to pick up my towel, soap and odds and ends, locate a nice hot bath for me at the Red Cross and meet me there with the above mentioned equipment so I could jump into a nice hot tub after work. You can well imagine how I appreciated that!

Johnnie was with me the night we moved from one billet to another in London. It was a not too clean place but we set to work and tidied up the room — then we set up our cots. They were really awful. A cot consisted of a long piece of wood with collapsible legs. For a mattress we had what we call three *English biscuits*. An *English biscuit* is something I would just as soon forget — but know you won't let me so here goes a very inept definition: — An *English biscuit* is something that is supposed be a mattress in three sections but ain't! Somehow or other, the next morning you seem to have lost at least one of the three and maybe you might even be marooned on the middle one with your head and legs sort of dangling. (I said it would be an inept description — best I can do.) Anyway, that same night what happens but the following: about 3 A.M. as my bed breaks down with a crash so I sleep on not only an inadequate bedstead but practically on the floor. At 5 A.M. we have a practice air alert and we certainly found out later no one needs any practice on that. And, to top it all off at 7 A.M. as I get locked in the latrine when the door knob falls off, who comes to the rescue — well, Johnnie, of course! She calls the janitor and "our little Nell is saved!"[17] Never will I forget that night.

I don't have to detail our experiences with the doodlebugs in London but I do laugh at Johnnie when she says I am the only one who got her to wear her "dog tags." But that is an army regulation — as if she didn't know.

Sometime later Johnnie and I were separated. She preceded me to Normandy about a month and I really missed her. Never thought we would get together again. But who do I run into during the first days of our roughing it — but Johnnie, standing in front of her pyramidal tent. We waved our arms madly and embraced each other like long lost brothers— or I should say sisters. She had saved a cot for me and even one for my friend whom I had "accumulated" after she had left me. That was Smitty.

From there we came on to Paris and as I write this I laugh as she and I go into our skit — you know slightly reminiscent of "Of Mice and Men." "Tell me again," I say. She says, "You don't know how much I missed you when I left you in London. I wanted you to be with me so we could laugh at the same things."— blah, blah.

That's the Army, Beck, little things that we do for each other and the experiences we struggle through make a friendship in a few minutes that might take years to ripen in civilian life.

Johnnie is a Secretary — steno in the Medics— different branch from mine but the same building. In civilian life — a Secretary for an investment counselor in Louisville, Ky.

Although I knew Smitty in London, we really became friends when we crossed the Channel. Never will I forget the night we slept on life preservers on mess hall tables. Nor can I forget the night we sat, cold and damp on board a ship carrying our heavy equipment on our backs and how Smitty was able to "snag" a cup of coffee and how we shared it.

The night we first landed in Normandy — do you think they had hotels for us— h---*** NO. Can I ever forget the look on Smitty's face or the comforting squeeze of her fingers when someone calmly announced: GALS — MAKE YOURSELVES AT HOME ON THIS FIELD — IT'S ALL YOURS FOR THE NIGHT. We didn't know if it was a battlefield or what. But we spread out our pup tents on the ground to keep out the dampness, piled our blankets on top of it, snuggled up and slept. When we got together with Johnnie in the woods, we found life was not too uncomfortable there but without Smitty I'm sure it would have been not quite so pleasant. When the tent began to sag at one end, we would all yell "Smitty!"— she knew how to take the pegs out and reset them to get the tent to hang right and keep out the rain. She knew how to split wood for our little stove — and —

Here in Paris— Smitty repairs our electrical appliances— our iron, hot plate, lights— knows how to wrap our perfume packages "break-proof." (She had enough experience in that having wrapped paintings, etc. for art exhibitions— at one time a million dollar exhibition!) What a gal! Smitty is a draftsman in our Medics, a rebel from Ga. and fresh out of college from civilian life.

Loddo and Bats are the Italian kids that are the rest of our quintet. I don't know them quite as well as Johnnie and Smitty but one thing I shall always remember about them — the way they say their prayers faithfully each night, kneeling at the side of their beds. Although they are Catholic and we of a different faith, it gives me a feeling of confidence — I know we are included in those prayers.

Bats is a statistician from Boston, Mass. and Loddo a Steno from Pa.— both hold the same type of positions here in the Medics.

So there you have it, Beck, "Portrait of 4 WACS," who are my best friends. What do you think of the kids?...

9. Keeping an Eye on Family and Friends Overseas: Paris
January–March 1945

As the last year of the war began, Mollie devoted an increasing portion of her off-duty time to helping family and friends back home keep track of loved ones in Europe. In addition to visiting Sally and Victor Fish, Mollie advised the family of a friend from Detroit, Sidney Cohen, who was reported as missing in action. She also kept her sister updated with the latest news about their cousin, Sammy, who was a combat soldier in the U.S. Army in Europe. Many of Mollie's letters demonstrate her attempt to strike a balance between keeping her family informed and shielding them (particularly her parents and other members of the older generation) from some of the harsher realities of war.

* * *

PARIS, FRANCE
5 January 45

Dear Beck:

I received your airmail of 23 Dec telling me about your being worried about Sidney and your V-Mail of 26 Dec telling me that he was missing in action. Received both letters the same time. Yes, I had been worried about him too as he had never answered my last letter or postal card. However, "missing in action" sure isn't the final word. I shall try to see if I can do any checking up around here and will write you more if I can. I am keeping my fingers crossed.

I guess I shall have to make this letter *confidential*, so don't even tell Mom and Pop about it. Just received a letter from Sammy (our cousin) and he is now in combat. The letter I have from him is 23 December and he was back in France after having been in Germany. He said it was pretty rugged but he sure is taking it all wonderfully well. Never really complains. He asked me not to tell his family about it. But I feel I can tell you but don't tell Mom and Pop because it would all get back to his family.— Now promise!

As Mollie was transferred from one location to another, she continued to keep in touch with Danny Raskin, the reporter at the *Detroit Jewish News*. His letter below mentions the war bonds campaign which the paper, together with B'nai B'rith, undertook in Mollie's name. The sale of war bonds was an important source of revenue for the U.S. government and helped to finance the war effort. The purchase of war bonds was presented by the government and regarded by many citizens as a patriotic duty.[1]

January 10, 1945

Thought you would enjoy reading this.— I answered it a long time ago— keep this letter for me — Mollie

(*On Detroit Jewish News letterhead*)
Hello Mollie,
We must attribute this long delay in my answering your wonderful letter to a sudden amount of WORK! Not Jewish News work, but advertising, a field which I have entered quite strenuously. And the first three months are the hardest when it is done on a free-lance basis. Coupled with my newspaper toil, or whatever it can be called, I was a trifle "on the ball" and it still hasn't stopped rolling! Forgive me? Thanks, dear!
Credit my lousy handwriting to the fact that typing has always been the (my) main source of displaying thoughts with words. But it is more personal, right, Mollie? Personal to the extent that I am probably the only one who can decipher it! The Bond Rally in your honor sold $165,000 worth — thanks.... M.C.'d one last night at the Jewish Center, given by B'nai B'rith...Gave your regards to Mr. Slomovitz [editor of the Detroit Jewish News] and Dena [Mr. Slomovitz's secretary].... Send theirs also.... Received their calendar and thank you for the addition to my "War-Time" souvenir collection.... Anything you send me for that collection will be greatly appreciated.... Your small picture goes in my private one, called "The Wolf's Den".... You're looking swell (I like that word — so informal) and I hope you are feeling the same....
I still am interested in knowing where you attained all that literary ability displayed in your magnificent letters. You should do them a favor and write something for a service paper — and I really mean that!
As for this sheet, S-H-E-E-T, you are the official correspondent in that

area for the "Listening Post" column and recognized as such. Gee! Doesn't that make you feel awful proud?—or just plain awful!...

Yours,

Danny

The reference in Mollie's next letter to bombing relates to a brief raid on Paris by German forces on the night of December 27, 1944. This was the first bombing in Paris since the Liberation. It was brief, caused little damage and only a few casualties.

Paris, France

14 January 45

Dear Beck,

...Re: the bombing—don't know if we are permitted to talk about it, but in as much as the paper's carried it, I don't see why I cannot confirm it.[2] Yes we were. It was very brief—thank goodness for that. Things are okay now and there is absolutely nothing to worry about.

...During the week I took the packages over to Sally and she was very happy to get them. By the way, she told me she sent back the money to her sister. Can't quite figure it out, but evidently, she does have enough to get along on. She was thrilled about the tea that was included in one of the packages. It seems that tea, which is most rare over here, costs in the neighborhood of $40 per lb. That is evidently black market prices. I am writing Mrs. Weissenburg about it all so I don't want to repeat it as I don't have time. Comprenez-vous [Do you understand]?

Sarah Cohen wrote me a V-mail and said that Sidney was missing in action since 3 December. In fact, yesterday received another V-mail from Sarah wherein she asked me to see what I could find out. I had already done that. In as much as Mr. and Mrs. C know nothing about it, I am enclosing Sarah's letter herein, as I fear that should I write Sarah direct, Mr. and Mrs. C would see the letter and I don't want to confuse things for Sarah. So, will you be careful in getting the enclosed letter over to Sarah—or else telephone or something. I shall leave it up to you.

The snow is rather deep around here now. You should see the snowball fights right on the main street—Champs Elysees.

By the way, Coleman gave me his sleeveless sweater. It is an OD [olive drab] color. It's too small for him having shrunk. It's very nice. I am wearing it now. It has a Bullock's Los Angeles label in it.

Am making this brief because I have a number of other letters to dash off and really don't have time....

PARIS, FRANCE
29 January 1945

Dear Beck:

I have received a number of your letters altogether within a few days—so shall attempt to answer them — as usual chronologically. For quite a while had not been receiving any mail — but even at that my correspondence is behind as I am quite busy — at work and otherwise.

...you ask me if I have gotten anything new — the answer is NO. I am trying to make up my mind, however, if I should ask you to send me my shoes that I had sent home (that is, if you still have them) or if I should ask you to send me some spectator pumps (if you could get some without a ticket inasmuch as I am overseas perhaps they would allow you to purchase them — good ones for me — not $3.95 brand). In other words I don't know if I want to be burdened with something extra to lug around with me because you see whenever we move, we must get everything we have into the same space as we had when we came. You cannot be bothered with a couple of packages here and there draped around your waist or an extra duffel bag. Do I sound confusing? Hope not! Anyway during the week Bricker and I went to a dance and one girl had on some very good looking pumps and of course he asked me if we are allowed to wear them. I guess we are. — So you see the guys sure notice every detail. Will let you know in my next letter whether you should get me some or just what. Okay?

...You ask me if I hear frequently from Sammy. I sure do and answer him right away. I have sent him a package, too.

****

...In fact, I wear G.I. wool socks every night to bed now. (WHAT A LIFE!) Every once in a while the heat goes off — lights go out — mais c'est la guerre, n'est ce pas [But that's war, isn't it]? But on the whole, Beck, things are very nice where we are.

Regarding Sidney. I saw the girl that looks up the records and she will look up the records again within a few days and will let you know the minute I find out anything at all. Does Mrs. Cohen know now? You know that girl who looks up the records (Lenore) thinks it is a better idea to tell the family that he is missing and then should he turn up, that would be wonderful, and if he does not, well then at least she will have had all that time to have had a chance for it to soften up a bit and it would not be as great a shock. I keep hoping that Lenore can give me good news.

PARIS, FRANCE
31 January 45

Dear

As much as I dislike doing it, here I am writing a carbon copy letter[3] to you but hope you will forgive me. Am busy at the office and otherwise, and have amassed quite a correspondence by this time but I feel I must catch up with myself and have taken this manner in doing so. Please forgive — but then I know a lot of things I have to say here are of general interest to my friends — so here goes: —

First of all, you should see the nice set-up we have where we can get hamburgers, coffee and light wines — which is really something. You see it is most difficult for army personnel to go into restaurants to purchase food — in fact we are really not supposed to. Now with this special set-up, it is really grand. A G.I. must have a WAC with him or he is not permitted to go in and no stags are permitted. The fellows say they are more interested in the WACs than the hamburgers — but we know differently! Anyway, we do kid the fellows. So you can see with a set-up like that French gals give us no competition at all. — how can they?

Our accommodations, etc. are still very good, however we are often left pretty much out in the cold so to speak — the heat may go off, the lights out and just when you are ready for a hot bath — ice water spouts forth. In fact, last night about 6:30 our lights went out in the hotel and the girls in my room and I decided it was a good idea to make the best of it and go to bed really early for once. So we did — then about 7:15 my friend calls me and insisted on my coming down to the lobby to see him and he mumbled something under his breath "WHAT A WONDERFUL OPPORTUNITY!" — wonder what he meant (oh yeah!)??????? Anyway, I had my hair up and didn't go down so he couldn't take "advantage" of that so-called opportunity.

Loddo (one of my roommates) — had her difficulties. However, she is being treated quite like a queen by us lately. You see she had a sailor friend connected with the navy mess hall. She has decided to break up with him, but we have been working awfully hard to convince her not to — after all he brings a dozen eggs and fresh apples, too, when he comes over to see her. When I tell you that we have had fresh eggs about 5 times since we have been overseas and fresh apples maybe 6, you can realize the fast talking we do. We keep telling her one evening going out with "Pete" once a week isn't too great a sacrifice. In the meantime, we hold her coat which she slips into it, we straighten out her bed, etc., etc. But she is a smart girl and suspects ulterior motives.

No doubt you are interested in our weather here. Reminds me a good deal of Detroit — snow, cold and rain, too. I thought our supply Sgt. was a bit "bats" when she issued us Arctic boots last July but now I really think it was a very good idea.

PARIS, FRANCE
3 Feb 45

Dear Beck:

Loddo and I went to a Dance at Bricker's Hotel last night. His boy friend had been pestering Bricker to fix him up with a WAC as he had not been out with an American girl in two and one-half years. He is a M.O.T. [Member of our Tribe — Jewish] — very nice — wears five battle stars on his ETO [European Theater of Operations] ribbon and has certainly been around in this war. Anyway, we all had a very nice time. The fellows sure cut in on us though. There were only about six WACs and the rest were French girls. The boys would tap our partners on the shoulder and say: "You wouldn't deny us the pleasure of dancing with an American girl, would you?"

Just before we went to the Dance two combat boys looked me up at my hotel. They telephoned me about 7 P.M. and were in the hotel so I went down to meet them. They are with our Cousin Sammy's outfit. They were in on a three day pass— which isn't exactly three days as it takes awhile to get into Paris. They were very nice boys and darn handsome too. They told me a lot about Sammy and how brave he is. By the way, this is confidential and don't say anything to our family as it will get back to his. Comprenez-vous?

They think that perhaps Sammy may get the opportunity for a pass to Paris and I do look forward to seeing him. I wrote him a letter and gave it to the boys to give to him and told him to let me know if there was anything I could get for him. We correspond very regularly. As a rule it takes only about five days for his letters to get to me.

During the week I had to help Loddo out as she had gotten rather involved with two dates in one evening — a sailor and a combat boy. After much coaxing I finally agreed to help her out. Went with the combat boy and was really glad that I did so that she didn't have to disappoint him. All evening he kept saying: "This is my idea of a nice evening — being out with Americans, etc." I let him hold my coat for me, open doors, etc., etc. Then he would say: "Gosh, I bet it wouldn't be so difficult getting back into civilian life." He had been over in France on D plus 5 (means D Day plus 5 days or June 11, 1944), which was pretty early in the game.

…just received a letter from Ross[4]— guess where in the h---** she is— she just landed in the Dutch East Indies. She is living in tents— wearing the type of clothes we wore in the woods and undergoes the type of living we did in Normandy. What a set-up! I guess I have been most fortunate all around. They have absolutely nothing to do as far as going places to see things....

In this next letter Mollie tried to explain to her sister her relationships with the two men she had been dating, The Sarge (Alex Korody) and Coleman Bricker. In subsequent letters she uses the term "etc., etc." or "my etc., etc. letter" to let her sister know that she is referring to the explanation she gives in this letter about her boyfriends. At this point Mollie was undecided about which, if either, of the two men she might consider for a long-term relationship. Both were Jewish, which was an important consideration for Mollie, but there were aspects of each one which gave her cause for concern. The Sarge's European upbringing and his apparent intention of settling in Europe to be near his family after the war raised the prospect that Mollie might not return to the United States to live if she married him. Coleman Bricker was wonderful company and he and Mollie seemed very compatible but he was several years younger than Mollie and he also had a girlfriend back in Los Angeles, both of which made Mollie uncomfortable.

> PARIS, FRANCE
> 10 Feb 1945
> 8:30

Dear Beck:

This afternoon I was able to dash off a quickie to you (V-mail with air-mail stamp) — in it I told you I would write more about certain things namely "etc., etc."

This paragraph is probably the only one that you can give out for public consumption as the rest of this letter is *confidential* to you, Beck, and if you like our own family — Mom, Pop, Jackie — I suppose you could include Sarah W. but only in the *strictest confidence*— pleeeeease. This part for public consumption!

Tonight about 8 P.M. our Cousin Sammy telephoned me. He is in Paris on a pass. I will probably see him tonight or tomorrow. He was in with a bunch of buddies. Will write you more detailed about that when I see him. He sounded very nice on the phone and very happy and not down in the dumps. Am very anxious to see him. Right now I am typing this in our Orderly Room, having borrowed the typewriter from the 1st Sgt (a WAC) and am more or less waiting for Sammy to pop in tonight or else sometime tomorrow will see him.

****

You sure are driving me wild with your misinterpretation of my so-called amours and, in fact, you have it all mixed up. Anyway here is the story.

The Sarge and I were very good friends in London. In fact, at one time when we went out — I remember quite vividly his saying: "Well, you will probably get married in Europe. — blah, blah." You see his real home is not the States. Anyway, I saw quite a bit of him there and when I was in the Forward

Echelon, he was not — so that is why I was able to write about him. You see we did not work together during that time.[5] Anyway when we came to Paris, he seemed to be busy with a lot of civilian friends. I sort of felt that he was going out with some French gals (However, I am sure that he is interested in me.) and then Bricker walked in on the picture way back in October. So I just didn't pay any attention to the Sarge at all. Of course, that "burned" him up. Since then he has asked me out many a time but it just happens that I am always very busy although sometimes I would have really liked to have gone out with him. Honestly, I could go out with Bricker every night as he is always making a date with me and in between times, he just drops over and telephones me from our lobby. Now Bricker is a wonderful guy and I am not kidding. However, he has a girlfriend back in L.A. Not officially engaged but he told me that he told her that if she waited for him, that would be fine, but he didn't believe in marrying her and then going off to war. When he first met me, he dragged out scads and scads of pictures— her and him, etc., etc. However, I really didn't care, meaning I didn't want to break up anything. Anyhoo, we became fast friends. He treats me wonderfully and is lots of fun to be with. He is a very clever guy and can converse on any subject — doesn't know French but gets around easier than guys that do know or even better than me and my 4 years of French. However, there is another fly in the ointment. You know how I feel about fellows that are younger than I am — well Bricker is. So I have never felt that I could be really interested in him — however, he is so darn swell, that one never knows. On his birthday I gave him a very nice little leather address book with a cute little card that Loddo made. He was very cute about it and of course said "Oh, you shouldn't have bothered"— but I think he felt good because one feels pretty sad when they are so far away from home and usually no cards and no gifts arrive at the appropriate time.

Anyhoo Bricker said to me that he had received a birthday card from his family and nothing from his gal friend. I said "Well, you know how the mail situation is— nothing arrives on time. It's probably held up somewhere." He said: "Well — my family's card got here, didn't it?" Several times since I have known him, he has said —"Well, you're over here and D —(that's his girl friend) is there." I sometimes think that he wants our friendship to be a bit more than just platonic — I mean in a nice way. Anyway, I know that he thinks I am a lot younger than he is. Well, that takes care of just part of the story.

Recently we had a Lt. come into our office, a doctor, he had been at the front. Well, the Sarge noted that the Lt. paid a bit of attention to me as he is a M.O.T. Anyway he is always asking me to go out with him (I mean the Lt.). The fly in this ointment is that he is married. Anyway the first time I did go out with him, I didn't know he was attached. He had only been in the office two days (worked pretty fast didn't he) and asked me to go out. He is always saying amusing things with innuendoes (don't know if the spelling is correct?) and of course, I always have a good retort. I know he gets a great kick out of practically everything I say. Well, the first time, guess where we went — to see the French version of "Snow White and the 7 Dwarfs." You know I had never seen it in the States. You know he thought I was 21 years old! Can you beat that?

Well, the next time he asked me out — I happened to not be busy and said I would go. Well, the Sarge later that same day asked me out and of course I had to tell him I was busy. But that's not all. While I am getting dressed to go out with the Lt., who phones — but Bricker — so I had to tell him that I was busy. The Lt. & I went to hear a famous French torch singer — she must be at least 50 but doesn't look a day over 30 — which is tops. Anyway, she is really gorgeous. Her name is Lucienne Boyer. I can't compare her to anyone in the States — perhaps a little like Morgan-Holman & Boswell,[6] all rolled into one. She wore a gorgeous Paris creation — a purple long-sleeved, full skirted gown with very intriguing pockets in the skirt. She has beautiful red-gold hair. Well, I enjoyed it all immensely.

But that's not all. — As we walked out of the theater — who should we bump into but the Sarge. Of course, he was stunned — we all laughed. The next day I walked into the office — who is sitting at my desk — well the Lt. and the Sarge is sitting at his and they are both talking together very peaceful like. I know that the Sarge was even more interested in me. The Sarge isn't too worried about that situation — the Lt. and me — as he knows I wouldn't ever get tangled up in such affairs. Anyway I just went because the Lt. is really very interesting, etc. However, I decided that perhaps he is a bit too fast or something and I had better not continue going out with him. But he does ask me continuously.

However, there's no feeling sorry for the Sarge as I know he had been chasing around. Anyway, the payoff is that he finally made a special, special effort (I mean the Sarge) and invited me out to some civilian friend's house. (This brings you up to date, as it is Wednesday night that I went). I went with the Sarge and a Lt. friend of his (not the Lt. from our office — of course). The home was not very nice on the outside but certainly was furnished beautifully on the inside. The hostess, a Norwegian woman, wore a red, fashionably cut street length dress with a dream of a neckline. The skirt was very full with black sequins. It was a knockout. There were three women there with their respective husbands. The women were all dressed beautifully, two were synthetic blondes. I felt sort of out of place with my dark hair. They all spoke French. They understood English very well but just a few spoke it so that you could actually understand what they meant. By the way, I knew the Sarge was trying to show me off.

The meal was excellent. We had a different kind of wine with each course. They brought different silverware with each course. We were served by two French maids—but very typical French maids, Beck—just like in the movies. We had some sort of milk cocktail in the drawing room. Then proceeded for our dinner. We had white wine, some sort of appetizer, a meat; red wine; some kind of meat which was very good—beef, I think, potatoes; white wine again; the French bread was very good; red wine; then some fromage [cheese] which was delicious; (don't forget the wine); then we had chocolate tart. The maids came around each time to offer us seconds on every course. Then we all proceeded into the drawing room and had coffee. When we finished that—what do they drag out but cognac. (PS—don't think I drank everything they offered—I sure would have been polluted.) However, everything was just grand. There was a French Colonel that sat next to me (by the way, he was unattached)—although he didn't speak English very well, I could understand him. (I think he understood my French.) He said to me in French: "Si vous voulez apprendre the langue Francais, il faut que vous couchz avec—" [If you wish to learn the French language, you must sleep with...]. Right then and there I chimed in (I'm not even at a loss for retorts in the French language) and said: "Oui, une dictionnaire vivante!" [Yes, a living dictionary!]—Don't know if my French is spelled correctly but you do get the idea, don't you? If not, let me know. (Ha.)

****

I think I have given you a good idea of what has been going on re: amour situation. Frankly I know the Sarge is interested in me as he often asks me if I would be lonesome living outside of the States.

Now, the Sarge has left to go to New York for a furlough as I wrote you in the V-mail dated the same as this letter. He will probably telephone you at your office long distance. Don't know whether he was kidding but he said he may go to Detroit. You might invite him to stay at our place—I mean should he show interest in his conversation with you. But let me tell you, he sure is a particular guy so everything better be spic and span.

****

Frankly I don't know exactly how I feel about it all. You see, the Sarge has an entirely different background and previous life—he is very unusual and I might say Continental in his ways. I just can't explain it. My roommates like Bricker better—he is more like us. However, I just don't know. I shall just have to let things work themselves out. (The Sarge is older than I am—several years.)

By the way, am going to get someone to censor this and tell them it is strictly personal and it sure is, n'cest ce pas?

I wish you wouldn't let the Bricker story out to our relatives as you know how things travel — they would probably have me married to him before he opened his mouth. Haven't heard from [Maurice] Kaye in ages, Beck. Think I shall have to forget that guy.

Dear Beck:

While I was writing my lengthy epistle to you — the kids informed me that Sammy was downstairs in the lobby. I immediately rushed down. Gosh, he looked good — nice clean kid — wearing those rugged combat clothes. He had two of his buddies with him. They sat down and talked with me for about an hour and then they rushed off to some kind of a dance. I will see Sammy tomorrow evening and will take him out to our little hamburger joint as I know he'll get a kick out of that — dancing, hamburgers, wine, etc. You probably can't realize how much simple things like that mean to us — but we all get a big kick out of that.

Mollie and her cousin Sammy Weinstein in Paris, February 1945.

Will try to take off Monday afternoon and do some little errands with Sammy in case he wants to buy something. He is going on a sightseeing tour that I told him about tomorrow afternoon. He can do that with his friends as I am sure they would enjoy seeing the interesting places here in Paris.

I understand he will be here until Tues. A.M. Beck, he sure has had a rugged existence and I don't mean maybe. He has been awarded the bronze star too. He gave me a few little trinkets — some German coins, his insignia, etc. We will probably take some snaps together.

I don't think his family knows that he is in combat so don't spring this letter with the details of his being in combat on them unless you know for certain they are aware of it. You cannot imagine what he has gone through and yet he is such a sweet kid and it hasn't left a mark on him. I hope to God it doesn't.

Paris, France
16 February 1945

Dear Beck:

Am terribly busy in the office not only because the Sarge went on furlough but otherwise ... in the evenings have washing and ironing to do, shining shoes, etc., go out a few times a week, then I am too tired to sit down and write — so instead get caught up on my sleep....

---

17 February 1945

Dottie[7] and I finally got in touch with each other. Saw her during the week. Couldn't get around to taking snaps. Will probably see her soon again. Talked over old times. First thing we noticed about each other was the three layers (shirt, jacket, overcoat collars — remember?). We sure laughed. None of her letters ever reached me — just her last one in December....

Paris, France
19 Feb 45

Dear Beck:

Just dropping you a few words to let you know I received two packages from you today....

Will probably see Mrs. Fish one of these days & take a few things to her. Am so terribly busy don't know exactly when I shall get to it.

...Am enclosing a picture (cover of New Yorker).[8] The Sarge is Alex & the WAC is me. The Colonel put it on my desk one day. I couldn't resist. The next day Alex found flowers on his desk. Ha! Ha!...

Weather is grand here now.

Cover of the *New Yorker* dated November 18, 1944, featuring a sergeant and a WAC (Alajalov/*The New Yorker*; © Conde Nast).

In this next letter, Mollie's friend Charles Knotts — the soldier she had met in California who was in a combat unit in Belgium and had fought in the Battle of the Bulge — was still hoping to be given some leave so that he could visit her in Paris.

February — 21 — 1945
Belgium

Dear Mollie,

Received your letter a few days ago so will take time to give you a report from this end of operations! Everything is O.K. I am getting along very good — lots of work and everything that goes with it.... We live in tents and after quite a lot of work we have them fixed up until it's pretty good except sometimes someone gets the stove smoking and it looks like Pittsburgh but with spring approaching things will be much better.

Well Mollie, I don't know if keeping your fingers crossed will help or not — I hope so though it's very doubtful at the present time — a few of our boys have been fortunate enough to get into Paris — mostly on business but I guess my chances at that are very small — if when someone is picked to go they would find out the fellows which have friends or relatives in Paris or wherever it may be and give them a chance to go but it just doesn't work that way — however something may turn up I always hope for the best.

Well Mollie I must close for this time and get on the job so here's hoping we can meet again soon. Until that time I'll be thinking of you very much.

Love,
Charles

Mollie and one of her friends attended a fashion show of hats which was a topic of widespread discussion and was reported in the press. They were asked for their opinions by a reporter and seemed to enjoy being the center of attention. However, the Director of the WAC, Colonel Oveta Hobby, was not pleased when a reporter asked her about hats during a press conference as she felt that the focus on clothing and fashion trivialized the work of service women in the European Theater.[9]

PARIS, France
1 March 1945

Dear Beck:

I really did have wonderful intentions — in fact had started a letter to you on 21 Feb but somehow got so busy that I just stuck it away somewhere — et j'ai oubli [and I've forgotten]. Anyhoo—I have been TRES busy—as usual at the office and otherwise.

...you say you are glad I am going to see Dottie. I believe I wrote you about the visit and I do hope I shall get around to visiting where she stays. She really isn't far from me.

...Your letter of 5 Feb.—the last time I checked on Sidney [Cohen] was 1 Feb. and I wrote Sarah that it was still "MIA"—missing in action. Will check again when I have a few minutes and can trail Lenore. It is good thing that Mrs. C. does know about it. However, Beck, you know there is still hope.

...I believe I told you Ruth Schaffer sent me a salami from Chicago. You would have died laughing though when I tell you that we used to hang it out on our little porch and it was certainly visible from the street. However, our C.O. [Commanding Officer] never said anything—rumor has it that she was formerly in the butcher business. What do you know???????

****

...Re: the furlough situation—are you kidding? I might add it will be a long time before I see you. We have girls that have been over for 20 months and if anyone will get priority—they sure will. Those gals have been in Africa, Italy, etc.—in other words some perhaps were in the same group as Ella. Don't know whether I wrote to you but I did bump into a girl that was with Ella in Africa. I noticed she was wearing four overseas stripes and Ella's group I know would be entitled to wear that many—so I took a chance and asked her and sure enough—she did know Ella.

********   *********   *********

...After a hectic Monday, Tuesday, and Wednesday until 1 p.m. (in the afternoon) when I went back to work—I decided Wednesday evening, which was last night, to take it really easy and go to bed after supper. Anyway, I told Loddo to wake me at 6:30 P.M. when everyone else finished with their baths and ironing. I would do my little chores after I rested—that would be from 6:30 P.M. till 8:30 P.M. I fully intended to sleep while everyone *piddled* around and finished their work. But, Beck, it always happens to me. There I was in bed practically asleep; Johnny had just finished her bath and was lying in bed; Loddo was ironing; Helen (new girl) as *Bats* is no longer with us, was lying on her bed resting—SO WHAT HAPPENS—A civilian French gal that Loddo looked up for someone in America—One of those correspondents I believe from French class or something—comes over. I was so d—*** tired and so was everyone else—but we had to entertain. I really think she thought we were quite nuts. Lying in bed and entertaining. I guess you couldn't do that in civilian life—but there we were. Loddo was at a complete loss—she had had only six months of French in school years and years ago and didn't know what to say or do. So—I had to come to the rescue. I—was the interpreter. So did I get to bed early—NO! The gal's name is Rene and she is in her last year of college—going in for teaching school. By the way, her visit to us was one of the most amusing I have encountered. You know I never use a dictionary (French English)—not that I am so good, but just that I don't have one. Anyhoo, I got stuck for a word and I used our telephone and asked our operator, who is French.—Well after beaucoup discussion and she had difficulty too—and everyone in our room went into hysterics—she finally came forth with the wrong word. Anyway, I struggled through and finally did get the *correct* word. What a life!

Guess this letter covers just about everything—just the high spots, Beck....

PS—Guess I didn't even tell you that I attended a fashion show of hats at MONNIER's.[10] A newspaper reporter encountered Loddo and me on the street one day while we were shopping and said—"You're just the girls I am looking for." This happened, I believe, one day last week. I guess so much happens—that I just cannot keep track of things. When the fashion show was over, Mme Monnier came up to us and said "YOU ARE NOT AFRAID FROM MY HATS, NON? And we said NO!

10. Tour Guide for Soldiers on Leave: Paris
March–May 1945

Mollie's friend and frequent correspondent Charles Knotts, a combat soldier who was stationed in Belgium, had written to her several times to say how much he wished that he could see Mollie in Paris but that he did not think it would be possible. Mollie decided that, having been in combat, Charles should have the chance to have some time off and see Paris, so without telling Charles first she wrote to his commanding officer, telling him that she and Charles were engaged and inviting Charles to visit her. Charles was not able to get a pass when Mollie first invited him to Paris because at that time his unit was in the middle of fighting to halt the German offensive known as the "Battle of the Bulge." But once soldiers from the unit began to receive leave again, Charles was given a 3 day pass to Paris, so the slight deception worked. In the next letter, written after his return to Belgium, Charles hints that he would like a closer relationship with Mollie than friendship and the exchange of letters. The fact that Charles was not Jewish meant that Mollie felt she could not enter into a serious relationship with him, but she nevertheless saved all of his correspondence.

* * *

March — 4 — 1945
Belgium

Dearest Mollie:

This finds me back again at the same old routine and I must admit that it's hard to take but I guess I'll be back in the swing again in short time — we arrived back O.K. Got here about 0200 and I was plenty tired and sleepy after all walking we did seeing Paris. I want to thank you again Mollie for all that you did to make our visit most pleasant — had it of been different I am sure I could never have enjoyed it as much as I did—I assure you that I appreciate it all very much—seeing you helped a lot as it had been a long time since we had seen each other and I had almost given up hope but one never knows what each day brings forth—who knows—the war may end someday—I only hope we may have the opportunity of meeting again but let's hope it's in the good old U.S.A.

I certainly miss the good W.A.C. chow—really it was very good and it helped out a lot—I bet one mess Sgt was getting tired of seeing us—it's a good thing we didn't have more time or we would have worn our welcome out. Mollie I must say that I enjoyed being with you very much and now that I am here I can think of many things I would have liked to talk to you about but I guess the opportunity never presented itself as maybe you wouldn't have been interested—that I do not know and maybe never will but I can think—can't I?

Well Mollie I must bring this to a close for this time. Here's hoping to hear from you soon. Thinking of you very much I bid you farewell.

Love,
Charles

---

6 March 1945

Dear Beck:

Happened to make a cc of part of a letter to Sarah W. ---- thought I would send it on to you. Believe it was dated either 4 or 5 of March.

Did I ever tell you I received Mom's latest batch of Korjeclach's. They sure were good. Still take them up for breakfast with coffee. Loddo likes them as much as I do with coffee. Tell Mom thanks.

[start of carbon copy of letter to Sarah] I don't believe I ever told you of the answer I received from Chas. to that fiancé business. After my letter of explanation, I received the cutest letter from him. In it he said, he only hoped that it would turn out like that. Then he asked me if I had any suggestions. I, of course, didn't want to commit myself as first of all he is not a NOT a *MOT* [Member of our Tribe], which is the main reason—other than that he is a very nice guy—good looking, tall, not a dummy, etc., etc. So we just let the matter stand but I told him I looked forward to his visiting Paris anyway. Well, three weeks ago when my cousin came in (and by the way we all had a wonderful time—I suppose Becky let you read my carbon copy letter) I had a feeling that Charles might be coming one of these fine days.

Well, Monday night of the past week I had decided to turn in early and was already taking my bath at 6:30 when Johnny burst into the bathroom — she yelled "Charles is here! I mean downstairs." I said: "Charles, who?" Then it dawned on me — my *fiancé*!

We talked on the phone and Chas. and his friend said they had to get
cleaned up and would come back in two hours. So Loddo and I got ready and
went down to meet them. The boys sure looked good. Charles introduced us to
his friend Dick Kramer. A handsome guy I must say, 6'1" and mighty rugged.
Anyhoo, we didn't know exactly where to go right off the bat. Charles said
"How about the Hamburger Place?" I said: "Fine — but how did you know
about it already?" Charles had a funny look in his eye — and then I realized that
I had written to him about it and of course he wanted to see it. So off we went.
Dick went with Loddo and I, with Charles. We must have looked mighty odd
trucking down Champs Elysees— Loddo about 5'2" with Dick, 6'1"— and
Charles 6'4½" with *me*. They really enjoyed it there and we had a very nice
time.

Tuesday morning I wrote Bricker a little note and carried it over breaking
our date for Tuesday night as I had to entertain Charles.

I invited Charles and Dick to eat their lunch and supper with us. We are
allowed to invite combat boys to have their meals with us— which of course is
most fortunate as it saves lots of time for them and us too. I told my Colonel
that my friends were in from the front and asked if I could have Tuesday afternoon and Wednesday morning off. He was very nice and said "Sure enough."

Dick and Charles were waiting for me lunch time and we all went in the
dining room — Loddo and Johnny with us. They enjoyed it very much — eating
with all the girls and having French waitresses wait on them. The waitresses
kept pouring coffee and *refueling* their cups until I thought it would come out
of their ears! But, of course, they are darn cute fellows.

The afternoon we went sightseeing. It wasn't too nice a day and don't
think we took many snaps. Anyway, with my sense of direction, it turned out
so that Charles was taking us on the tour. He would orient himself with the
map — and then I would act as the interpreter and ask the French people how
to get there. Dick and Charles got the biggest kick out of my French speaking
so that they kept asking me to ask the French people questions. Anyway, we
saw: the Louvre Palace, Palace des Invalides, Tomb of Emperor Napoleon, Arc
de Triomphe, Place de la Concorde (where the guillotine stood during the
French Revolution), and the Opera.

We were certainly tired when we got back for our evening meal. I gave
them soap and towel to wash up and they sure looked good — nice, clean shining faces. After supper — Helen (our new roommate) went with Dick. (Loddo
and Johnny went to see Smitty in the hospital — by the way she is okay now
and home with us.) I, of course, went with Charles. Dick wanted to go indoor
ice-skating. We took a horse and buggy transportation to the Palais Glace —
but darn it — no ice skating. Anyway the ride was fun. Then I took them on a
merry chase by subway. Went to the Olympia and saw three vaudeville acts—

Charles Knotts and Mollie in Paris, March 1945.

chorus girls — out of step as usual, a magician and some acrobatics. Then we went to the Allied Club[1] and heard Glenn Miller's band and each had a glass of beer. Charles doesn't dance — so I danced with Dick. They tried to cut in on us but Dick gave everyone an emphatic "No!" for an answer, which settled the question. Then we went to the Red Cross for donuts and coffee.

The boys really had a good time and Helen and I did too. Dick and Charles knew I had Wednesday morning off and wanted me to be ready at 7:30 a.m. for sightseeing and inasmuch as they had to take their jeep out of the garage, we could go sightseeing for a while with the jeep. I convinced them that 7:30 was too early. They came by at 9 am. It was a wet and dark morning. Dick wanted perfume for his sister or girl friend (?). Went to Rue de la Paix and got some nice perfume. He spent 750 francs. When we got back to where Charles was with the jeep — he wasn't there. We waited around and sure enough he got back. Was tired of waiting for us so he went on a little ride to look the situation over. Honestly, it was the funniest thing to see Charles drive the jeep. His knees would come up through the spokes in the steering wheel. We went to the Eiffel Tower and got off the jeep. Charles had to stand underneath the Tower as his Uncle had done in World War I. He wanted to be able to tell his Uncle he had done that. We took some snaps. Don't think they will come out though. Charles wanted to buy me a souvenir bracelet but he had promised to make me one from V-2[2] so I wouldn't accept the one he proffered.

Then we went back to the hotel for lunch. When we got through the boys walked me to the office as they had parked their jeep in the garage a few blocks away. So there I was walking down the street with the two boys, their mussette bags were slung over their shoulders. On the way I ran into our Lt. and Major. Said goodbye to the boys in front of our office — hated to say "goodbye." Don't know when I shall be seeing them again. They were "kidding" me — wanted me to go with them to Belgium. They both said they had had such a wonderful time and didn't really expect it. After I said goodbye I stood in the doorway and watched the boys walk off with their mussette bags swinging from side to side. Then I plunged into our revolving door. When I got upstairs — the Major and Lt. said: "Some guys!"

Well, that just about covers the Charles situation — except for this. Charles told me he received my invitation a week before he received my letter of explanation. It seems that his C.O. [Commanding Officer] brought a paper in and stood at the foot of his cot — Charles being a big guy looked over and said: "Sir, that looks like it belongs to me." And, it did. Charles showed me the paper and there it was in black and white — all that fiancé business — invitation to Paris by WAC so and so. It was awfully cute. Charles said that he asked his C.O. right then and there —"Well, when can I go to see my girl friend." But, of course, he couldn't then as the German counterattack was in full swing. I

asked Charles if he was startled, angry or something when he first received it —
but he just smiled and I guess he was more pleased than anything else.

So there you have one phase of my life here....

PARIS, FRANCE
8 March 1945

Dear Beck:

Just beating out a quickie to you....

By the way, is my bathing suit still good? If it is, would you send it on to
me? Otherwise do you suppose you could buy me a new one? I am really not
too heavy in weight — so don't think you would have to get me a size 40. In my
birthday suit I probably weigh about 112. — Of course, you know my legs have
developed some — I think my arms, too! Wanna see my muscles?

Last night Bricker and I saw a stage play. It was excellent — Yellow
Hands — with Cedric Hardwicke[3] in person. Very well done and we enjoyed it
immensely. Expect to attend the opening of our Stage Door Canteen, which
will be this Saturday. Used to be a popular café — but now our Army has taken
over. In fact, that is the place that Bricker and I went on our first date.

I almost missed that booklet in the Korjeclachs box regarding Jack
Winokur Veterans Post.[4] Why doesn't somebody tell me those things? I first
heard about the post a short time ago through reading one of those Danny
Raskin's columns. I shall write Aunt Surka and Uncle Abe for membership in
the post.

Just received an airmail from Ruth Schaffer dated 25 Jan. I received it 7
March. Not hot on mail service. Eh? Her brother is overseas. Sounds very
much as though he has a very tough assignment. Did she write you of it?

That's all for now....

The next letter is one that Mollie received from Ted Kaminsky, who was
the boyfriend and later became the husband of Mollie and Beck's close friend
Sarah Weinstein (Nash). Ted was stationed in France and later met Mollie
when he visited Paris on a pass. As the letter makes clear, Ted did not have a
favorable opinion of WACs. This was not an unusual attitude on the part of
American servicemen. The creation of the Women's Army Corps had been
controversial and was accompanied by a great deal of disparaging press cov-
erage, including reports and cartoons which suggested that women were only
joining the Army in order to find a man. These prejudices on the part of servicemen were usually dispelled when they had the chance to meet a WAC
and see that she was contributing to the war effort,[5] as indeed was the case
with Ted Kaminsky.

Dear One Rank Higher Than Me:[6]

Not having ever written to a WAC and not even knowing one I thought that it would be all right if I did write to one just to find out if they can read or write. I've heard so many stories about the poor girls that I thought it would be high time for me to find out if the stories are true and then write to the folks at home (Detroit) and tell them not to listen to the stories emanating from the mouths of gossipy USO hostesses or hostages or whatever you may want to call them? Jealousy isn't it?

I damned near had a chance to visit Paris about a week ago but lost out when a staff sergeant drew an ace. I had a *king* and for about 30 parts of a second I thought that I was it. His story and the stories of others who have been to Paris (slumming) are quite interesting. Tell me. Are there any decent people there besides Army personnel? Do the armchair commandos stationed in Paris have a rough time or do they also dig fox holes and police up the area plus about a daily dose of calisthenics. Some rumor coming up the front lines say that it's trying for some of my buddies to get shoe polish. Could that be true? What a rough time they must be having. Incidentally before I forget Sarah Nash[7] gave me your address. Seems to me we are all from Detroit. How about dropping me a line and telling me what part of Detroit you are from etc. etc. Could you? Will you?

Sincerely yours,
PFC [Private First Class] Ted

In this next letter to her best friend Sarah, Mollie describes an evening spent showing two combat soldiers around Paris. They were eager to see the more exotic side of the nightlife which Paris had to offer, and did not hesitate to splurge on entertainment and champagne when they had the chance.[8]

PARIS, FRANCE
16 March 1945

Dear Sarah,

...I must tell you about my latest escapade and inasmuch as it is going to be rather long, I may as well start now. By the way, am making a carbon copy of this letter, which I shall send to Becky. This was a rather different evening in my army career so I want Becky to have a record of it, too.

I believe I told you that a Sgt. George Greenberg (New York) from the Field Artillery had looked me up and I was "entertaining" him the early part of this week. His friend Jack was with him. Anyway, he wanted to do something entirely different the last evening — not be with a lot of G.I.'s — wanted to go to one of those real Frenchie cabarets. He left the planning up to me. (I am getting to be a real "operator"). Anyhooo, we invited the boys to have dinner with us the last evening, which was Tuesday. Then Loddo and I got ready, put on our faces, etc. In the meantime, I told the boys that the "Little Boys' Room" was straight down the hall and then turn left. I told them one had better stand guard because sometimes one of the gals might venture in. They, of course, laughed.

At 7:30 P.M. we were all ready and started out on our big evening. We were going to the famous Montmartre[9] district, which, I understand is similar to New York's Greenwich Village. We went by Metro and got off at Pigalle.[10] Then we set out to find the famous Bel Tabarin.[11] We really didn't have much difficulty in finding it. I talked with one of the waiters— in French — and the place didn't open until 9 P.M. and the "spectacle" was on at 11 P.M. — which, of course, would be too late for a couple of Cinderellas like Loddo and me because we had to take the last Metro at 11:15 in order to make our darn old bedcheck. However, we were not too disappointed as there were many other famous cabarets for us to track down and besides they wanted to hear me speak (?) French. The next place we went to was Chantilly — which was a similar set-up. We ambled by the Paradise but decided to forego the information quiz there as it was a bit dark and eerie. All of a sudden it dawned on me — what about MOULIN ROUGE. (You must have heard of that place, Sarah. I believe it used to be only a theater.) Well, that's where we ended up. The place opened at 9 P.M. and the various acts began at 10 P.M. That set-up was much more to our liking.

MOULIN ROUGE is a very interesting night club. It has many little tables surrounding the dance floor. Then on the platform to the right is seated an orchestra of only string instruments; they play tango, rumba and music of that type. On the platform to the left is the wind orchestra; they played fast music, more on the jitter-bug order. The entire length of the room to the right and to the left — that is the wall — is mirror, which has trees painted on them. This gives an illusion of a forest and certainly makes the room appear huge.

When we walked into the room, we hardly knew where to look first — where to walk — and least of all where to sit. George spied a table with Champagne in a bucket and he insisted we "plunk" ourselves down right there. We asked an officer who happened to be sitting at a table next to us if the Champagne meant that the table had been reserved. He said no— that it meant you had to lay out 600 francs on the spot when the waiter came around. George said that was fine.— So we sat there. When the waiter came around — the Champagne popped for us and George was relieved of 700 francs—100 for the waiter "pour boire" [a tip for pouring the beverage]— ask Becky she knows. Our first drink — we drank a toast in Italian, Hebrew, French and English — all to our health, and then we settled down to watching everything going on —

dancing, drinking—George told me about himself; Jack told Loddo about himself. We danced and it was very nice dancing to that smooth music. Occasionally I would be wriggling the wrong hip in the rumba number and then George and I would burst out laughing. He was trying to finish up telling me of his life's history and would notice I would be "shaking" the wrong hip. So he decided I couldn't concentrate on both things at the same time—his life's history and my rumbaing. When it came time for the floor show at 10 P.M., we thought we were going to be seeing something pretty risqué (maybe that came on later—who knows???)—but it turned out to be just the same type of thing that we have back home, but, of course, everything in French—including the jokes—and frankly, they were a bit too fast and idiomatic for me to catch on. But we enjoyed it anyway.

In some of the numbers a striking-looking French girl—gorgeous red hair, beautiful eyes—wearing white flannel slacks came out to sing. She was the type that "mugged" a lot. A lot of the soldiers were interrupting—making remarks and she kept saying: "After—you will talk wiz me after." She was really very cute. After singing a number and a half, she gave up and told the guys at the table next to us—who were doing all the heckling—to take the mike—and that they did. They sang a rousing "Roll out the Barrel"—two combat boys and an officer. Then when they came back to the table, I think we witnessed one of the most touching scenes I have ever seen. There was a slight intermission and I turned around and noticed the combat boys and officers at the table next to us. The officers had their glasses raised to the combat boys and said "Here's to the Combat Men!"

I guess I forgot to tell you during the course of the evening we had another bottle of Champagne—although I told George we really didn't go in for that much Champagne, he insisted and said: "When do you think I shall get a chance to be back in Paris?"

Well at 11:15 we made our mad dash for the Metro and got back to our Hotel in time. We talked for a little while with the boys in our lobby and then bid them goodbye and wished them good luck. We all had had such a very good time—one to remember. George had me write out the names of the Cabarets we had visited so he could show off to the rest of the boys.

Guess that's about all for now, Sarah, and do give my best regards to everyone....

In this next letter, where Mollie recounts a visit from her cousin Norman, who was also serving overseas, she points out the contrasts between old-timers like herself and her friends, who were well-versed in Army slang, and relative newcomers such as her cousin.

PARIS, FRANCE
19 March 1945

Dear Beck:

Suppose you wonder if Norman got in touch with me. Well, he sure did. The following day after he telephoned me at the office he popped in. He was very fortunate in getting a pass so quickly. It seems that he told the Sgt.-Major where he is that he just had to come in to see his cousin, who is a WAC and it happens that the Sgt.-Major is a MOT, too. Anyhooo, Paris is sure getting to be a reunion spot for us Weinsteins. He ate dinner with us; went to the hamburger joint (don't think he has been away from the States long enough to really appreciate the hamburgers); then we went to the Stage Door Canteen. Ran into Bricker there. Then Bricker and I (Bricker left two of his pals at the Stage Door Canteen) took Norman to the Red Cross so he could get the information in order to get back to his place. With Norman's knowledge (?) of French, which is *rien* [nothing], I had visions of his getting lost so that's why Bricker and I took him exactly to the spot. We had to go by the Metro to get to the Red Cross and Norm had never been on it before. I sure got a big kick out of Norm though because he is so *darn* green about being overseas, etc., etc. For instance, when we talk about our *Hershey bars*—we aren't talking about our candy rations—we are talking about our overseas stripes. Norm saw the two that I wear on my left sleeve and remarked about them. But of course, he didn't know that we call them *Hershey bars*. I asked him where his *Spam ribbon* was. He didn't know what I was talking about. Our European Theater ribbon

Mollie with her cousin Norman Weinstein, left, and friend Coleman Bricker in Paris, March 1945.

Drawing by Smitty of the "little houses" (public toilets) in Paris.

that we wear over our left pocket is called that by the G.I.s. Guess you know why — we had to eat enough Spam to earn it! (But frankly, Beck, we never did have much Spam — but we laugh about it anyway.)

— Continued — Mollie

Part II of my letter of same date.

Dear Beck:

Hope you receive this letter with the Part I. Resume of Part I letter is that Norman came in to Paris to see me last night. Another thing, Norm was certainly shocked about those *little houses* [outhouses used as public toilets] on the various corners....

****

Must tell you about this little incident that occurred on inspections in the office Saturday. We were having inspection by one of the Colonels that I know. Well, when the inspection party came around and someone yelled "ATTEN-TION," we stood up and waited while they inspected around; the ledges, file drawers, etc. Then the Colonel stopped in front of me and said: "That is your name, Miss Weinstein?" That almost floored me. Usually they ask some rather difficult questions.

You want to know what I answered back????? "Corporal Weinstein, Sir!"

Guess this covers just about everything....

As Mollie wrote in her "etc. etc." letter to her sister dated February 10, 1945, the Sarge went to New York on furlough and intended to get in touch with Mollie's family while he was in the United States. As this next letter reveals, he did indeed phone Mollie's family in Detroit but unfortunately Beck was not at home to take the phone call and instead the Sarge spoke to Mollie's parents, who did not speak English very fluently.

PARIS, FRANCE
20 March 1945

Dear "Jackette:"

...Guess I haven't written home in a little while — really have been awfully busy. In your letter, you tell me about Alex's telephone call, etc. Yep, it's too bad Becky didn't get a chance to talk. Just received a letter from Alex and in it he tells me he called and speaks of Mom getting excited. He seems anxious to get back to Paris.

...Norman was in to see me last night. This coming Thursday he will be in again and will probably spend the afternoon together too. He will have a half day off. If it is nice, we shall take pictures if Bricker's camera doesn't fall apart.

...Another guy looked me up — Tech Sgt Emil Klein. It seems that his wife knows someone who knows me but he doesn't know who it is. Anyhoo, he is from Detroit.

The weather has been perfectly gorgeous and I don't mean maybe. Now I know what they mean by "PARIS IN THE SPRING."

The following letter refers to Seder, a family dinner during Passover, an eight day Jewish holiday in the spring when Jews throughout the world commemorate their ancestors' flight from Egypt and escape from slavery. During the first two days of the holiday, families conduct a Seder, retelling the story of the flight from Egypt during a traditional meal.[12] Jewish service personnel during the war were only allowed to attend one Seder. Since Mollie wanted to attend with her cousin on the second night, she had to turn in her invitation for the first night Seder.

Paris, France
29 March 1945

Dear Beck:

Have been busier than heck — also, haven't received any mail in quite some time. Maybe because I'm a bit behind in my correspondence — je ne sais pas [I don't know]. Anyway, haven't heard from you in some time…. Haven't received the shoes yet. We received our date dresses — but I really don't like mine. It seems that size 11 fitted me well — except a bit too long but then when we received the darn dresses, they didn't fit too well. Mine is too tight across the shoulders. Am having it altered.

Today is my day off & I am waiting for Norman as he will be in this afternoon. This evening we will attend a Military Seder. I had an invitation for one last night when most everyone I know was going to attend — but when I told the Chaplain I wanted to attend the Seder on Thurs with my cousin — I had to turn in the one for Wednesday.

Sunday night Bricker got some tickets to see Lily Pons & Andre Kostelanetz[13] at the Opera House. It was impossible to secure tickets because it was a G.I. performance (& everyone wanted to go) — but Bricker got them anyway. He had gone Saturday on one ticket that he won in a drawing at his hotel. Anyway, he took Loddo & me over to the Opera House & we went with another fellow who hadn't seen the performance. The other fellow is a MOT. His father's a rabbi. Loddo went with him. Anyhoo — Bricker waited for us — It was simply heavenly — Pons sang all the favorite numbers — "The Bells," "Ave Maria," "The Dancing Doll," "Estralite," "Summertime," etc. There was a 110 piece orchestra. *Wow.* Theodore Paxton — famous pianist, played "Rhapsody in Blue." *Couldn't have been better*!!!!

Monday night a number of us WACs visited an Army hospital to see the boys.[14] I brought several nice games along & left them. I played checkers with one of the boys — real cute blond boy. I wanted to leave my checker set there but he said *NO*, keep it & bring it along & play with the boys. I won 2 games & he one!!! He really got a kick out of it. Some of the ambulatory patients were walking through the ward to chow (a snack about 8 P.M.) & when they saw us WACs there — they stopped & said they could eat anytime — but couldn't talk to American girls all the time. So they hung around & talked instead of going to eat. To top it all off — Norman works at that hospital & when I walked in on him — he almost fainted. It's not too far from Paris — I cannot tell you where though. Anyhow, we were taken by truck.

A couple days ago, a friend of Sarah W.[15] looked me up. He telephoned me just now. Will probably be over in about a half hour. His name is Ted Kaminsky. Don't care too much about his type — but I'll entertain him anyway. — However, he had written me a darn cute letter, which I answered (equally as cute — I think!) but he didn't receive it. He may come to the Seder tonight — don't know yet. Our cousin Sammy's two friends, Irving & Saul, will probably be over tonight. Things get mighty involved — don't you think? To top it all off — am so busy at the office — I don't have time to whip up a letter at the typewriter. Gosh — what's this WAC coming to?

One of these days will send you Charles' letter for you to read (& keep) — really sounds serious — but it's a darn cute letter. Guess I wouldn't get tangled up with a *goy* [a Gentile or a non–Jew] though. No need to worry.

Received a letter from the Sarge. Guess he's anxious to get back.

...Ted K. did show up & was very nice. Went to Seder — 6 of us from Detroit — more later.

The next letter is from Maurice Kaye, the Air Cadet whom Mollie met in California. She enjoyed his company when they were both stationed in the United States but until this letter had not heard from him for some time.

"Italy"
4 April 1945

Hello "Shorty"

Notice new address. It is my permanent one. The 15th Air Force. Met a few of my classmates from Santa Ana and advance. Some have been here for some time and have a few missions to their credit. Went to town yesterday to bring in some cleaning. We have no facilities whatsoever for any laundry or cleaning. The road going to town is sort of a tobacco road and discourages going in. Too bad you aren't in this vicinity. No women around here at all. You can see how bad off we are.

Write soon
Good luck,
"Kaye"

PARIS, FRANCE
5 April 1945

Dear Beck:

Have been busier than h —— but was most fortunate in being able to borrow this typewriter from our Orderly Room — in fact the 1st Sgt. was very nice in permitting me to borrow this — even though it makes lots of mistakes.**---/// Loddo just asked me if I wanted to go out on some "USO activities," she happens to have a couple extra fellows, but I was adamant — "Nope, I said, can't do it tonight." Can you beat it, Beck, the number of dates we refuse! I seldom have time to write in the office and don't have much time in the evenings to write either; it's too gorgeous — "Paris in the Spring" is certainly all that they say it is.

Tomorrow night Loddo, Helen (our new roommate) and I are going to a dance at Bricker's hotel. Bricker has beaucoup pals. It was a funny thing but

Bricker asked me about two weeks ago to go with him. I usually don't like to go anywhere Friday evenings anymore because we have to get ready for a silly inspection both at the office and at our hotel for Saturday. So the way Bricker asked me about going—I just couldn't refuse. He said: "Do you think you could tell in advance whether you would be too tired to go to a dance two weeks from tomorrow, April 6th." I laughed and laughed and then said: "Okay."...

Sunday evening on our return from seeing Sally and Victor [Fish] (which I wrote Mrs. Weissenburg), we noticed the Metro was terribly crowded. In fact, we almost decided to walk home. We did take the Metro to Place de la Concorde but decided to walk from there. The streets were crowded, sidewalks, roads, everywhere. Then we stood in the middle of street and edged our way among the crowds—straight down we would see the Arc de Triomphe—a sight which I shall never forget. It was about 9:30 P.M. and Beck, the Arc was floodlit. I don't believe you can visualize the Arc de Triomphe brilliant with light. One has to see it to really appreciate it. Anyway, Bricker and I walked through the milling crowds up to the Etoile (where the Arc is) and gazed upon that magnificent sight. Truly it was like a dream. I understand it was floodlit for the first time in five years. The Cathedral of Notre Dame had been floodlit too but we didn't get to see that. I understand there were liberation ceremonies.

Yesterday, Bricker and I went to Versailles. The Hall of Mirrors is not quite as impressive as I expected it to be. You know that Hall of Mirrors was the room where the Versailles Treaty was signed in WWI. I have a very nice book on the exterior views of the palace—courtesy of Bricker—will send it home when I get through looking at it. The "Battle Room," which portrays the various battles of Napoleon, was most impressive.

Of all things, Beck, we had a French guide and honestly I don't know anything re Versailles—that is the reason. Maybe I had better study up on it in the books or get a good old American or English guide. Bricker laughed at me all the time and said I had better brush up—

Guess that takes in about everything—Oh—Sarge came back yesterday—came in the office and I was off with Bricker. Ha. But I saw him today. Sure had a swell Florida tan. Seemed glad to be back, too.

Nope, as far as I can see it—don't think I'll get a furlough. I really could use it, but we are too busy. I believe they do have a rest set-up for the guys but not much of a set up for the girls.

Must really say "au revoir"...

The following letters show Mollie's concern for her cousin Sammy who was wounded in action.

PARIS, FRANCE
12 April 1945

Dear Beck:

Before I go any further — I know that Sammy has been injured in action. A friend of his, a Medic, who has been corresponding with me *preparatory* to coming in to Paris to see me (but now won't be able to because he is no longer near) wrote me that he was able to help Sammy. However, he gave me absolutely no details. I don't believe he is able to reveal same in his letter to me. I immediately got my "G-2"[16] working and am in the process of having Lenore look up the records for me. Expect to hear from her this afternoon.

Last night Norman came into Paris. His morale was lower than heck — had received the news from home that Sammy had been injured. I told him that I was looking it up and will let him know as soon as possible. I told Norm to keep writing to Sammy anyway, and I wrote to him the same day I received the news from his friend. The mail will be forwarded no matter where he is. I told Norman there was no use worrying about it. The only thing we can do is find out where he is and if at all close, to see if he can get a pass to visit. It is rather difficult for me to get any kind of pass out of Paris for any distance. You see they really don't have provisions for WACs to get anywhere. But Norm would be able to more readily than I. We hope and pray that he is not seriously injured.

I guess I told you that Sgt. Knotts (Charlie) is in the hospital in Belgium — he did not give me any details either, saying he could not at the moment.

Will probably mail this letter the last thing in the afternoon — hope I can add some good news about Sammy.

Yesterday noon.
15 April 45

Well — Beck, you can see what happened — I just didn't get to finish this letter — forgot what my train of thought was beginning with "yesterday noon"…

Lenore looked up the information on Sammy and he is now in England. Don't say anything to his family — but I understand he is seriously wounded. The kids probably know it but don't think Aunt Hilda knows about it. I don't know if Uncle Hymie knows. I have written the Registrar at the hospital where Sammy is for more information including how long he will be there, etc. If it were possible I would try to get to see him, but don't know how long he will be there. Norm is coming in to Paris today and we'll see what we can do. However, I really am waiting to hear from the Registrar. Have written Sammy at the hospital too.

Today I attended Services at the synagogue. It was something special — for Pres. Roosevelt, memorial services.[17] Most impressive. The Army personnel were on the ground floor and the civilians on the balconies. We all feel the loss of Roosevelt very deeply but as Chaplain Nadich said — not in the exact words — but — a philosopher dies but his work and thoughts live on. They took movies, too, during the services.

     ✳✳✳✳✳✳✳✳✳✳✳✳✳✳   ✳✳✳✳✳✳✳✳✳✳✳✳✳✳

Guess I have hit the high spots for you, Beck. Really have lots to write about but darn it — no time to write it....

PS Forgot to tell you I received the shoes. They fit well and are darling. Thanks a lot.

Dear Beck:

Here's a copy of letter I recd today, 16 April, from Milton Hickman, who is Sammy's friend and the boy that was with him on pass to Paris. Am sending copy of this to Norman. I haven't heard from Sammy, though. You can pass this on to Sammy's family — but please with restrictions — if Aunt Hilda doesn't know — for goodness sakes, just don't shove this in front of her. Give it to one of the kids. I shall answer Milt's letter within the next couple of days. You can see I have beaucoup correspondence with service people. Today I received the bathing cap and stockings, also lipstick. Just swell. I sure appreciate all the running around you do for me Beck.

---

8 April 1945

Dear Mollie:

Received your letter and the snaps a few days ago, thanks.

I suppose you have heard from Sammy. I don't think he will be out too long, unless some complications arise. I would have written about it before, only I don't think that it would have passed. Some of the fellows in the platoon heard from him and he seemed to be getting along fine.

We really have a good deal now. I can't tell you what it is, but I like it much better than before. I hope Sam gets to come back with us because he has earned the chance to take things easy.

This country where we are in [Germany] is really beautiful. I suppose some people would spend a lot to get to see it, but as far as I'm concerned we have better in the States. Most of the houses we have stayed in have been modern, so far so good. I hope they continue to be that way.

One can hardly realize the number of Poles, Russians and a few Italians that the Germans have had over here for slave labor. The roads are full of them....

Thanks again for the pictures and if there is anything you would like in particular out of this country, I'll try to get it for you.

As always,

Milton

---

18 April 1945

Dear Beck:

Just received [a] letter from Sammy today. I made two copies and sent one to Norman. I am keeping one; am sending you the original as I know Uncle Hymie would want to see it in his own handwriting. One certainly has to admire Sammy — the way he takes everything. Many fellows become bitter and act as though the world is against them — but gosh Sammy is just wonderful.

Have written several letters to Sammy that he evidently hasn't received — in fact, wrote two of them this past week to his new address. He will probably receive them shortly. I shall answer this latest letter very shortly. You don't know what a relief it is to receive that letter from him.

Must make this short — am very busy.

In this next letter, Mollie makes some suggestions for her sister to pass on to the family of their friend Sidney Cohen, who was listed as missing in action in December 1944. By this time his family had received a card indicating that he was a prisoner of war, although Mollie had not yet been able to confirm his status through her own sources. It was later confirmed that Sidney was a prisoner of war.

PARIS, FRANCE
27 April 1945

Dear Beck:

Am busier than heck but just felt I had to take off a few minutes to run this quickie off to you....

Regarding Sidney being a prisoner of war. I contacted Lenore today and will know very shortly whether or not they have any record of that and will let you know or else I shall write Sarah Cohen how she should go about tracing the matter further. As I see it — I should think that she should contact the local RED CROSS where she is and show them the card she received and ask them what she should do. After all, they are supposed to be able to help you in such matters. That is indeed good news about Sidney and I hope that is the case and that he is getting along well. I shall see what information I can secure.

This next letter is from Mollie's cousin Sammy, written in response to one of the many letters from Mollie that he finally received. As he notes in the letter, he was finally old enough to vote — twenty-one was the voting age in the United States at this time, although young men were drafted to serve in the armed forces from the age of eighteen.

April 29, 1945
102 Gen Hosp
England

Dear Mollie,

I just got your letter dated the 18 April, and was very glad to hear from you again. It is your first letter I received from you also. I am so happy to know you're seeing brother Normie. He's really a sharp cat, and can dance much better than his kid brother, Sam.

I'll be looking forward to see those pictures you both took. I bet you look like a million, after all you're my wacky cousin, so you got to be sharp. You dig me there don't you Mollie??

Yes, Cousin dear you're tops, I don't know of any other cousin that beats you. In other words, Cpl. you're it....

Cousin dear, I have around 15 letters to answer. My mail is finally catching up with me. So please excuse this short letter. I don't know why I call this a short letter, because all of my letters are about the same. You figure it out.

Thanks a lot for keeping the family up to date.

Your loving cousin,

Sam

...PPS Today I'm old enough to vote. It's my birthday.

PARIS, FRANCE
30 Apr 45

Dear Beck:

Have a couple of minutes to spare so am dashing this off to you.... I am enclosing the WAC picture that you liked — it's "pour-vous" [for you].

...I forgot to tell you — the orange that you covered with paraffin did not come in good condition. The paraffin covered the orange very well, but the orange was moldy anyhooo. However, dry your tears, Beck, lately we have been receiving oranges a couple times a week. In fact, last week we received them three times in succession, which is a record. By the way, I brought one over (and Loddo gave me hers too) to Sally and Victor.

I wrote Sarah Cohen Kurland today telling her that Lenore just looked up the records on Sid. It is still Missing in Action. I told Sarah the best thing to do was to contact the International Red Cross in Detroit and have them advise her the next step. That is what I was told around here. I also told her if there was anything she wanted me to do in the matter, let me know and I would do my best.

A parade was planned in Paris to mark the third anniversary of the formation of the WAC and Mollie and her fellow WACs spent the weeks before the parade rehearsing. Technically the anniversary which was being commemorated was the establishment of the predecessor to the WAC, the Women's Army Auxiliary Corps (WAAC), which was created on May 14, 1942, when President Roosevelt signed the bill authorizing their formation. The auxiliary status of the WAAC created a number of problems, however, because the women who joined were not regarded as members of the armed forces and therefore not entitled to the full benefits of military service, although they were subject to military discipline and regulations. In July 1943 the auxiliary status was removed and the organization was renamed the Women's Army Corps, but May 14, 1942, continued to be regarded as the founding date of the WAC.[18]

PARIS, FRANCE
4 May 1945

Dear Beck:

Just got back early from lunch so I could rap this off to you. Have been very busy and have done a lot of things but honestly don't have time to write. You see we now have drill in the evenings about 4 nights a week and the other three I just don't have time to sit and write. I suppose you think we are practicing for the VE [Victory in Europe] day parade — well, we are not. It is a parade for May 14th, 3 years for the Women's Army. No doubt we will parade down the Champs Elysees. Frankly, I don't relish it — you see we are very much out of practice. Anyhow, they are trying to get us back into the swing.

The enclosed stamps — I don't know the value of them — were given to me by Bricker. I think they are a "liberated" German collection or something....

      ***********   ********

I note what you say about my being home September. Frankly speaking — if I should get home in 1945 — I'll really be doing something. So — Beck, don't get your hopes up high for September because it won't be. Anyhoo—I must admit that the war news is excellent.

Norman told me he heard from Sammy and he is "reconditioning" or something. I wished he had brought that letter to me. It sounds as though he is convalescing at the hospital. Evidently he is getting along fine. I guess I would not be able to get to him because by the time I would get my furlough he would no longer be there. Then, of course, I could not find lodging like the boys do—just anywhere. If I would get a furlough—it would probably be in July and of course, that depends on a lot of things.

Did I tell you that I heard Emil Ludwig[19] speak? It was an excellent lecture—on the character of German people, etc., etc. If I have time I might drop Mr. Slomovitz [the editor of the *Detroit Jewish News*] a note on that as I owe him a letter but just haven't gotten around to answering same.—By the way—got to hear the "spuuch" through the courtesy of—guess who?—Bricker. Loddo, Bricker and I went. It was in the morning—on our day off.

Must sign off....

As VE day approached, Mollie received news from two of the combat soldiers she knew who had been wounded: her cousin Sammy and her friend Charles Knotts. Sammy was being sent back home, probably due to the severity of his injuries and the fact that fewer troops were needed in the European theater as the war in Europe wound down. The injuries that Charles had suffered had been minor in comparison and after release from the hospital he was sent back to active service.

May 1, 1945
102 Gen Hosp
England

Dearest Cousin Mollie,

I just received the letter you wrote to the 102 General Hospital and I am answering it for them.

You see cousin dear I am going back to the *good old* U.S.A. You could have knocked me over with feather when they told me so. 'Twas I happy to hear that news, you can just imagine how I reacted. So there won't be any need for you to come. I want you to tell Norman the news, and tell him not to say anything to my folks. He can tell them I am doing fine and etc.

I am so happy Mollie I can hardly write a letter [makes a scribble]. You see what I mean!! I hope to God this war would end soon, so you all can go back to the *good old* U.S.A.

Love to all,
Your cousin Sam
PS I'll see the family for you.

---

7 — May — 1945
Germany

Dearest Mollie,

Well I guess this is it! The long awaited V.E. day so far as we know at present & that the remainder is brought to a speedy end. I received your very nice letter yesterday, had been some time since I had heard from you but there was a slight delay in the mail, I imagine that you all will celebrate, & how! Gosh I'd like to be down there, have one for me, will you? Well at the present no one knows what will happen next, all one can do is sweat it out.

...So you know where 30th Gen[20] is at, well I had my fill of the place, was in 23 days, had my ear drums punctured but they are O.K. now, one of them still has a slight opening but doesn't bother me any. Can you read this writing? I doubt it as I am doing it in quite a hurry & using my knee for a desk so can you overlook the mistakes?

Well are you going home? I hope you are fortunate enough to do so but it all takes time so you may or you may not, anyway — I'll hope for you if that will help. O' yes how about your home address again, I did have it but have mislaid it somewhere. Well Mollie I must stop for now as I have an urgent mission so write soon.

Love always,
Charles

As this letter from Charles Knotts demonstrates, with the war in Europe officially over, the American men and women serving in the European Theater of Operations began to think of returning to their homes in the United States. As Mollie discovered, however, the U.S. Army still had much work to do to help restore order to the countries in Europe which had suffered in the war, and the WACs were needed to support that effort.

11. VE Day and After: Paris
May—July 1945

VE (Victory in Europe) Day was declared as May 8, 1945, the date which formally marked the surrender of Germany to the Allied powers and the end of the war in Europe. Celebrations took place on that day all over Allied-held territory in Europe as well as in the United States, but the day was marked with particular joy in Paris, which had so recently been liberated from Nazi occupation.

In the next letter, Mollie describes the hectic and ecstatic atmosphere of VE day in Paris, when civilians and soldiers celebrated together and, as Mollie writes, "Everyone was just going wild." But, although the war in Europe was over, the U.S. military was now needed to assist in the transition to peacetime in the territories that had been controlled by Axis forces. The conflict continued in the South Pacific throughout the spring and summer of 1945, and Mollie and her friends did not know where they might be sent next. As Mollie points out in the next several letters, those who signed up for military service during World War II made an open-ended commitment and no one could predict when they might be demobilized. The Army devised a point system to determine when individual soldiers would be eligible for demobilization. Points were awarded for such factors as length of service, service overseas, medals and other commendations received and participation in combat operations.[1] Soon everyone in the Army became obsessed with calculating the points they had earned and trying to estimate when they might be released from duty.

* * *

Bois de Boulogne, Paris
Day after VE Day

Dear Beck:

Here I am in the lovely Bois de Boulogne.[2] It is Loddo's and my day off—

most fortunate, too, because last night we did not have bed check for the first time since we've been overseas.

It was a great celebration and one to remain forever in our memories. As Loddo and I are sitting next to the lake and beneath the beautiful trees — writing — a jeep with four G.I.'s stops at the roadside. They have just yelled, "Hi Yanks!" and Loddo and I both look up. "What cha doing?" they say. We yell back — "Writing to the folks back home." They yell back, "That's a heck of a thing to be doing in this beautiful park." "We can't think of anything better *we'd* rather be doing. How about you?" we say. They yell back, "Oh, we'd rather sleep." I yell back, "What a hangover you must have." They laughed and rode on.

Well — back to the celebration. The streets were jammed. It was practically impossible for any vehicle to get through. GIs were driving trucks and jeeps with people crowded all over the vehicles, as best they could through the crowds. Every once in a while a crazy jeep driver loaded down with GIs, French gals, and WACs, too, would maneuver his jeep through a crowd and whiz around the block, he'd have a siren going & flags waving in the breeze. What a sight! A couple officers tried to get Loddo and me into their jeep — but we didn't feel like risking our necks. Everyone was just going wild.

This took place in the afternoon. In the evening Loddo and I ventured forth — all spiffed up in our date dresses and dress shoes. We didn't want to be with anyone but ourselves (will explain later). We got tangled up in many a crowd. In fact, as we stood in front of the Red Cross, a G.I. grabbed me & swept me off my feet. My legs were kicking in the air; my arms waving; & I was red as a beet. He just wouldn't let me go. All the people — French & Americans, stood around & watched & laughed. He was wearing 49 shades of lipstick &, of course, wanted to wear mine. He insisted on what he called "An American kiss." But I said — "In France, we do as the French" & with that I kissed him on either cheek. The crowd laughed & the G.I.'s roared. Finally he let me go.

We left that spot toute de suite [very quickly] & let the crowds push us along to the Place de la Concorde. It didn't make any difference where you wanted to go — the crowds just swept you along with them.

A group of French boys & girls sneaked up on us, encircling us with a conga line & there we were stuck again. They kept yelling, at us — "kiss the one you wish." Loddo thought first & grabbed me & kissed me a la Francaise. We really surprised them. Everyone watching us — laughed and laughed.

We finally managed to get back to the Etoile (where the Arc de Triomphe is located) & almost was smothered in the crowds. The Arc was floodlit & the flags of the Allied nations were flying in the evening breeze. (I didn't tell you that it was a gorgeous day yesterday & incidentally today too. Just like one of those beautiful days we spent in Florida.)

Although I could write on & on, Beck, I just don't have the time nor the patience to scratch along with my impatient hand, as a lot will have to go unsaid.

This part of my letter will have to be confidential — please, Beck.

The postal card that you'll receive from the Sarge will no doubt be self-explanatory — but Beck I didn't say "Yes" and I didn't say "No" [in response to his marriage proposal]. And to top it all off — [Maurice] Kaye is now in the picture — along with Bricker, of course. Charles is definitely out and always has been. The other day, the Sarge came back from Germany and brought back a little souvenir. Guess what? A little picture (painting) of two love birds. *WOW.*

Things are very involved, Beck. Gosh, I just don't know what to do. You should see how interested everyone is in the situation — at the office, too. Of course, they don't know about the other guys. However, just to make things particularly "mish-mash" [a Yiddish expression meaning complicated or mixed up], Bricker phoned my office yesterday and the Sarge answered (WOW!). I couldn't go out with Bricker for VE day — nor could I go out with the Sarge.

Now to continue my amour situation. Kaye has flown only 2 missions and now with the war over in Europe — will probably go to the South Pacific. Must write him today — don't know what I shall say.

Oh well, it's just as bad to have a couple of offers as to have none at all.

Well … I've written Mrs. W. [Weissenburg] about the $25.00 which I delivered to Sally [Fish]. Did you tell Mrs. W. not to send any more packages directly to me? Frankly, I don't know what the Army will do with us, but please don't think just because VE Day has been declared — all I have to do is run out to the docks and grab a boat home. The Army doesn't operate like that!

Did you receive the Roth family[3] letter I sent you? Are you allowed to send chocolates to them? I know they would like that. You could send hose for her — any wearing apparel. She is small — a size 12 would be large enough. You might send some cute things for little Georgie. He is about the same size as Victor. Socks, a little striped sweater, etc.

We are watching a lot of the French people stroll by. It's all very interesting and enjoyable. I'm thinking back to the first day of my service and honestly speaking — I've never regretted being in. I've a wealth of experience in so many things that civilian life could have never given me. However, now that we can see the beginning of the end, I am not sorry that I shall have to give up this nomadic existence and return to normalcy.

We (Loddo and I) are watching a group of huge planes flying low. It's so wonderful to feel that every plane flying over is friendly.

Am wondering how the front line boys took VE Day and how about

Detroit? Must close now, Beck. Hope Mom, Pop, and Jackie are well and give my love to them....

PARIS, FRANCE
12 May 1945

Dear Beck:

Received a very nice letter yesterday from Sammy [Mollie's cousin, who was wounded]. He is in very good spirits.

Have you heard any more about Sid Cohen [the family friend who was reported missing in action]?

...Thursday night Norman [Mollie's cousin and Sammy's brother], Alec Bratt (his cousin) and I went to a Jewish place for supper. It was a restaurant. They evidently have some connections. Anyway it was good. My Commanding Officer let me out of drill that night because I told her I wanted to be with my cousin. I was surprised that she let me go. Anyhoo, last night was our last practice for our parade Monday.[4] No doubt there will be something about it in the papers, etc., back home. We will parade down from the Champs Elysees to the Place de la Concorde and there will be ceremonies at the Arc de Triomphe. There will also be French WACs and English WACs.

...Not receiving mail lately.— Of course, I am behind a bit in correspondence, too. Evenings are too nice to stay in and am still busy at the office. Don't think because that VE Day is declared that it's just *fini*— because it ain't.

Yesterday, I had to ask the Colonel to let me off for a while in the morning to act as an interpreter between Loddo and the man at the optical shop. He doesn't speak a word of English. Then later in the day, we stopped at the tailor shop and there was a WAC Lt. who was in quite a mess trying to grab off her two shirts and jump into her jeep — she was in a h--- of a hurry and couldn't make herself understood. She looked at me helplessly and asked if I could speak it. It seems the time before she was given two shirts that didn't belong to her and the tailoress wanted her to return them and wouldn't give her anything else. There were three skirts involved in the deal somehow and she wanted at least one of them for the big parade Monday. So— you can see what a mess that was. Well — I got it all straightened out and everyone was happy. It was really very simple. But I guess I won't go into that now....

PARIS, FRANCE
14 May 1945

Dear Becky:

Today we had a most impressive parade — 3rd Anniversary of the W.A.C.

Mollie, first row, second from the right, marching with her fellow WACs in the parade in Paris marking the third anniversary of the formation of the Women's Army Corps, May 14, 1945.

The US Army band played for us & were very good. All the boys said we girls looked "sharp"! We wore OD's [olive drabs], new WAC overseas caps, yellow scarves & yellow gloves. We marched down the Champs Elysees from the Arc de Triomphe to the Place de la Concorde — distance of about 1½ miles. You might even see pictures of our parade as there were lots of photographers, also newsreels were taken.

This afternoon Smitty, Loddo & I went on our roof & really began our sun tanning. I've got a pretty nice tan already. When we came downstairs after our sun siesta, we ran into our dining room (mess hall) in our slacks & ate supper. Gosh — I felt just like South Haven.

If we are still here in July (who knows??), I will probably go to the French Riviera with Loddo.

From the looks of things, etc., I don't think I'll be seeing you in 1945 — if I do — it will be quite a surprise. If they stick to the point system, — well I ain't in the running!! Oh well.

Just received a letter from Sammy. He is in excellent spirits. He wrote that

The residents of Room 220, Hotel Reynolds, Paris, on May 14, 1945. Back row, left to right: Mollie, Johnnie and Helen Lushok. Front row: Smitty, left, and Loddo.

he was going *home*.... He said for me to tell Norman — but he didn't want Norman to tell his family — so, Beck, govern yourself accordingly....

From time to time Mollie would receive a letter from her sister Beck's boss, John McNeil Burns. Mr. Burns took a close interest in Mollie's wartime experiences and would sometimes write to her to offer advice or encourage–

ment. The anecdote that he relates in this letter suggests that many Americans, both those serving in the armed forces and civilians back home, continued to have an unfavorable opinion of WACs.

May 17, 1945

Dear Mollie,

…You may think it strange, Mollie, but I know you through the reflection of your letters—much better than I would if you were here — nearly all of which Rebecca reads to me, and in which I have gotten in to the habit of looking forward to them almost as much as she does….

Now, Mollie, I want to talk a little bit about yourself and your letters. You see through Rebecca I keep track of your WAC friends as well as Bricker and some of your other associates and doings. You need not be a bit embarrassed or disturbed about that because I have said you do not realize it but I feel that I know you. The letter which you wrote describing the 4 friends making up your quintet, was a masterpiece. It conveyed an intimate picture, not only of them and such part of your life as you described in London, on the ship to Normandy, your arrival there and later of your life in Paris, but sentiment you expressed for the Catholic girls who knelt at their bedside and said their prayers for you and the girls of a different faith was a touching picture.

For some reason, probably because WACs come from every strata and fill so many different jobs that the impression was around that the GI Joes had an unfavorable impression of them. I think that has since been largely dispelled. Where Jack Burns[5] has been, he has had the impression of them that they were just a lot of grease monkeys, willing to raise a little hell if the opportunity presented itself. Jim, Janet's husband,[6] had somewhat of the same idea not having met your type at the time, and then came your letter of which I had read about Smitty who you met in London and who wrangled a cup of coffee and shared it with you that dismal night when you slept in your clothes on top of mess hall tables crossing the sub infested English Channel. The hints of your life in Normandy, that required what the men would call "real guts" and your cheerful attitude about it when you reached Paris. I sent a copy of the letter on to Jack and one to Hugo, Betty's[7] husband, who was living at the time under trying tropical conditions in Guam, doing his own laundry and sleeping in a hut infested with huge banana rats which carried off his wrist watch because of the leather. I was at the home of Paul Allens[8] on Sunday evening, when some remark was passed about the WACs merely seeking adventure. I produced a copy of your letter and read it to the assembly. There was a hush and then the exclamation that you were a fine girl, different from the ordinary WACs. Then the admission and conclusion that their impression had been all wrong. So, Mollie, your letter went a lot further than you ever anticipated.

She [Beck] has a strong hunch that you are about to be moved. We all wonder just what your work is, where you are going and when you are coming home. I know that you will be swamped with the queries of interested friends. When you do get back, I would like very much to have a quiet dinner or visit with you and your sister as my guest. Let's look forward to it.

John McNeil Burns

By this time a few things had changed in Mollie's life in the service. She had gone up in rank again and was now a sergeant (T-4), a rank which reflected the level of her skills and the value which the Army placed on them. Rather than tell her family directly when she had received a promotion, she would mark her new title on the envelope to see if they noticed. Censorship had become more relaxed and was no longer performed by the officers that Mollie worked with, so she felt freer to write in more detail, especially about her continued involvement with the Sarge (Alex Korody), Coleman Bricker and Maurice Kaye. Everyone she knew seemed to have an opinion about her romantic relationships. Her co-workers assumed that she and the Sarge were on the verge of announcing their engagement, while her fellow WACs felt that Mollie and Coleman Bricker were more suited to each other. The situation was further complicated by the fact that the Sarge and Coleman Bricker did not realize that Mollie was seeing both of them at the same time. Although Mollie had not seen Maurice Kaye since they were both in California in 1943 and early 1944, he continued to write to her and she seemed to regard him as a potential romantic interest.

Mollie had received word from her sister that their friend Sidney Cohen, who was reported missing in action in December 1944, had contacted his family and that it was finally confirmed that he had been a prisoner of war. In the weeks after VE Day, Mollie began to indicate in her letters home that she might be sent to Germany next, although this was a place that she had no desire to see.

Paris, France
18 May 1945

Dear Beck:

The Sarge gave me a German drinking mug, souvenir de German — It was sent off in a package about a week ago. No doubt you'll be receiving it in the not too distant future.

Don't know whether I told you that Wednesday evening Bricker and I went swimming — indoor pool at the Columbia Red Cross. Really was wonderful. Then we went for hamburgers.

...another letter from Kaye. Ho hum!

PS — I understand censorship is now relaxed so we can tell a lot of experiences and places we have been to that we were not permitted to before. Wish I really had time to give you a spiel....

Paris

23 May 45

Dear Beck:

Look — please get this straight the Army sends you where they want to. They don't ask you where you want to go. From the looks of things I won't be going home for some time and as I said before should I get home before Xmas 45, that would be really something. I am not counting on it one bit. Comprenez-vous [Do you understand]? I am not packing up at the moment — and anyway when and if we do move, it will be fast — and I don't think it will be the S. Pacific, however, it might be Germany. Frankly, I don't particularly relish that but if it is in the cards — guess I shall just go along.

****

Saturday night went to a wedding of the guy and gal from our office. Very nice affair. I am still undecided — everyone at the office has me all sewed up with the Sarge. In fact, I understand the first words of our Colonel were: "Where's Mollie and K------?" (K------ is Alex's last name) upon his entering the reception of the bride and groom. The reception was held in the recreation room of a hospital and it was very nice. We went there by jeep — Alex, Smitty and her friend.

Sunday night I went with Bricker to see Maurice Chevalier.[9] It was a French theater. I bet there weren't more than 15 army personnel there. Everyone kept watching us. We were sitting in the second box from the stage on the 1st floor. It was a great thrill to see Chevalier. As soon as he walked on the stage everyone applauded. I did, too, and then I just sat there with my mouth wide open — don't know why but that's how it affected me. He is all gray, quite heavy but still light on his feet and as charming as ever. The whole program was very French — not a word of English. At one time he sang about half a song right at us and gosh — everyone looked our way and I know I blushed.

Tuesday — was my day off and I went with Bricker to see La Malmaison where Napoleon and Josephine lived. It is the cutest place and we went through with a French guide. He took us there personally. I shall send you a booklet on it very shortly — when I get through reading about it. The guide took us through the 1st floor and that was all. When we started to walk out — Bricker said: — "Shucks — I wanted to see the second floor — that's where the bedrooms are!" — I laughed and laughed — anyway the pictures in the booklet really look just like what we saw.

I still hear from Kaye — need I say more? But I am not counting on anything — anyhoo.

****

...Just to make things more interesting — am going to a party tonight with Alex. Did I tell you that my Colonel gave me two bottles of Champagne — German stuff — and I understand it is very good. I gave one of the bottles to the other gal in my office as she had given hers away to her best friend who happened to be the bride. So now I've a bottle of Champagne to celebrate one of these days.

****

...That's all for now.

Paris, France
24 May 45

Dear Beck:

...You also tell me to say *Hello* to Norman when I see him — I shall. Say *Hello* to Sammy [who by this time was back home in Detroit] and wish him and also his girl friend the best of luck. He sure is a swell kid and I don't mean maybe.

...By the way — as you probably can tell from the tone of my letters we no longer have censorship right here at the office. You see our own officers used to read all the mail we sent out — I mean our personal letters. However, now there is only base censorship. That means we can seal our own letters and then someone at some central spot — I don't know where, probably goes through and reads an occasional letter in a certain number that is being sent out. So — now I can be a little more free about my personal affairs. No doubt you figured the above out — that was why I couldn't write very much.

There is such an undercurrent of stuff in my office — that is, about my personal affairs — that it really is amusing. We had a very nice party last night — beaucoup Champagne — honestly my Colonel I am sure thought I was going to make an announcement — engagement or something. Guess it is up to me. — My etc., etc. letter still stands pat. Comprenez-vous????

Beck — forget about my getting home real soon because I just know that won't be the case. In the first place I don't have the points and in the second place the Army isn't asking us anything. It's true that when I first got into the WAC that overseas duty was voluntary but just after I came overseas things were changed and that's the way it has been ever since...

Anyhooo, I refuse to get excited about it and will let things ride and see what happens. Gosh — that's the only thing you can do.

Must close and get back to work. Yep — even though the war is over in Europe we still have work and don't let anybody kid you and say that all you have to do is pack up and go home — 'cause it ain't true. and, I vas there, Charlie!!...

PARIS, FRANCE
29 May 1945

Dear Jackie:

...I note what you say about the Army arranging tours of Europe for the service men. Hell's bell's — as for me I don't know what you are talking about. I am as busy as ever and certainly no time for tours. I may get the opportunity for a week's furlough at the French Riviera but doubt that very much. As far as my coming home shortly — forget it. I am afraid the Army has other plans and they certainly don't consult me — sooooooooooooo — it looks very much like Germany.

By the way, WACs can get out if they are forty — and of course a lot of the gals that sure didn't look it, are admitting it now. I think "Johnnie" will probably be getting out on that — however, she certainly doesn't look that age. "Loddo" might be getting out but certainly not soon but she does have the required points. That leaves "Smitty," "Helen" and myself. But even having the required points, the gals won't be getting out for some time yet as there is plenty to do. Well — I guess that takes care of that!

Hope everyone is well at home — Mom, Pop and Beck. I am feeling fine....

PARIS, FRANCE
30 May 45

Dear Beck:

Am very busy but just had to take off a few minutes to tell you I received the shorts and sweat shirt today. Sure was wonderful mail service, n'est-ce-pas [isn't it so]? Thanks a lot....

Also, received a very nice package from you that arrived in perfect condition — the cheese, nuts, crackers. The crackers arrived in amazingly good condition and very few were broken, which is remarkable. Thanks again. Very nice to have the tea. I gave one of the boxes to our maid — as through her we get our shirts done — which we all appreciate so much. They won't take any money for it — instead prefer things that they cannot get — soap, ciggies, etc. You know tea is about 40 bucks a pound or something like that on the black market and that is about the only way they can get it. Really the actual franc means so little here.

Re: the points necessary to get out of the WAC — well, they have stopped accumulating (I mean the points) as of 12 May. So — I have just 37 and that's all — no more and no less. I have been hearing rumors that we may be getting a battle participation star for our service in London during the Doodlebugs — but that still wouldn't give me the 44. So — you all can take it or leave it. Oh well — I guess Germany will be next. Whatever rumors you hear, Beck, just discount them. The army hasn't consulted me. As I explained to you when I first came over it was voluntary — that is, overseas. But it isn't any longer voluntary. We are in it just like the boys and don't let anybody kid you. As far as I know, at this moment S. Pacific is not on my itinerary. — And, as I said before — no trips, other than perhaps a furlough (which I don't think I shall be able to get — d*** it) for seven days to the French Riviera. I do feel like I could use the furlough — especially now having the bathing suit, shorts, etc. Oh — well — I'll just let nature take its course. I've learned to be very philosophical about everything — so--------

Yes, I am happy to hear that Sarah Cohen recd word from Sid. Really is wonderful.

PARIS, FRANCE
4 June 1945

Dear Beck:

No doubt you have noted my falling off in my correspondence, but Beck, I can hardly find time to write. However, I do like to receive mail and it means a lot to me, but as for my keeping it up — guess at this moment I am more or less tired with the struggle of keeping everyone posted and consequently have relegated practically all my letters (with the exception of some of the boys in service) to my "inactive" file. Every once in a while I look at my darn file and decide I should answer a few letters but I just can't make it — seems as if I get sort of tired of trying to give people a picture of life overseas. In fact, I am almost getting to the point where I feel this is real over here and you back home ought to give me a picture of things. Confusin' isn't it but I think you understand, especially when I say don't get your hopes up high on seeing me this year. I am sure it won't be 1945. However, don't for one minute get the idea that I am depressed, because, Beck, I never have been. By the way — there is no need for you to "read between the lines" because our mail is not censored in our section where we work so I can certainly speak my mind.

Before I go into the real story, I shall have to preface it with a few little incidents that occurred during the week—furnish you an atmosphere worthy of the tale I have to relate.

During the week Bricker called me and we didn't feel like doing anything particular—I believe it was Tuesday evening. It was a beautiful day and the evening promised to be the same. So—we decided to go for a walk and so we ended by walking along the River Seine. We noticed a launch going up the river and we discerned 2 people in khaki waving like mad at us. They were motioning for us to remain where we were and evidently they were going to come by to pick us up. Well—we remained glued to the spot and sure enough the boat came up and it was the police patrol boat and the two Frenchmen, who were evidently patrolling the waters had already invited the Major and WAC who were in the boat and who had been waving to us, were now inviting us to join them for the ride, which we did. It was a most delightful and refreshing experience boating up and down the River Seine. The people along the banks waved to us and we waved back. Viewing the Notre Dame from the River, was most impressive. Everything seemed too perfect for words and then—bingo—it began to rain. However, even that didn't dampen our spirits because rain brought additional beauty to the surroundings for, there, suspended in the heavens was the first Parisian rainbow I had ever seen. (Let me pause here and reveal a secret to you—no different from a rainbow back in the good ole USA. That's a fact!) We finally reached our destination or rather the Frenchmen's destination and after a bit of scrambling got off the boat. We thanked them most profusely and wished we had had some cigarettes to give them but unfortunately we didn't carry any as Bricker and I do not smoke. However, the other couple did have some to give them, which they were happy to accept whereas they certainly wouldn't have accepted money. However, sometime we hope to go back there and bring them something.

Well—a couple days pass and one noon at the office what do I see but my friend the Sarge walking in with another one of the boys carrying three of the most gorgeous roses in a little bouquet. The Sarge said—(ahem) "The boys thought you would like these." I, of course, thanked them for it and thought it was very nice of them. However, when the Sarge walked out, the other boy said—"Confidentially—I had nothing to do with it—it was the Sarge's idea."
XXXXXXXXXXXXXXXXXXXXXXXXXXXXXXXXXXXXXXXXXXX
Now I come to the real draaaaama. Honestly I don't think they could cook up anything better in Hollywood even in their colossal features.

Friday evenings I usually stay in to get caught up on my ironing and shining of shoes and arranging my things—besides we have inspection on Saturday. Well at 7 P.M. the Sarge called me. I really thought he had left the country as he was going to Switzerland—which would take him two days to get to and was going to see his family for 3 hours at the border. Anyhoo, the Sarge said he wanted to know if I could see him — I told him I wouldn't be ready until 8 P.M. Well — he said he would wait in the lobby.

Lee (the girl that works with me) had just returned from London and was in my room. Well — I told the Sarge that Lee was in my room and he said he would like very much to see her as she had just gotten back from our London office. So Lee went down.

In the meantime Bricker telephones me. He wanted to confirm arrangements for our Sat. day off. He was also in the lobby. I was taking a bath and couldn't get to the phone. Anyway, Smitty had a date with someone and was supposed to meet them in the lobby so she went down. Well — that just fixed me dandy. The Sarge knows Lee and Smitty, and Bricker knows Lee and Smitty. Oh — what a situation! And to think all these months nothing like that had ever occurred — with the exception of the time that the Sarge saw me with the Lt.

Lee came dashing upstairs, opened the door and said: "Wish I could stay to see it through. Wonder how you'll get out of it. I talked to both the Sarge and Bricker." Smitty came upstairs and very cheerful like said: "Oh boy you should see the Sarge glaring at Bricker and vice versa. They are both at opposite sides of the lobby but they recognize each other."

Well — what was I to do? What would anybody do? Helen, our roommate, was in the bathroom combing her hair and laughing to beat the band. "Tell me, Helen," said I, "What in the heck does one do now? I know you've been in such predicaments before."

"Introduce them to each other," says she. And by cracky that's exactly what I did. As I walked out with the Sarge, he said: "who's that fellow?" I explained very briefly — Los Angeles, etc. Then he said "OH!" then he said — "You didn't have a date with him tonight?" I said "No."

Then later on the Sarge said: "Do you have your program planned for tomorrow?" I answered: "Yes." Then he said: "OH" again.

Anyhoo — we had a very pleasant evening but, Beck, my ETC., ETC. letter still stands pat.

You are probably wondering how come the Sarge didn't go to Switzerland. Well, he had just received a French wire which he showed me that his family were going to Marseilles on their way to Palestine. He didn't know what his next move would be and wanted to talk with me, etc. Yes, Beck, he is interested.

Well — Saturday — Bricker and I went to the Bois de Boulogne about 1 P.M. and I packed a nice little lunch with the cheese that you had sent me and I was most fortunate in being able to *hook* an extra tomato from our mess hall. (We get them about once a month.) Anyhoo, I made up the most delightful and delicious cheese and tomato sandwiches. Helen had some cherries that a civilian had given her so she was very kind and let me take some for our little lunch. We also had a couple of chocolate bars. We found a nice little spot with a waterfall bubbling in the background and parked ourselves and watched the Parisian surroundings. We took some snaps and I do hope they come out.

PARIS, FRANCE
6 June 1945

Dear Beck:

...By the way, I meant to ask you many a time — you are keeping my letters that I send home to you — aren't you?? Let me know....

Yep, today is a holiday[10] but I am the skeleton force. Is it a holiday for you? ... is it a holiday for everyone???

PARIS
8 June 1945

Dear Beck:

...You also tell me you received the Sarge's card. Please don't complicate things by writing, which I am sure would happen. However, I shall tell the Sarge that you said "Thanks" and that you thought it was very nice of him to think of doing it. Things are much too complicated already. In fact, I just heard in the office thru the grapevine that they are expecting me to announce a [wedding] date. — Of all things! I've a date with Bricker tonight. He is taking me to a dance at his hotel.

By the way, the Sarge finally did get off to Switzerland to see his family. Expect him back in a few days.

I really wish I could tell you the whole story in the detail that it deserves because you sure would get a kick out of it. By the way, the Sarge probably will get out of service way before me because he has enough points.

Oh well — I'm letting things ride at the present moment.

PARIS, FRANCE
12 June 1945

Dear Beck:

...the prices they ask are just too silly so I don't even bother about it anymore. Not that the stuff they have to sell is even anywhere near what they ask for it — it's all black market prices. I've told you how the prices run. Just the other day I happened to see a dress and honestly it wasn't worth one more penny than $8.95 (I'll grant you that $8.95 priced dress probably back home is $16.95) but it sure isn't $75.00, which that particular dress was priced at.

...I expect to get over to see Sally shortly because when and if we get ready to move, I sure won't have time to go visiting. It may be the last time I get over to see her as I am very busy. I doubt that I'll even get the furlough. However, one never knows in the Army. (I'm referring to the Riviera deal.)

These next letters are the last ones that Mollie wrote to her family while she was living in Paris. By this time, several of Mollie's friends and family who had served overseas in the Army were back home, including Sidney Cohen, who had been a prisoner of war. The relaxation in censorship meant that Mollie was able to tell them about her next posting. Charles Knotts continued to write to Mollie from Germany, hoping that they would see each other when they were both back in the United States, although Mollie always knew that she would not consider a serious relationship with him. As we see in the last letter in this chapter, Mollie finally finds out about her much-anticipated furlough in the South of France just before her office was transferred to Versailles, a few miles outside Paris.

PARIS, FRANCE
19 June 1945

Dear Beck:

Recd your V-mail letter of 13 June today. Glad to hear from you. Haven't received any mail from anyone in quite some time. By the way, next time you write anything about my ETC., ETC. situation, please don't write it in a V-mail. You see V-mails come to us not in envelopes.[11] Comprenez-vous???? Re: the situation — I don't have to work on anyone — I just have to make up my mind. I'm letting things ride though....

Looks like everyone will be home much before me, Beck. I know for certain I cannot be released for some time — darn it! — By the way, did I tell I may get another 8 points in the way of a battle participation star for the Forward Echelon. That will make my total 42. However, Lee, the girl in my office has 62 and still does not figure on getting out until perhaps November and then that is just a guess. Please give my regards to all the veterans — Ella, Helen, Sid, Sammy and any of the others. — I attended several excellent concerts with Bricker — Jascha Heifetz[12] and Alec Templeton[13] — just wonderful. Saw Eisenhower[14] and DeGaulle[15] a couple times this week. Have been darn busy....

Coleman Bricker and Mollie at the Paris zoo.

PARIS, FRANCE
25 June 1945

Dear Beck:

...we never know what is going to happen next here, but anyhoo, we are still in Paris. Thank heavens for that.

...Don't know whether or not Loddo and I will get to go to the Riviera. Everything is so uncertain. You know we are supposed to go there the first week in July. However in the Army nothing is certain. Maybe that's why I don't know what to write and so I just don't write.

...Bricker and I had some more nice snapshots taken when we went to the zoo....

Still in Paris
28 June 1945

Dear Beck:

Just a quickie — Have been very busy — at the office and otherwise.

Frankly, Beck, I don't think I will even have the opportunity of getting out [of the Army] perhaps for a year. Stenos and typists have been declared essential in this theater whether you have enough points or not.[16]

Last night saw Laurence Olivier[17] in a George Bernard Shaw play — I believe it was called "Arms and the Soldier." It was excellent and we had fine seats. I was rather disappointed in Olivier. He certainly isn't quite the romantic figure I thought he would be in person. Perhaps it was the role he played. (Bricker and I went — again.) Ahem!

It's quite certain that we will be moving. Bricker will, too, but not the same place. I am still keeping my fingers crossed re: my furlough. Bricker thinks he may get one, too....

June 30
Ebrach, Germany

Dearest Mollie,

Well at last I have finally heard from you again. I had delayed writing because I was afraid you had been shipped back to the states. Two letters! How nice it is to hear from you again. Honestly our mail has been coming very slow in fact we haven't been getting any.

Well you asked if Germany was as beautiful as pictured, yes it is, there are some very pretty places inside Germany. We have been doing disarming work and that consists of traveling a lot so we got to see a lot of the country.

So far I don't know my fate, I have only 74 points but we are supposed to receive two more battle stars. If we do and they drop the critical score I'll make it out. If that doesn't come through I guess I'll be on my way to _____? Well, whatever may be the outcome, Mollie, I think we by all means have a date in the good old U.S.A. which isn't G.I., get what I mean?

Love always,

Charles

PS I almost forgot to congratulate you "Sergeant." Good going Sgt for you deserve the best I am sure. If I was your C.O. [Commanding Officer], I'd have you wearing eagles or stars.[18]

Paris, France
1 July 1945

Dear Jack:

Am just dropping you a line to tell you I received your V-mail of 11 June. As you can see by my handwriting — am busier than heck — am packing to go to the French Riviera for a 7 day furlough. Am trying to answer everybody's mail tonight, too — have about 30 letters to write. The reason I want to get them off my chest is that while "Loddo" & I will be at the Riviera our office will move — I just can't cart the letters all over with me so I'm answering everyone very hurriedly. Our office is moving to Versailles — & then to Germany....

12. In the Palace Stables: Versailles
July–August 1945

By the time Mollie returned to work after her furlough on the French Riviera, her office had moved to Versailles. The first letter written to her sister was on Bastille Day (July 14th), a national holiday in France which marks the anniversary of the storming of the Bastille prison in Paris during the French Revolution in 1789 and the beginning of the modern state of France.

Mollie found the living and working conditions in Versailles to be very different — and much more rugged — than Paris. She had a lengthy journey each day to and from work. There were no French maids and cooks to look after the WACs as there had been in the hotel in Paris, so more of her time was taken up with routine chores. The group of close friends who had been with Mollie since her early days in the Army began to break up: although she and Loddo were still together, the other WACs remained in Paris, were sent elsewhere or were demobilized. Mollie was also separated from Coleman Bricker because he initially remained stationed in Paris and then was transferred to a location about twenty miles away from Versailles. They began to correspond but did see each other occasionally when their off-duty time permitted. Mollie and the Sarge continued to work together after the office moved to Versailles.

About the time of her move to Versailles, Mollie sent her family a newspaper article (although she did not identify the newspaper it came from) which described the work of the U.S. Medical Intelligence (including her office) since the end of the war in Europe, reviewing the German military records which were being uncovered in the spring and summer of 1945. These records were among those used extensively by war crimes and intelligence investigators in the months and years after the war. Mollie's office was also involved in assessing whether the "scientific experiments" conducted by the Nazis were of any scientific or medical value. The conclusion was that the Nazi experiments made no contributions to medicine or to science.[1]

* * *

Versailles
14 July 1945 (Bastille Day)

Dear Beck:

Very busy at the office — just returned to office yesterday from our furlough to Nice. As you can see we have moved. What a nutty set-up. It's not
going to be too permanent I can see that — or at least I hope it's not permanent. We work at the "Petites Ecuries" — translated — it means the small horse
stables (of the Palace). Not too bad though. But here is the catch. We live
about 8 miles from here — a place called "Butte Rouge." We have double
bunks. Loddo sleeps under me. I just about kill myself every time I have to get up to the top one. Sorry I didn't go in for acrobatics in my younger day.

Our happy little family has been split up. "Johnny" has gone home (age you know — however, she certainly doesn't look over 40 and I am not kidding). No doubt you will receive a long distance phone call from her. She's a swell girl and if you feel like inviting her to spend a little time at our house — do so. I think she has a friend in Detroit. — "Smitty" is on temporary duty at some school doing some spe-cial drawing. Helen remains in Paris for the time being. Thank good-ness — at least Loddo and I are together.

Mollie relaxing off-duty at Butte Rouge, July 1945.

I suppose you want to hear all about Nice. Gosh, Beck, I really have "beaucoup" to tell but I don't think I have the time to detail it all. Sufficient for the time being to say we had a marvelous time and it was really "out of this world." You know I've been keeping a brief diary since April 1945 and haven't missed putting an entry — but when I look back on my little book now I see I missed out on the 7 days I spent in Nice. Just didn't have time to write in it. Whadyaknow???? ...

Forgot to say in the above paragraph (no. 3) that Bricker was at Nice, too. He sure did the operating for us and we took in all the tours and even a sail boat ride on the Mediterranean.

PS — We don't live in a hotel anymore and eat out of mess gear. Rather hard to get used to roughing it again after that gorgeous hotel. Did Sammy [Mollie's cousin, who visited her in Paris, and by this time was back in the United States after being wounded in action] tell you how nice we had it? Them were the days!

PS 2 — *USFET* stands for "United States Forces European Theater"[2]

Paris, France
17 Jul 45

Dear Mollie,

Just to let you know I didn't make OCS [Officer Candidate School] Board[3] either. Perhaps it was for the best. I have always let the Army take its own courses on my behalf and up until the present I haven't had any real regrets. Incidentally, we were just given the Battle Participation Star for the Normandy Campaign. Isn't it a farce? Well, I won't say I can't use the points. I also checked up for you on the same star. It seems Det. "A," WAC Det. HgCmd, ETO [High Command, European Theater of Operations], was granted the Normandy Star, but it was later revoked. However, Fwd Ech, Hg CZ, ETO [Forward Echelon, Communications Zone, European Theater of Operations] is listed, so I suppose that's your second star.

Here's that rumor again. We may still have to move. The place is still Maisons Laffitte. Boy! What a big month I have. It is about 9 miles outside of Paris in the opposite direction from Versailles. We still don't have to stand reveille. This morning I noticed the girls drilling in front of the Windsor. We can see them from our mess hall.

Well, that's all for now. I must do a little work today. See you Thursday. Regards to the girls.

Sincerely,
Coleman

My Birthday 1945
Work at Versailles
Billeted at Butte Rouge
F R A N C E

Dear Beck:

Encore busy but I just had to take off a couple minutes to run this off. Guess I wrote you "thanks" for the little package.... Well — that little soap dish sure comes handy. When I go to Paris I put a little bar of soap in that soap dish and carry my little towel and few other little things in my little WACKY bag. Very handy. It's much better than carrying a big soap dish. Of course, I could sponge on the kids I know in Paris but it's much better for one not to get into such a habit — don't you think?

Regarding a request for food — Would like the following: how about some sandwich spread — pickles & olives, tuna (if you can spare — otherwise — *PLEASE* don't), crackers. I really mean it, Beck, don't send stuff that you cannot spare — I mean canned stuff. I told you that way Loddo's father sends glass jars — remember?? He puts it in a can and stuffs it around the edges. However, nothing that you have sent me has ever broken, anyhooo.

Just went downstairs — everyone in our division had their picture taken — group photo. Hope we'll get them soon — will of course mail one home to you.

Am going into Paris this evening and will celebrate with — guess who — Bricker!

The Sarge just returned from Switzerland, today. Ahem!

Guess I told you how wonderful the Riviera was — perfect weather, too. By the way, a lot of people have asked me which is more glamorous, picturesque, etc.? Hate to admit it — but must — the Riviera has it over Calif. and Fla.

Am a little behind in my correspondence but one of these days will get caught up. Seems that everyone will be home before me — I mean Sid [Cohen], Sammy [Mollie's cousin], Ted [Kaminsky], etc. Did you know that I am essential? Woe is me — Yep — stenos at this point in the game are that!

...Also "thanks beaucoup" for that great big birthday card. Pretty cute.

Don't mind so much living out in the country — plenty of fresh air and the food is better out here — that's not too bad. By the way we eat our noon meal at Versailles with the boys and use our mess gear — guess I told you that. It really is sort of fun — the boys always waiting for us to go with them — saying they want to take us out to the Ritz for lunch. Ha!

Believe I've covered everything in your letters and put you up to date on things at this end.

20 July 1945
Work at Versailles
Billeted at Butte Rouge
F R A N C E

Dear Sarah:

Suppose you'd like to hear all about Nice (The French Riviera). I really wish I had time to detail the beauty of that place to you and the wonderful time we had there.... In the morning we'd go touring; afternoon swimming in the blue Mediterranean; in the evening night clubbing. Wow! Bricker was there — too — ahem.

Loddo and I roomed together and a couple of cute gals that we know very well were with us too. We had a most wonderful time. Nothing G.I. — really back to civilian existence. We'd put our shoes outside our door at night and presto in the morning, they were shined. They'd slide the newspaper under our door in the morning, too. They'd press our clothes for us. All — thru the courtesy of the govt — not bad. We just paid 100 francs when we got there and that was that. The Red Cross tours were free. So — all in all — was inexpensive to say the least.

Loddo's future brother-in-law, who is a Lt., was there. He is officially assigned as a manager of a hotel — or I should say three hotels. He did have difficulty in going out with her as Nice is a recreation area for enlisted personnel only — even though he is stationed there. But leave it up to Loddo — she got around it anyhoo.

Yesterday — of course — was my birthday. Those things sure creep up on one. I went into Paris and met Bricker at my old hotel at 8 P.M. There he was waiting for me. He handed me two packages. One was the most beautiful corsage — 5 red rosebuds. The other was Je Reviens Perfume and Je Reviens Cologne, rather substantial size, too. We went to the G.I. night club in the Montmartre district. Had champagne — ahem! We had a very nice time. One G.I. came up to Bricker and asked if he could dance with me — Bricker gave his okay and so we took off. He was really the smoothest dancer — used to do regular ballroom stuff. Gosh — I was out of practice for that kind of terpsichorean [dancing] art. He said to me — "You know I've waited 12 months to dance with an American girl." I laughed and said: "That's beaucoup SNOW, but I like it. However, it's too bad you picked on me 'cause I cannot do your fancy dancing justice." Anyhoo, we had 4 dances together and then walking back to our table he said: "Perhaps you and your friend and I can get together another time." — Oh — Ho. Course I didn't bother to take him seriously. Though he meant it.

Later in the evening just before we were ready to leave, an excited G.I. came to our table and said: "You're a medic, aren't you?" I said that I was. Then he said that some girl (French) had passed out — not from drinking. He

wanted me to go with him. I said that I was just a steno. But I went along anyway.— Well the gal was stretched out on a table. There were about thirty people hanging right over her. Someone had placed a cold cloth over her temples.
Really I didn't know what was wrong. She complained about a pain in her right
abdomen — in French. Gosh — I'm not a doctor — in fact my work doesn't concern diagnoses — I've forgotten what I did know about making diagnoses
(ahem). Anyway — I told them all to get away from her and just let her girl
friends and two other boys stay with her. I asked if they had notified a doctor
or called an ambulance and they had done that. There wasn't anything I could
do. So that was that. I felt rather inefficient about the whole thing. But what
would you have done? One of the G.I.s who was with the girl said that he
thought she threw the "fit" (which it wasn't) for his benefit. He was very nice
looking — but I do think he was flattering himself a bit. The whole thing was
too involved so in parting I gave him a bit of advice — says I — "Well, just don't
get tangled up in anything, compris?" He said: "No, Maam, I won't get tangled
up."

By this time Bricker and a couple of other nice guys who had been talking
to us at our table were beginning to wonder what happened to me. They were
going to send out a scouting party. However, I returned in the nick of time.
When I got back it was time to leave as I had to catch a bus that leaves from
our hotel back to Butte Rouge and still had to make the METRO to Hotel
Windsor. One of the boys came up to Bricker and asked if he could dance with
me. I hated to say no because it was time for me to go— and I don't think the
boy believed me as it was quite early about 10:45 P.M.— but such is life when
you're a country hick.

You asked me about the Sarge. Today, he returned from Switzerland. Yep,
he is still here.

Guess that just about covers everything. Haven't written Beck about the
above — so you can let her read it as I don't want to repeat myself. You might
let Beck keep this letter so it can fit in with my *episodes* that Beck has on me.

Guess that's all for the moment....

After just a few weeks of working and living away from Paris, Mollie
discovered to her surprise that she was enjoying life in the countryside,
although she continued to go into the city for evenings out. At this point
there was a great deal of uncertainty about where she might be sent next,
when and for how long, although she expected a transfer to Germany soon.
Many other American soldiers who were in Europe in the summer of 1945
were in the same situation, as the Army tried to determine where it would
need different types of personnel, both to administer postwar Europe and to

fight the ongoing war in the Pacific.[4] In addition to the uncertainty about longer-term arrangements, Mollie went through a number of short-distance moves from one accommodation or building to another which required time-consuming packing and unpacking. Once the unpacking was done, of course, Mollie then had to arrange her possessions in accordance with the Army's strict requirements.

26 July 1945
Work at Versailles
Billeted at Butte Rouge
F R A N C E

Dear Beck:

Received your letter of 16 July the other day. That was the one saying you had not received any *real* letters from me in some time.... Today I received your letter of 19 July. So you can see the mail service is not too good. In it you say you haven't heard from me in a long time.... You ask about [Maurice] Kaye. Yep, I still hear from him. However, he expected to go back to the States any day now and then on to the CBI [the Pacific theater — China-Burma-India], or he may go direct to the CBI from Italy. He cannot possibly get out [of the Army] as he doesn't have enough points nor does he have enough missions.

Last night I went into Paris and met Bricker for swimming at the Red Cross Pool. One of the other boys in my office [Karl] met us there. We had great fun and enjoyed the swim immensely. Course Bricker and I wanted to go to the Hamburger Joint after the swim as we had appetites — but I had a problem — how could I sneak Karl in with us as no stags are allowed into the Joint. I just couldn't see Karl parting from us at the Red Cross and we go on to have those nice hamburgers and so I said "Come on along and let's see what we can do." (It's practically impossible to get a last minute date, especially to ask a WAC to go just there — she thinks it is the hamburgers company you're interested and not her!) When we arrived at the entrance of the Joint, the MP [Military Police] looked at us and sized up the situation. I told Karl to wait outside and Bricker and I went in. We ordered two extra hamburgers and I splashed them with catsup on one side and mustard on the other side and wrapped them up in Kleenex and then put them in my little "ditty bag" that contained my swimming equipment. Bricker dashed outside and in front of the MP and said: "Mollie would like you to carry this home for her." Then out of the side of his mouth, he said: "Couple in there for you." You see we're not supposed to take any out either. Well today in the office Karl returned my swimming equipment, etc. and told me how much he enjoyed those hamburgers.

By the way, Ted Kaminsky just telephoned me. He is a patient in a hospital not far from Paris and is awaiting evacuation. He will probably get in touch with me Saturday morning — if he is still there. You see he is scheduled to leave very shortly. I shall be off Friday evening and all day Saturday. I will be staying at a special WAC hotel for girls that live out of Paris. Bricker and I will probably go to the show. Saturday morning Bricker works so that's the time I expect Ted to call me at the WAC hotel. I sure hope he does. Don't know if he will be able to leave the hospital to come to Paris to see me. Sometimes they do permit the patients to go into Paris. There is nothing too radically wrong with Ted so perhaps he will be able to do it. I want Ted to look you up.

Expect to see Bricker later in the afternoon as he has that off. Then we expect to come out to Butte Rouge to eat our evening meal out there. You see the fact that we have "good mess" spreads around Paris so I do want to invite Bricker for at least one meal at our place. The wide open spaces are pretty nice and for once I almost feel as though I could live in the country and enjoy it. Can you beat that? All the gals have always kidded me because I am strictly a city kid and I've kidded them and said life was too dull in the country — Oh me!

Of course, you want to know more about the *ETC.* situation. I cannot unravel it myself — so there! I am doing nothing about it anyway at the present so you can tell Mom to get that glass out of her eye. (Ha! — Ha!) A lot has happened but it is too lengthy to go into it at the moment. Probably could write you a book. Sufficient to say — that I find "nothing definite" best at this time. Comprenez-vous [Do you understand]?

By the way, I shall be moving — rumor has it within 10 days to Wiesbaden, Germany. — Bricker, I think, will be leaving Paris, but he doesn't know where at this time. Surely will miss him. You should see the cute letters he writes. — Don't believe I wrote you about spending my birthday with Bricker. Sarah has the letter on same.

You probably wonder why I haven't been writing. First of all, the mail service isn't too good. Secondly, things are very much up in the air around here. We've packed and unpacked our silly duffel bags and that takes time. We've had to get our clothes in order and then before you know it, we have to pack again. We just get our room nicely arranged and they decide we have to move into another. Then, going into Paris takes in the whole evening. Then, too, we are busy at the office. So there you have the full story.

That's all for now and hope this letter makes up a bit for your not hearing from me....

As Mollie indicated in her letter above, Coleman was anticipating his transfer out of Paris and the very next day he learned that he would indeed be moving to the outskirts of the city, but in the opposite direction from Versailles.

Paris, France
27 Jul 45
Fri Morning

Dearest Mollie,

...When I returned to the office, the Colonel was in the midst of delivering a speech. The text — movement to Maisons Laffitte on Saturday or Sunday. He told how the first Allied Airborne Army headquarters had been there and made themselves very much disliked. He said the French would probably resist us a great deal because of the actions of this other group. He also said that if the Chief of Staff hears any complaining that person would be given an assignment directive to the CBI tout de suite [very quickly]. Well, that's all I know about that. ... I'll tell you more after we move.

Sincerely,
Coleman

Paris
28 July 1945

Dear Beck:

Had an overnight pass at the enlisted women's hotel [the Patio Club] as pictured on the other side [of the postcard she was writing on]. Now that I don't live in Paris we get such passes. It's very nice. I have a delightful room to myself. I've checked it (see check mark). This is an actual picture of the "joint." I'm sitting (at the X) writing to you. Bricker's meeting me for lunch. He is leaving Paris next week....

Mollie continued to hear from Charles Knotts, who was still in Germany and increasingly dissatisfied with the living conditions of his unit in comparison with those of the recently defeated Germans.

July 29
Sunday
Germany

Dear Mollie,

...You mentioned on the card that you probably would be leaving Paris soon ... but if you were here a while you would see that it is no good. It's too bad you had to leave the hotel. I bet you all hated to leave, didn't you?

Well you see I have a new address since you last heard from me, I am supposedly on my way home.... I lived better in combat than I am now. We are stuck out here in a field in tents. Imagine that, conquer these _____ Nazis and then end up like this. It makes a guy wonder what it was all about as if someone has sympathy for some of these people. We could be living in some Nazi's house if they had the guts to kick them out but the way I look at it is that as far as they are concerned they are done with us as it doesn't matter much what we get. So with a start like this what can we expect in civie life. I am pretty well disgusted with the whole thing myself. They have inspections and look for everything and say they are making soldiers out of men with five and six years service who are on the way out. The only thing we are hoping for is that it isn't long until we will get out of here. I have 84 points so I am not worrying too much about it.

Glad to hear you had a good time on your rest leave as we call it. We are under the 9th Air Defense Company and they have a couple of places the guys go. I could have had a pass to Paris a few days ago but then I had received your card that you may be leaving soon so as I had already seen Paree I gave it up.

...Well Mollie I'll have to close for now so write soon and I hope we meet in the U.S.A. soon! *Virginia*!

Love,

Charles

The anti–Semitic graffiti that Mollie mentions in the next letter indicates that not all the French welcomed the liberation of their territory by the Allied forces. Marshal Philippe Petain, praised in one of the slogans that Mollie saw painted on a wall, had negotiated an armistice with Germany in 1940 when he was France's vice-premier. The terms of the armistice gave the Nazis control of the northern and western part of France, including Paris, leaving the rest of the country nominally independent under the leadership of Petain and a government based in the city of Vichy. In reality, however, Petain's regime collaborated extensively with the Nazis and cooperated in the persecution of Jews living in Vichy-controlled France. Petain fled to Germany after the D-Day landings but was sent back to France after the liberation to stand trial for his actions. Petain's trial began in Paris on July 23, 1945, just days before Mollie's letter was written.[5]

30 July 1945
At the office, 5:15 P.M.
VERSAILLES

Dear Beck:

Over the weekend — as I wrote you in my postal card — I stayed at the Patio Club (for enlisted women). I ran into a girl there who was on a three day pass. She is stationed at Wiesbaden and says it's not too bad there. She says if you mind your own business, things are okay. The scenery and climate are both very nice.

Went into Paris last night. Smitty met her friend and I went with Bricker. Went to the Hamburger Joint — Loddo and her friend were there, too. We really had a grand time. Went dancing there.

Bricker moves today — gosh — don't know what to say about it.

...you ask if the entire office moved to Versailles. Yep — the Sarge is here, too. This, I do know for sure, though, the next move we make there will be changes. I feel very badly about some rumor that I've been hearing and which I feel sure to be true — Smitty and Loddo will probably remain in Versailles....

...Please send me some leather for repairing shoes, especially heels for my civilian shoes. I understand it is difficult to have civilian shoes repaired — that is, procuring the leather in Germany. The army will not take care of civilian shoes for us. Send me a piece about 10 inches by 10 inches. Should be ample. I don't contemplate wearing out those civilian pumps but it would be handy to have in case I should spring a hole in those pumps. After all I go to dances frequently and that should wear shoes out more than back home.

...By way of interest, the other night Bricker, Smitty and I were walking around where we live — which is the country and we came upon a large estate all fenced in with a brick wall. Painted in bold letters was the following — "Vive Petain" "Mort Aux Juife" ["Long Live Petain" "Death to the Jews"] — and there were a few other remarks, which had been sort of washed away.

You ask me if I should like a diary. If you can get a nice flat one — not a five year one as I am sure it would be too bulky — I would appreciate it. Do they have diaries for one year and something not too cumbersome? You see we like things that are compact. For instance, that was a nice French dictionary you sent me but yet it was bulky — I like something rather flat. If you cannot find something like that, please don't run your feet off looking for same.

...You see our water is pretty hard and it is difficult to get the soap out. Perhaps, too, you can find some special soap for hard water. I remember when we came across on the ship from New York to England, we had some very nice Jergens soap for hard water. It really lathered up beautifully. About 3 or 4 bars would be enough.

...Am enclosing some German insignias that are worn in the Sleeve of the German uniform.

Guess I didn't tell you out here at Versailles we have German PWs [Prisoners of War] who wait on us during our noon day meal. Some of them try to smile at us—but "Wir machen keine aufmerksamkeit." [We pay no attention] Comprenez-vous?—So that's that.

Course every time I think about the way our boys fraternize with those frauleins in Germany—I get so d---**/// mad.

By the way, Beck, you have never told me whether you are keeping all my letters. I hope you are. Please let me know. Everyone's been teasing me about writing a book—so maybe someday I might want to use a couple letters for reference. (Ha! Ha!—don't think I'd ever get beyond paragraph No. 1.)

Here's a picture that I've never had the nerve to send as both Johnnie and I look so goofy in it. Bats looks pretty nice. It was taken last year in August when we were in Normandy. I had thrown it in amongst some papers and forgot about it—just popped up the other day. That's the tent we lived in. Did I ever tell you that we were near Valognes when we lived in Normandy?

Maisons Laffitte
31 Jul 45

Dear Mollie,

Well, here I am finally located in my new country home. We were worked like draft-horses moving the rest of the office. My hands are blistered and my shoulders ache. I guess I need it though. After moving our section, we had to help several other sections because their boys goofed off.

Last night, I unpacked my duffel bag and put my stuff into a cabinet I confiscated. There are 5 of us in my room including Dave Woods and Dick [friends of Coleman that Mollie had met]. It is just a bit crowded. It will take us some time to really clean the place up. Last night the water was turned off making it difficult to clean up. We had to run back and forth with helmets of water from the house next door. I managed to get cleaned up after that race. Incidentally I am on the second floor. I hate to admit but the average fellow here says that he likes it here and is satisfied with being away from Paris. I won't give you a chance to say that I am stubborn, by not siding with the boys. All I will say is that this place has possibilities but as for myself give me the big city. We are a short distance from the center of town. The town is typical French with dirty buildings and streets. The residential section is similar to Malmaison with 15 or 20 room homes surrounded by high iron fences. We have a large backyard, I say backyard because that's the way we do at home. I should say grounds. There is a tennis court which needs cleaning up. Our room has a veranda that can well serve as a sun porch. As a whole, the place is well run down but it could always be worse. We are about a ten minute walk from the office.

Here's a little note for Smitty. Tell her I said the mosquitoes attack in air fleets, bombing squadrons and whole air forces. You ought to see Dave. He looks like he has chicken pox; he has been bitten up that much. The Seine River is about ½ mile from our house and close by to the office. It is very dirty and smelly.

Today we had a good laugh in the office. I took your picture out and set it up before me. Every time Lt. Griffiths would come over to my desk, he would turn the picture around. Finally I said, "She gives me inspiration." He snaps "The wrong kind of inspiration."

Well, Mollie, that's all for now. I don't have a phone number to give you just yet, but I'll let you know soon. Hope you are well and happy. Regards to the girls. Guess I'll hit the hay.

Sincerely,
Coleman

Aug 1
A.A.F. [Army Air Force] day
Germany

Dear Mollie,

Well as this is air force day and we are at ease except that I have been on C.Q. [Charge of Quarters] I have Beau Coup time so decided to write you a few lines.

It has been quite cool here for a couple of days and living in tents is nix good. However, am hoping tomorrow is warmer.

Well the way rumors are going around here we may leave here sooner than expected. The general opinion is somewhere around the middle of this month. I hope so anyway.

I told you in my other letter that I was up for a furlough to the U.K. [United Kingdom]. Well they are supposed to be cancelled so I am going to Berchtesgarten (I missed it), anyway it's Hitler's redoubt.[6] It should be interesting. I am supposed to leave the 3rd. I suppose about the time I get ready to go they will continue with furloughs to the U.K. I would have liked to visit London again. I made them all but Berlin. I did get within about 55 miles of Berlin once and the Russky's stopped us. We had some Jerry [German] motorcycles riding around. Maybe I didn't tell you. Well when we were up at Zeitz near Leipzig [cities in Eastern Germany which came under Soviet control after the war], we had to move when the Russky's took over. The people were certainly scared of their coming. They were always asking the fellows when the Russky's were coming. They were close to the Russian line and had heard some stories of how Russky's treated Germans.

Well Mollie you beat me over here to this ETO [European Theater of Operations] but if nothing happens it looks like I'll beat you to the U.S.A. Well, I'll have a grand reception then for you when you land.

I will close for now so write soon and I wish you luck. Are you in line for staff [promotion]? I am in line for "Civilian."

Love,

Charles

PS I am not bragging Mollie but I do feel good about it.

---

2 Aug 45

Versailles (At the Office)

Dear Beck:

...tell me about Mom's statement that I should keep the perrrrrrfuuuum now that I work in the horse stables. Ha! Ha! ...

Regarding Xmas packages to me — please don't bother about sending me anything that comes in the Xmas category yet. I just as soon you would fulfill my requests and that's all. Frankly, I don't know when I shall be coming home. Everyone is very close-mouthed about the whole thing. You can imagine how much work we have when we are even taking on personnel now. Phooey, and such!

Am quite certain of going to Wiesbaden, Germany within a month.

I told you that Bricker was moving — well he did, but I received a telephone call from him last night. Am meeting him in Paris Sunday evening. He sure doesn't stray long from the fold, eh what? Re: the situation ETC. and ETC. — everything is up to me. So that's that. Guess I am a goon----agree?

Note: Another change of address as per envelope.

Mollie continued to act as a liaison between friends and family in Detroit and their loved ones — civilians or service personnel — who were in France. She would sometimes even receive letters like this next one, from people she did not know personally but who had heard about her from other acquaintances and wrote asking for her help. The writer of this letter knew the Weissenburg family in Detroit, who had asked Mollie to find their relations in Paris who were refugees — Sally Fish and her son Victor.

Beck: I answered this letter recently but thought you might enjoy reading it.

Mollie
August 1945

Detroit, Michigan
1136 Atkinson Ave
April 15, 1945

Dear Miss Weinstein:

My son Sgt. Martin Nadler who is in France wrote me all about the fine time his buddy had while visiting Paris all due to his acquaintance with you. And I want to thank you for your interest in our Jewish boys.— My son Martin tells me he is looking forward to a visit in Paris and will look you up when he gets there — if and when — it was through me that they reached you as I gave him your address having received the same from very good friends— The Weissenburg family in Detroit.

I am now visiting them and taking the liberty of writing these few words to you and hope someday to have the pleasure of meeting you and your folks— in Detroit.

I come to you with a special request hoping you may be able to do me a favour while you are in Paris.— My other son, P.F.C. [Private First Class] Leon Nadler #16161371 is in the hospital with a wrenched back somewhere in France.— He has been there about 10 weeks. All the time that he has been there he receives no mail from home. I have sent 2 cables to him but he did not get them up to the present time, while we do get his mail. He is very much depressed as he does not hear from us. No doubt you could obtain the location of his hospital and communicate with him advising him that we do hear from him and that we write daily to him and that we are in good health.

He is supposed to be receiving therapeutic treatments but at the hospital where he is, it seems they do not have the necessary equipment. I wish he could get to Paris in the Hospital you are in.

Anything you can do for him will be very much appreciated. We are very anxious that he knows we are well and that we receive his mail — and very sorry that he does not get our mail....

With the kindest personal regards and wishing you good luck and many thanks to you, I am

Your truly
Louis Nadler

---

3 August 1945
Versailles (at the office)

Dear Beck:

...Today, Loddo and I were really smart. Don't know how long we shall be able to get away with it — but this noon we went back to our Billets in the shuttle bus for lunch. The meals are so much better out where we live and also Loddo hadn't been feeling well — think something disagreed with her at our mess hall — so we thought we'd take the chances and go out there. We really had a humdinger of a meal — delicious steak, fried onions, French fries, stewed tomatoes and butterscotch pudding. We would probably get conked on the head if they caught up with us — but we don't care.

Must sign off for now....

Although Mollie addressed this next letter to her friend Sarah Weinstein (Nash), she made a carbon copy of it and sent it to her sister. The stories Mollie tells of the chance meetings of friends and acquaintances and the planned meetings which fail to take place reveal the many daily uncertainties that plagued military personnel at this time. Everyone in the Army was subject to last-minute changes of plan to their travel, work and accommodation arrangements.

Versailles at the office
6 Aug 1945

Dear Sarah:

Received your newsy letter of 30 July and was certainly glad to hear from you. Somehow all the mail has dropped off around here. No one seems to be getting any — including me!

Enjoyed your letter very much — laughed about your wondering what BEAUCOUP SNOW meant. Let me see what would be the best way to explain it to you — Oh I know. Here 'tis. If Sgt A hands Cpl B lots of compliments that Cpl B doesn't believe — Well, she says to Sgt A: "that's beaucoup snow." In other words— Comprenez-vous? I believe the expression SNOW is used back in the States. However we picked up the BEAUCOUP here in France.

Yesterday I met Bricker in Paris and we went to the night club in the Eiffel Tower. (I was supposed to meet him at 7 P.M., thinking that he was working and I was off. I get there at 4 — the Windsor Hotel — and here he had been waiting for me since 1 P.M.— was taking a chance on my coming in early. He didn't have to work. He was unable to get a phone call through to me at my billets. What a life!) It was the second night of its existence. Really is a snazzy place with the cool Paris breezes wafting through that 1st platform of the Tower where we were. I ran into someone that I had been waiting to see for some time — a friend of my cousin Sammy. He is from Detroit — fellow by the name of Irving Klein. It was really a "co-inky-dinky."

Some Sgt that I didn't know came up to me and showed me a WAC's name on a piece of paper and asked me if I knew her. I did not but from the address, told him I thought she had left Paris and was probably living at Butte Rouge where I was. I gave him the address but he said he couldn't make it that night as he was in on leave and had to return the next morning. However, he might be able to make it sometime later. It seems that two years ago he had a date with her at some camp and she was shipped overseas and so he was aiming to catch up with her. — I told him to wait just a minute and I'd ask some other WAC that I spied in the Club and thought perhaps she might know the girl. Well as luck would have it, that WAC was the other girl's roommate. Isn't that cute? (This all happened at the Eiffel Tower night club.)

Another interesting incident occurred there. Some fellow came up and asked Bricker if he could dance with me. 'Course Bricker said yes. Well — while we were dancing the fellow kept saying "You sure look familiar to me and I am not handing you a line." I thought he looked familiar to me, too. I said: "I think we have seen each other at the Allied Club in Paris." — You know when I got home last night I finally figured it out. I had met him in Normandy a year ago and we were in the mess hall line. He happens to be a MOT [Member of Our Tribe]. Sure was a smooth dancer; tango and rumba. Not that I am so hot — but he just made me put my tootsies just where he wanted me to. He was leaving for Berlin the next day.

That was for Sunday.

Well today I get to the office bright and early and one of the boys said something about one of the jeeps having to go to the 1st General Hospital. That's where Ted Kaminsky was. Anyhoo, I went along (The Sarge went too). When we got there, I inquired whether or not Ted had left. You see Ted had warned me that he would be leaving any time for the States. I took the chance and darn it (but fortunately for Ted) he left by plane just the day before. Anyway, we ate our lunch out at the hospital as it was after 12 noon — so I ate with all the guys.

I guess it just wasn't meant for us to meet again on this side. Last week Ted came in to Paris on Sunday and looked me up at the Patio Club but I had left the day before. Oh well — that's the army!

Do give him my best regards when he looks you up as I know he will come in to see you.

At this time, both Charles Knotts and Coleman Bricker were writing to Mollie frequently and wanted her to know how much they cared for her and thought about her when they were apart. In the case of Charles, the fact that he was not Jewish meant that Mollie was not prepared to enter into a serious relationship with him, however much she liked and respected him. As for

Coleman, Mollie clearly enjoyed his company and regarded him as a possible future husband, although she did have doubts about the age difference between them (in particular the fact that he was younger than she was by several years) and about the extent of his attachment to his girlfriend back in the United States.

Aug 6
Outside, Ansbach

Dear Mollie,

Well another lonely day, raining and nothing to do so as I received your letter you wrote while in Paris on pass decided to spend a bit of time this afternoon in your respect.

Hope everything is going alright with you. We are still out here in tents & right now it isn't so good because it is cold up here today.

We haven't found out much about leaving here or when we are supposed to ship out. It may be a long time according to the S. & S. [Stars and Stripes newspaper]. I hope that if we do have to stay here someone gets on the ball & does something about the conditions here.

We are across the highway from an air strip, R.45 and a week or so ago some WACs were assigned to the base. Already some wild stories have circulated around, in a couple of cases not so wild I don't think. I don't know why I am telling you this, maybe as a forewarning, anyway Mollie when & if you do come to Germany you are going to see plenty that right now you wouldn't believe. You tell me if you haven't after you are here a while. It's a sad sight at times.

I don't know what you think Mollie as I have never asked you, I guess I always felt there was no use but just the same I have always had the highest respect for you & although I never attempted to reveal any particle to you I have cared very much for you. Maybe I am being a bit foolish in telling you this, I don't know. If I am, tell me, will you? Just the same though you can't blame a guy for saying what he thinks that is if he doesn't think too much. Maybe I have thought too much but regardless Mollie I can assure you that you have been very dear to me.

I have made a very poor attempt at trying to tell you this but I felt I had to tell you how I felt.

Well Mollie I have said enough, maybe too much. I have often wondered what would happen if I did tell you. Well Mollie put me straight on the subject, will you? It will be better.

I'll close for now so write soon.

Love,

Charles

Maisons Laffitte
6 Aug 45

Dear Mollie,

I caught a truck directly after leaving you last night and made a fast trip back. Believe it or not, we were back in less than twenty minutes.

Your letter was on my bed when I came up to my room. Your letters are just as cheerful as you are. I can hear you saying "There he goes with the snow-job again." I wonder what the girls will do when you have moved on and are not around to cheer them up and give them advice. As for myself, I don't have to say how much I enjoy your company and wit. Your kind are hard to find and to equal, believe me.

I really had a swell time last night at the Tower Club. I don't know how your feet can take such a beating and yet you come back and ask for more after dancing with clumsy me. I was almost speechless when you asked to dance to "Long Ago and Far Away" with me. That gesture meant a lot to me, Mollie, and I won't forget it. I suppose it is easier to put this into writing than into words.

...I started operating as soon as I got to the office this morning. I am going to be off every Sunday now. So if you don't mind, I would like to spend Sunday at your place if you like. I would come out early Sunday morning or if you stay over Saturday night, we could go back Sunday together. I still have a half day off for this week. Are you going to ask for an afternoon off to attend to your business? I will probably phone you by the time you get this letter. How's about coming in and going swimming Wednesday evening?...

Say hello to the girls for me. Hoping to see you soon.

Sincerely,

Coleman

In the next letter, Mollie refers to the Soviet Union's declaration of war against Japan on August 8, 1945, three months after the Allied victory in Europe and just two days after U.S. forces dropped the first atomic bomb on Hiroshima on August 6th. There was no announcement at the dance that Mollie attended about the Americans' use of this new weapon against the Japanese.

Versailles (at the office)
9 August 1945

Dear Beck:

Last night Loddo and I decided to give the guys in Versailles a break and attended a dance at the Hotel de France. Really wanted to see the ballroom, which is very impressive. The floor is really smooth. However, the things that really impressed me were the chandeliers that were suspended from the ceiling — the most gorgeous things I have ever seen; cut glass, edged in gold. A number of the interesting incidences occurred but nothing spectacular that is personally. There was one very nice fellow (married) who works at the Surgeon's Office with me and whom I have known for over a year. I asked him to rescue me every once in a while, which he did. You know how at a dance you get tangled up with jerks — well this guy Phil would disentangle me when I would give him the distress signal. — Must say, though that one spectacular thing did occur and that was the announcement of Russia's declaring war on Japan, which was announced on the dance floor by the band leader. I am wondering how that announcement and the certain (I hope) early defeat of Japan will affect us individually.

By the way, yesterday I asked my Colonel for the day off as we moved from one billet to another at the Butte Rouge and I also had to go into Paris to do a little clearing up on personal items. He was very nice and let me take off the whole day. I caught the 9 A.M. bus with Smitty and we landed in Paris. I stopped into WAC Personnel and checked up on my records to be sure I was credited with those additional 5 points. I told you I wasn't sure I would get them — Well, I definitely have 42 points now. Anyway, I am still considered essential as a steno. — Then Smitty and I went to the QM [Quartermaster] store and bought some moccasins that we were permitted to buy — one pair each. They are nice for slacks. — Then Smitty and I rushed back to Versailles on the train and made it in time to catch another bus back to Butte Rouge. We met two of Smitty's friends (guys) from her office and they ate lunch with us at Butte Rouge and then helped us move.

We were going to room three in a room (Smitty, Loddo and myself) even though our C.O. [Commanding Officer] had said there would be only two in a room. However, she knew how we palled around and inasmuch as we had written a personal request for it, she consented. But at the last minute I felt sorry for another gal who had been with us temporarily at Butte Rouge so decided that I would room with her — she looked so lonesome when she realized that she would have to find somebody else. So now I am billeted with Lois Hutchins — Smitty and Loddo in the room next to us. Lois is a very cute gal and very nice — hails from Oregon. She has just been overseas 3 months.

You ask me should you send me any packages because of my impending move. You can go ahead and send me stuff because it will get to me anyway.

The latest dope is that we may go to Frankfurt instead of Wiesbaden. Anyhoo, it is a toss-up. We are supposed to go by 1 September. However, nothing is definite about our situation — other than Smitty and Loddo will remain back and should we make the move, I shall go forward.

By the way, the Sarge is off to Switzerland again....

Still not getting any mail — wonder what's going on — received about 4 letters in two weeks, not exaggerating either....

Re: the ETC. and ETC. situation — just tell Mom not to worry. I've got the situation in hand and don't know what to do with it — other than just wait. I can really go out when I want to. Must admit that the Sarge *isn't* a stinker; just very, very different — maybe too much for me. I could really go out with him if I wanted to any time. Incidentally, I don't think he will go forward with us as he has enough points to go home. He will probably return to the States. Threatens to go to Detroit "to buy a car." — So you see he is still interested.

Am still seeing Bricker, though.

No doubt if I were home and could see things in my own surroundings, I wouldn't feel as I do. Guess I am not the only one in such a situation.

By the way, some time ago I made a bet with Loddo that Japan would give up by 19 August — might happen, eh? I also told her over a year ago that the war would be over by October 1945. Gosh, that's pretty good guessing, isn't it? Sure hope that it all comes out as I've predicted.

Just recd a cute letter from Bricker. One of these days shall send you one of his letters to me.

In the last few letters she wrote from France, Mollie was anticipating a move to Germany very soon and even used V-mail (which she disliked using because of the lack of privacy) to write a quick note to her family to let them know that she believed her departure to be imminent. But after being told she was due to leave almost immediately, plans changed and more than a week later she was still in France. Mollie was very reluctant to go to Germany, chiefly because she had no desire to live and work among the people who had so recently been the enemy and who had caused so much suffering for the Jews of Europe. She also had personal reasons for dreading the move, as none of the friends she had made during her Army service would be going with her, but in spite of her reservations she took a philosophical approach and was determined to make the best of it.

Versailles
11 August 1945

Dear Beck:

...Am still not getting any mail — pourquoi [why] — ??? Nor does anyone else around here. Sure wonder what the hold up is.

By the way, Captain Cleary, who is the Administrative Officer of our Division is leaving for the United States tomorrow — don't know what date he will actually depart — but anyhoo he is from Detroit. Loddo works for him and he was not in today but she told me that he would drop in the office tomorrow (my day off) so — I wrote him a little note and asked him to call either home or your office whenever he had time. I've known him since April 44. PS — He is married.

By the way, just heard that I am supposed to be leaving for Frankfurt by plane very shortly, however, am trying to swing a deal for a substitute for me. The way I look at it — when I get to Frankfurt, I have a feeling that our office will dissolve shortly — then I would be shoved into something new, which means the new set-up would begin to depend on me and I would never get out of this Army. If I thought I would remain with my Colonel and would actually carry through with the same set-up, I wouldn't mind. However, things aren't too definite other than this is the latest.

Yes, I heard about Japan's defeat but it won't affect our stay here — that's what they tell us. However, it is great news, Beck.

By the way (again) haven't heard from [Maurice] Kaye in ages — sure isn't very dependable, eh? The Sarge is still in Switzerland. Am expecting to see Bricker tonight. Loddo and I are going into Paris and will stay at the Patio Club. Will probably go on double date to the Eiffel Tower Club. Sunday, Norman [Mollie's cousin] will be over to have lunch with me (I hope he can make it) at the Patio and probably Bricker will be there, too. Then I have to rush back to Butte Rouge as I am CQ for the evening. Bricker said he'd come over and keep me company. No doubt most everyone will be running into Paris Sunday evening and I shall have to stay at Butte Rouge. Oh well — will probably knock myself out Saturday evening at the Tower Club.

Forgot to tell you this but during the week one of the boys' outfits got tired of having so few WACS attend their dances so they decided to bring everything to our place and hold a dance for us on our own grounds. It was rather nice, however, even then not many WACS wanted to bother to stay for the dance but went off on their own business. Three WAC Lts. ran through our billets trying to convince the girls to attend the dance right on our own porch. I had washed my hair and the Lt looked at me and said "Did you have to?" I was standing in my fatigue dress with my hair fuzzy-wuzzy. I laughed and said that it wouldn't take long to dry. I hadn't really intended going to the dance but felt sorry as there were so few girls and scads of guys. WELL — the pay off was that the orchestra pulled out because they felt there weren't enough remaining to dance to their efforts.

Anyhoo, someone pulled out a nice radio and it was most enjoyable. (Loddo had finally convinced me to attend.)

PS … Loddo and Smitty aren't going to Frankfurt — nor is Lee — nor is the Sarge — in fact, it looks like just the Colonel and me from our set-up. So you can see what would happen to me. Am sure I would get sent somewhere else after the final break up. Would rather stay back with the people I know. But I did tell the Colonel that I wouldn't mind going if there was a real necessity and if we would continue — otherwise — I didn't care to go and if I could get out of going would like to. Anyway, everything is up in the air — but mostly in my disfavor. Oh well.

---

12 August 1945
Versailles

Dear Beck:

I must write you this "quickie" to let you know I am leaving — this time I am sure — for Frankfurt Saturday A.M. — Not by plane. Don't have the 44 points and am essential — D/**n it! — So they say.

I sent you today an envelope with a couple of magazines…. By the way, in the envelope I also included a picture of the Sarge. However, I am keeping Bricker's picture with me. Ahem!

Shall be sending little things home — souvenirs and stuff that I have kept with me — because we shall no doubt be doing a lot of moving. So — hereafter when you receive a package or large envelope from me, please look through it carefully.

There are a lot of changes around here; however, I seem to be stuck with remaining in [the Army] for a while longer. I have no desire to, but there is nothing I can do about it. I tried but couldn't get very far.

Anyhoo, I have my duffel bag packed because I felt this was the real thing. Shall be going to Paris tonight — will see Bricker. — Must get back to work. Nuts!…

Maisons Laffitte
20 Aug 45

Dear Mollie,

…We had quite a mental bout and as far as I am concerned, I got a lot off my chest in that haphazard talk of beating around the bush. After all the talking we did, I guess the situation is still the same "status quo." I think I said everything that I had to say and yet I don't think I said very much at that. I feel like a dope, honestly. Maybe it's because I haven't had any experience in these matters, as you put it. My concern is that I don't want to hurt you in any manner. Possibly it will take one more discussion starting earlier that this last one and without any drinks to loosen my tongue. Did I surprise you with my direct questions? You jumped like a scared rabbit and told me not to yell so loud. I guess I was just as excited. Mollie, I hope I don't sound like I am trying to "pass the buck" as such and say "oh, well, she's leaving so the heck with her." I don't do things that way. My feeling is that I just took things for granted and didn't stop to think what the outcome would be. Well, I guess we have hashed this over enough for one week and give it a try the next time I see you.

This morning my colonel called section chiefs and officers in for a meeting ... and that he expected us to be in the states by Christmas. Sounds great, doesn't it?

Well, I'll have to cut this short. I hope you can come out here this weekend. Say hello to the girls.

Sincerely,

Coleman

---

20 August 1945
Versailles

Dear Beck:

As you can see I am still in France — don't know when the exact date of our moving will be but we shall move. Still working at the office. The Colonel has already gone to Frankfurt. Frankly — I haven't even packed yet because this Army is so indefinite that for all I know we might hang around here for quite a while yet — in fact, all we hear are rumors. You can ask anyone who has been overseas just how crazy and upsetting rumors are. One person says they know for sure you are leaving tomorrow and the next guy says it was just cancelled and you are leaving a week from tomorrow. Half of the kids thought we were leaving today and packed — so now they must unpack. What a life! (I haven't packed yet.)...

By the way, the Sarge brought me back a gorgeous watch from Switzerland. Incidentally, I paid for it — that's the only way I wanted it. It is a little round-faced watch with Roman numerals on it. The gold is a dark pink — or something. It has a brown suede band. It is a darling watch and one that I would have picked out for myself. — I don't know how he got it — but he did — you see Army personnel are allowed only a certain amount of money that they can spend in Switzerland, which doesn't include the price of a watch. I believe they are allowed only $35.00. My watch cost $37.00 wholesale.

Just this minute received your letter of 14 Aug telling me that the Japanese War is over and expecting me home soon. It's a funny thing though — when I studied about the World War I in school, I figured that when the Armistice was signed, the war was over; everyone packed their bags; left what they were doing and grabbed the first boat home. I am afraid that was a gross misconception. That is not the case. Everything is going along quite as usual and I don't expect to be home shortly. No — Beck — I have not volunteered to stay any longer. I was not asked.

I feel that now the war is over that I have fulfilled my duty; I did replace a man; now I am ready to go home — but the Army is not ready to send me. 'Course I could make myself unhappy about it all, but that would be pure dumbness on my part. I have decided to take it all philosophically — "What is to be is to be." And, I can say this genuinely — I have not regretted being in service nor having been overseas. In fact, Beck, not knowing where I stand regarding going home, I believe I shan't say any more about it. When the time comes, I naturally will be ready to go and will let you know. So let's leave it there.

Not long after she wrote this letter to her sister, Mollie was finally transferred to Germany. Her next letter home was written from Frankfurt.

PART FOUR : GERMANY

13. With the Army of Occupation: Frankfurt
August–September 1945

After the war, the U.S. Army's role in Europe changed; it became an Army of Occupation in Germany in order to control the population and stop any significant resistance to the new post war order.[1] In its new capacity, the Army continued to need the stenographic skills of members of the Women's Army Corps[2] and in August 1945 Mollie was transferred to Frankfurt. This was an assignment that she did not want. She had no desire to be in Germany, "formerly Hitler's world," as she described it. But as she kept reminding her family in her letters, the Army did not consult her on assignments. She simply had to obey orders and make the best of it.

Frankfurt did not have the glamour and allure of Paris and Mollie found it very different. She traveled the countryside and saw the destruction that this war brought to the German people and their towns. Many of the cities were in ruins with very few recognizable standing structures left. Mollie also encountered DPs (displaced persons) in Germany. These were civilians who had been uprooted as a result of the war. Many lived in camps while they tried to find family members and a place to settle. Often they had no homes to return to, either because their homes had been destroyed or because they feared returning to towns and villages which were now under the control of the Soviet Army and later became part of the German Democratic Republic (East Germany). The presence of thousands of DPs in post war Germany created an additional drain on the already meager food supplies.[3] In spite of the widespread destruction all around her, Mollie's accommodations in Frankfurt were luxurious in comparison with much of what she experienced throughout the war, especially in Normandy. She was in a nice apartment building and had excellent meals prepared and served by civilians.[4]

Speculation about when Mollie and her friends might be discharged from the Army was a recurring theme of the letters in this chapter. During this time, the Army was constantly changing the number of points required for discharge as it juggled postwar military needs for personnel with the logistical challenge of separating large numbers of soldiers from the armed forces and transporting them back to the United States from their overseas postings. The frequent changes to the rules created confusion and resentment among the troops waiting to be demobilized.[5] The intricacies of the point system became one of the most common topics of discussion among U.S. service personnel as well in their letters to their families back home, as male and female soldiers alike struggled to explain why they were still overseas weeks and months after the war had ended.

When Mollie first arrived in Germany, Bats was the only one of her friends in the WAC who was still with her, although Smitty was later transferred to Frankfurt. Mollie was also separated from the two men she had dated on a regular basis in France: the Sarge (Alex Korody) and Coleman Bricker. By this time Mollie had received proposals of marriage from the Sarge and from Charles Knotts, the combat soldier to whom Mollie had pretended to be engaged so that his commanding officer would allow him to visit Paris. Mollie felt that she could not marry a man who was not Jewish and so she gently declined Charles's proposal. Mollie had a continuing complex relationship with Coleman Bricker. Coleman and the Sarge took every opportunity to remind her how much they cared for her. Although Mollie clearly felt close to each of them, she decided to postpone giving a definite answer to either until she was a civilian again and back in Detroit with her family.

* * *

Maisons Laffitte
Sun, 26 Aug 45

Dear Mollie,

Just came back from seeing, "Along Came Jones," again. Nothing else to do so I went to the movies. I spent the afternoon in Paris with Lou.... Near the station is a zoo and museum I never heard about previously. It's called the Museum of Natural History. I dragged Lou around the zoo and then decided to look inside the various buildings. They have a tremendous collection of zoological specimens.... You would have probably kicked me for dragging you to such a place.... We decided to go to the Red Cross for cokes and then return to Maisons Laffitte for supper.... After waiting around awhile, Bernie Garfinkel came along in a command car and we made supper with time to spare.

The dance was held last night as scheduled. I hung around for refreshments as usual....

...Let me know if there is anything that I can do for you. Take care of yourself. Don't let me hear of you starting any riots about the fellows fraternizing.[6]

Love,
Coleman.

Frankfurt, Germany
27 August 1945

Dear Beck:

Well, here I am in what was formerly Hitler's world and I must say the Yanks have certainly taken over. We left Gare de L'est, Paris, at 12 noon on the 25th August on a hospital train and arrived in Frankfurt at 6:15 P.M. 26 August 1945. We had wonderful accommodations on the train — the beds were not litters but regular hospital beds with springs. There were only 8 of us WACs traveling and we occupied two adjoining cars. We had so much space that we used an upper and lower berth; one for reading and writing room and the other for a bedroom. We had expected to eat K-rations but instead were pleasantly surprised to have regular hot meals prepared by an excellent cook, who knew how to make dehydrated potatoes just as creamy and fresh-tasting as a good old real live spud.

Our billets are in the section of the city that is not too beaten up. It seems that part of Frankfurt was left largely untouched as it had been marked for the Army of Occupation. It houses not only us— the WACs— but a great number of DP's, largely Polish. The Germans had been given a few hours notice to leave and presto had departed. Although the European War has been over for some time, there is a great deal of cleaning up yet to be done. They are still digging through the debris in the bombed buildings.

Our living accommodations are excellent. There are six of us to an apartment. Reminds me of the apartment back home, except for the very German looking pictures and paintings on the wall with German inscriptions. Another thing that is different is *K* and *W* on the water taps [Kaltwasser and Warm] — in France we had *F* and *C* (froid & chaude). Guess we shall get used to it though.

Bats and I are rooming together — not bad!

...Guess who I ran into as soon as I walked into the mess hall — Dottie Dicks![7] She has been in Frankfurt about 10 days.

Our mess hall is about 4 blocks from our billets but that isn't too bad as we get all dressed and ready for work and then go off to eat. I understand it isn't very G.I. out here. I believe you know what I mean. We don't have reveille, retreat, we don't march to work in formation; nobody cares whether our buttons are shined or not, etc. That is what being G.I. means.

We are supposed to go to work by trolley car. Bats and I were standing near a corner trying to figure out what direction we should go and some Major came along in a staff car and asked us if he could help us. Well — the next thing we all knew we rode in his car. It's about 15 or 20 minutes ride. We were about two blocks away from our office and my Major happened to spot us. Gosh his eyes just about popped out. No doubt wondered how come we were riding to work in a staff car. Just a lucky break that's all.

...I am using an honest-to-goodness German Continental typewriter....

---

28 Aug 1945

Had to leave the other typewriter — left work a little early yesterday. Bats and I went out with two of the boys that run the hospital train. Went to dinner on the train. Then up to the American Red Cross here. Really not much to do. Then went back to our WAC billet and sat on the lawn in deck chairs for a while. The boys were leaving the next day for Paris.

A weapons carrier called for us this morning and took us 8 medic girls to work. However, this noon Bats and I had to hitchhike back to the billets and get back to work the same way. Of course, we don't have any difficulty in getting a ride. The boys are very nice to us.

Frankfurt is still quite a mess even though they say it has been all cleaned up. As I mentioned before, they are still digging through all the debris and all the bricks have been piled high so they make a fence around what used to be buildings.

Before I forget, don't send me anything else at all, I don't know if I am too optimistic but I think it is more than rumor that we shall be home for Xmas....

No doubt the Sarge — his name is Alexander Korody — will be contacting you. I have a feeling that he will. He is expecting to leave for the States 10 Sept. — that is, if there are no changes in plans. I have not made up my mind [about whether to accept his proposal of marriage] but I must see my friends back in the States and out of uniform. Anyway, Beck, Alex's parting words were this — "You know how I feel about you." — And, he just shook hands with me. He has done all the chasing of me — anyhoo, he said he had my home address.

Must say that Bricker is swell as ever and we had a most wonderful time the "last time I saw Paris."

Of all things — Charles [Knotts] —'member him — gave me a "beat around the bush" proposal and I wrote him a very nice letter but told him on account of religion, etc., etc., but he still may look up our family on his way home when I wrote him. He is a very nice guy. — I really mean it.

...I told Bricker that he is welcome to come to Detroit any time and that I would like to see him there. He, of course, invited me to Los Angeles.

As far as [Maurice] Kaye is concerned — he is the most indefinite thing I have ever run into. Guess he is more indefinite than I am. I haven't heard from him since he said that he thought he was on his way to the South Pacific, which was a long, long time ago. I just could never count on a guy like that. However, he is a pretty funny guy and usually pops up at the wrong time....

Just had a meeting with the Colonel and the enlisted personnel — sounds encouraging for HOME BY XMAS!...

Frankfurt, Germany
30 August 1945

Dear Beck:

...Am quite certain I shall be home by Xmas 1945. I don't know if they will give us a discharge or just a 30 day furlough and back to the Army for a later discharge. No need to worry that I'll volunteer. Yep, I have "did my duty" and certainly wouldn't volunteer to remain in. — Just showed my Colonel the report card and he kidded me about it — especially at what I had in the back — 50 times tardy — he said that I came by it honestly — now he could see!

I think Bats and I may go to Wiesbaden on Sunday. That is if the weather is nice. One of the boys in my office has access to a vehicle so we shall go swimming if it is nice.

As I said before there isn't much to do in Frankfurt. Course you can have as many dates as you want but there are very few places to go to. There are dances every nite — if you want to go.

The food is very good and we have plenty of it. They don't clamp down on us as far as strict army regulations— which is nice and relaxing for us. Our office building is very nice and our billets are excellent — so we have nothing to complain of. Did I tell you we have luncheon and dinner music (a six piece orchestra — German) every day? Have you heard the song "Symphony"? It is really smooth. First heard it in Nice and now every time they play it, I feel I am back at that gorgeous French Riviera. WOW!

Every time we go out on the street, we see army vehicles (trucks) herding PW's [prisoners of war], DP's back and forth. Must take some pictures of these beat up buildings. It is still a mess and yet they tell us Frankfurt has been cleaned up.

Feeling fine....

FRANKFURT, GERMANY
31 August 1945

Dear Beck:

...Re: Bricker. He worked for Civil Service in an office. He also worked in some large grocery on weekends. It seems he had to contribute quite a bit to the family. He has two years of College. Materially, he doesn't have much. But he does have a wonderful personality and everyone likes him. I do have a great deal of confidence in him and he sure is dependable. As you can tell from the letters he wrote me (I mailed them to you during the week), all his friends like me and we sure get along beautifully.— As Bricker once said to me if the fellows in his outfit thought I was a heel or anything, they sure would "expectorate" on all the WACs. I can remember way back to October when I was the first WAC to enter their lobby and attend a movie there and all the applause the boys gave us. Do you remember my writing that? I sure do have wonderful memories of Paris.— But of course it has to be more than that and I want to be home. You live under a slightly different tempo and tension overseas.— so being home for a decision like that is necessary.

Sunday, Sept 2
Ansbach

Dearest Mollie,

I received your letter yesterday that you wrote on the train starting for Deutschland! Well, what do you think of it? I hate it worse every day.

I am supposed to go to Chainnin (spelled wrong). Anyway it's a leave center down in France. I am supposed to go the 7th if nothing happens....

Well we finally moved into a house & out of these tents which is quite a change. Several of the boys are leaving. I believe that this week they will take all 85'ers [those with 85 points] out then it comes down I guess. Well, I still have 79 but supposed to have one more star coming as I should get caught in the "next draft" as we say.

Yes Mollie I know how it is to have to leave friends because I have had to do it several times especially when I was shipped into this outfit leaving my old one. I left many good friends....

Mollie I guess I didn't look at it as you do & I am sorry but I had to tell you how I felt. I refrained from mentioning it for a long time because I didn't quite think it would do, but I assure you Mollie that you are very dear to me but I guess that's as far as it goes but I'll always remember you.

Well Mollie I will close operations for the time being & be sure to tell me what you think of Germany....

Love,

Charles

Frankfurt, Germany

3(?) Sept 1945

Dear Beck:

...If you don't think things are complicated just listen to this.------My Colonel just told me that the Sarge is coming up for a few days—then with a wink in his eye, he said that he (Alex) was lonesome back at Versailles. MY! OH, MY!

By the way, this morning Bats and I were supposed to "fall out" for drill, but when the time came, we pretended we hadn't heard anything about it. The first Sgt. just came over from the States and we VETERANS (AHEM!) refuse to play soldier. No doubt we shall hear about it. Anyway, we didn't drill today....

Frankfurt, Germany

4 Sept 1945

Dear Beck:

Haven't been getting hardly any mail lately from the States, but I guess that is to be expected on account of our moving. Have been receiving mail from Versailles from Smitty, Loddo, and Lee and also from Bricker. By the way, the Sarge was here today but had to return to Versailles. Flew both ways....

Last week I had stayed in Tuesday and Wednesday evening and decided to see a show with one of the gals on Thursday—so what happens—someone looks me up at the billets. It was a Sgt.—tall—he talked with BATS but didn't leave any name or message. Wonder who it was!!!!

Sunday evening I went out to the A.E.F. [Allied Expeditionary Force] Club with two of the boys from our office—fellows that had been with our Medical Intelligence office in Germany while I had been back in Paris—very nice boys. The A.E.F. Club is very nice—they serve snacks, juice and beer, which is quite a rarity as most places just have Cokes. They had an excellent band there. I know you'll laugh at this—there were 6 WACs and 2 Red Cross girls and about 250 boys. I am not exaggerating one bit. It was impossible to dance a full dance with one fellow. Honestly, I felt like I was a "dime-a-dance" girl. There was one fellow who was quite a dancer—smooth and jitterbug, too. He kept cutting in all the time. I'm not much of a fancy jitterbug-ger, anyway he took me off to the side—out of the circle of the dancers and taught me a few of the intricacies

Mollie and some of her colleagues from the office pose in front of the rubble of a bombed building in Wiesbaden, September 1945.

of jitter-bugging. To top it all off — don't think that guys didn't try to cut in — even on my dancing lesson! He was a very cute fellow — a corporal stationed about 75 miles out of Frankfurt. Said he might get back again and took my address. He was awfully funny and kept calling me "Callahan" and I said: "Nope, that's wrong. It's O'Weinstein." You guessed it, he's an Irishman. He wears a Purple Heart and has been overseas two years.

Monday, five of the boys that work in our building took me out to Wiesbaden in a weapons carrier. Altho that town is pretty much beat up, too, it is much nicer than Frankfurt. The Red Cross there is beautiful — in fact, nicer than anything in Paris. We took some pictures and I shall send them home when I receive them from the developers. — Am feeling fine....

Mollie received the next letter from Joe Beaton, the Irish corporal who gave her the dance lesson described in the letter above. Joe Beaton's letter expresses very eloquently the feelings of a combat soldier who had survived the most difficult days of the war and regarded a return to his home and civilian life as a precious gift which he was eager to enjoy to the fullest.

Salmunster, Germany
Sept 5th 1945

My darling sweetheart — no that's too informal, Dear Sergeant Molly — no that's too G.I., Dear Friend — nope too cold, I know.... Hi Callahan!

You see, I told you I'd drop you a line (or should I say a *note* because good l'il WACs stay away from those bad boys with "lines"?) I finally caught a ride home but it was the next morning after the dance about 10:00. I spent the night in the transit barracks in Frankfurt. It was much too cold and dark to try those 60 kilometers home. I got home in time for dinner so I didn't miss much time hitch-hiking on the road.

I wanted to tell you though — thanks, honey I had a swell time. I only hope I didn't scare you too much with all that chatter. Actually, I'm not such a talkative fellow as I may have seemed. But you can't really understand what being at that dance meant to me. Honestly it was the first American dance I've been to since I came overseas twenty months ago. I was as happy as a lark and I guess I showed it a little more than somewhat?

Heck, all I want to do the rest of my life is have a good time. I came pretty close to bringing down the curtain on the biography of Joe Beaton in the Ardennes[8] last winter and from here on out I'm going to enjoy the life I almost lost. It wasn't much fun day after day in fox holes for almost eleven solid months and when I prayed for help and courage in those dark hours, I vowed should I ever get out alive I'd live as some men only dream they would. The little things—little things I've missed I'm going to have again. The jingle of a nickel, a few pennies, dimes or quarters in my pocket. The vibrant rhythm of life in the "Big Town." The rush, honey & jam, the noise, the music, the symphony of seven million souls working, laughing, crying—living in one corner of the earth that is heaven to me—home!

New York City to a stranger seems cold, aloof and distant to them but it's not really. You see, these people never want to lose time. You've got to be "on the ball" to get around. It seems like life hangs on the next few hours. So you've got to make every minute count. Molly, how I love that town and how I've missed it. I'm wise enough to know it's not Utopia but it's as close to it as I can make it. "Be it ever so humble_____"

Gee, here I was going to write you and extend my solicitude and thanks for a very charming evening and I start out like a Junior Chamber of Commerce. Excuse me please, but you know how it feels to be away from home yourself so I need not explain any further.

I hope what I have once enjoyed will not be the last. I'd really like to see you again and you can bet the very next time I go AWOL [absent without leave] to Frankfurt I'll give you a buzz. Heaven knows how I'll find you with the aid of Providence and a couple of MPs [military police] maybe I can find you again.

Be a good girl. Work hard but most of all stay as sweet and as kind as you are.

Yours always,

Joe

Frankfurt, Germany
5 Sept 1945

Dear Beck:

Just thought I'd whip out a quickie to you. Not so busy in the office these days. Am really certain of being home before Xmas. Perhaps even the latter part of November. Things are moving pretty rapidly around here. Don't know whether I told you "Bats" met one of her pals from the States and moved out so I am saving the bed for Smitty. There are just four of us in the apartment now. Three of the kids—which just leaves me alone in the apartment—have been advised they will be leaving for the States the end of the month. Wow—just like that—course they have the required points. Now with the recounting of points, I now have fifty and I am eligible to go home—whenever that will be—

By the way am receiving no mail. Since I have been here, just recd one letter from you and one letter from Sarah....

Beck, it would be funny if I get home in October because I always did say "October 1945." Anyway, Loddo will be home by then for sure. Do you know she once said to me: "If I'm home in October 1945, I'll surely believe anything you ever tell me"....

Maisons Laffitte
7 Sept 45

Dear Mollie,

I received your letter dated 4 Sept 45 last night and I can't tell you how happy I was to hear from you.... Your letter boosted my spirits no end, believe me. What with all this point business and over age discharges and more rumors, I have been feeling quite blue. The announcement today that all men with 70 points and over will be out of the theater by the end of December is the best thing I have heard yet. I believe that I'll be home for my birthday. I always said you would be home for Thanksgiving and from the looks of things I may be right. You said October I believe and that may prove right. I dropped by the Windsor and phoned Marti and Helen. Marti said she, Loddo and Vickie expected to go to 16th RD [a staging post on way to being discharged] about the 19th of this month.... I'll have to phone her one of these nights before she leaves.

I haven't written you since 29th Aug. expecting a letter from you in the meantime. Not much happening around these parts. I am still unaccustomed to this life of a country gentleman. I walk around like a tiger pacing back and forth in a cage.... Need I say, there's no reason to go into Paris any more.

Last Saturday afternoon, I decided to see Norman [Mollie's cousin]. I didn't have any trouble getting out there. Hitchhiked just like you did. He was surprised to see me and even asked where you were. He didn't know that you left the week before. He thought that postponement was indefinite....

Incidentally I want to wish you a Happy and Prosperous New Year. Please send my regards to your family.

...I am glad to hear your surroundings are quite pleasant to say the least. Your office sounds like a playground with that escalator. If I get a chance I'll try and call you. I would like to phone you very much, but you know the Army, so I don't want to make a promise I wouldn't be able to keep.

I don't have to say I miss you too, because you'll never know how much I do. Hope you are well and happy. The boys all say hello. Let me know if there is anything that I can do for you. Write soon.

Love,
Coleman

In the next letter, Mollie mentions visiting a building occupied by the U.S. Army which was previously the headquarters of the I.G. Farben group. The Farben group was established in 1925 as the result of a merger of the largest chemical companies in Germany. It reached its full strength during the period of Nazi control but was divided into its original components after the war. The building itself, in northwest Frankfurt, was very unusual: nine stories tall, made from travertine stone with marble-lined corridors, it was one of the best known landmarks in the city. During its use by the U.S. Army, it was surrounded by security fences and patrolled by American guards.[9]

The previous year, as part of her contribution to the war effort, Mollie decided to work on the Jewish New Year and Yom Kippur rather than observing them as holidays, but in 1945 circumstances were very different. On Rosh Hashanah, Mollie went with a group of other Jewish GIs to the Westend Synagogue in Frankfurt for High Holiday services and to witness the synagogue's re-dedication. Mollie felt this experience was one of the highlights of her overseas service. Although it suffered bomb damage, the Westend Synagogue was the only Frankfurt Synagogue to survive the war. Other synagogues were destroyed by the Nazis on Kristallnacht (or the Night of Broken Glass) on November 9 —10, 1938, when hundreds of synagogues and thousands of Jewish businesses and homes throughout Germany were damaged or destroyed. The Westend Synagogue was spared only because Nazi party members used neighboring buildings and did not want to risk damaging them.[10]

Frankfurt, Germany
7 Sept 1945

To Weinstein Family:
Witnessed the Rededication of the Great Synagogue of Frankfurt tonight. Can truly say this is the beginning of a Happy New Year. Happy New Year!!!

Frankfurt, Germany
8 Sept 1945

Dear Beck:
...Last night two of the Jewish boys and a Jewish Captain from some of the other offices in our building went to services for Rosh Hashanah with me. The Captain got a jeep and first we went off to eat. We ate on the grounds of the I.G. Farben Building (this is within the COMPOUND AREA I told you about). It is the most impressive office building I've ever seen. Have you seen any pictures of it?

The services were conducted in a synagogue which was spared in the fires set by the Nazis Nov. 9, 1938, in nearly every synagogue in Germany. The New

Year's services were combined with a rededication of the synagogue. Chaplain Vida (Army) and Dr. Neuhaus (Frankfurt civilian rabbi) conducted services. The services were certainly well attended by our Army and Navy personnel. There were a lot of high ranking officers there, too. As for the civilian Jews, there were very few left to attend from this once large community of 34,000 Jews. Beck, these Jews were not dramatic, nor did they *carry-on*, but one could discern readily the untold suffering they had experienced these many years. They held their heads high — and we were all proud to be a part of them.

Yes, the Germans watched us walking in the synagogue and out — they were hanging out of their windows eyeing us carefully. Not one remark was passed; nor did they even speak amongst themselves, that is, while we stared back at them. This was a great day and one I shall never forget. Although I really didn't want to come to Germany, it was worth it just to see all this.

...I wrote you I thought I'd be coming home Xmas— perhaps I might even make it sometime in November. Seems unbelievable.

Re Bricker — Yes he is a swell guy and I guess you understand the situation by now — eh? By the way, would like very much to go to Paris on Temporary Duty (fly if I can) — maybe straighten things out too. Expect the Sarge will be leaving sometime this month. Would rather make my trip to Paris in early October. Must start "working" on the Colonel. However, at the moment he is away, visiting German cities. Smitty is trying her darndest to come to Germany on T.D. [Temporary Duty]. Don't know if she will be able to make it or not. With the lowering of points, she, too, will be eligible to go home when I do so they probably don't want to bother to reassign her. Loddo is leaving the 19th of Sept. Guess she will be home for sure in October. WOW — how do you like that for my crystal gazing accomplishments?

...HERE'S WISHING MOM, POP, JACKIE AND YOU — A HAPPY NEW YEAR. Please convey same to our relatives, en masse. Friends, too.

As the following letters from Coleman Bricker demonstrate, he was feeling lonely now that Mollie was in Germany and they could no longer see each other on a regular basis. He took every opportunity to keep in touch with Mollie's friends who were still in the area and to write to Mollie to let her know that he wanted to continue their relationship.

Maisons Laffitte
10 Sept 45

Dear Mollie,
...Anyhow, about 1:30 A.M., Bob wakes me up to tell me that Loddo was at the dance and wanted to see me at early chow.... After lunch we walked to the

house where our WACs are billeted. She really liked the house and raved about sleeping in a real bed. She told me about Smitty going to Frankfurt on T.D., also about Bats moving out on you. Most of this, you wrote in your letter which came in Sunday night.... What did you have to leave Paris for?

...When I got back to the house last night, I walked into the day room and there on the table waiting for me was three envelopes all from you. Really put a brightening touch to cold and miserable week end.... I noticed on a general order that Colonel Howard [Mollie's Colonel] was awarded a Legion of Merit. I can't see any reason why he could not have recommended you for a Bronze Star. You certainly earned his Legion of Merit for him. You don't need the points now, but they would have certainly given you a higher priority on getting home....

I hope you were able to get Smitty into your room when she came in on TD. Wish I could swing a TD deal but of course without the aforementioned accommodations, I guess Smitty is probably back already. I am going out to Butte Rouge for supper with Loddo, this coming Friday so will let you know about that later.

...Hope you are well and happy. Regards to your family.
Love,
Coleman

Maisons Laffitte
12 Sept 45

Dear Mollie,

Last night I received the cute poem you sent and was very glad to hear from you. The poem was very nice and if you had handed it to me in person I would have probably been speechless and nervous and shifting my feet. Are you asking me if I am on the spot again? I'd probably answer yes and lower my head again. Boy! What a jerk I am and don't I know it. Well, there is no denying it. I wish you were here too, or I there.

I took the afternoon off yesterday and dragged Lou to look up the address you left with me. After walking almost in a circle, and asking a few questions, we found it. The outcome of the visit is that this lady you asked me to find was deported by the Germans sometime ago. Lou talked in French to the concierge and I in German to her son to find out the story. They said that they haven't had any word from her since she was taken away. It's really quite sad. I am returning the letter you gave me. What do you want me to do with the box of tea?

...I suppose you heard that the point score is to be lowered to 70 on the 1st of October. The reason is that the Army shipped home too many low score personnel and have them sitting around in the states. So now they have to discharge them, so the public wouldn't yell too loud. I always figured something like that would happen. You really get the bum breaks by being overseas.

...Did you have to turn in your Paris Assignment card when you left? We were supposed to turn ours in when we moved out here. I told them I lost mine. Now they decided that we are in the city limits of Paris and are going to issue new ones. Well, I guess I will have one for a souvenir after all.

That's all for now, Mollie.... Well, I hope you are well and happy. Take care of yourself.

Love,
Coleman

In the next letter, Mollie tells her sister more about the difficult living conditions in Paris during the winter of 1944-45. At the time, Mollie did not dwell on the problems and hardships of everyday life, in part because of the restrictions imposed by censorship but also because she had not wanted her family to worry about her, but now, looking back on the experience, she wanted those back in the United States to know that she and her fellow WACs had not had an easy time. With no heat and no hot water, many of the WACs became sick and it was estimated that in one unit 25 percent of the women had chilblains.[11]

Frankfurt, Germany
12 Sept 1945

Dear Beck:

...In other words—don't send me nuttin!

...Guess I shall have to bawl you out, too. I get the goofiest letters from people saying: "Well, you've got 42 points, why don't you get out of the army"—and no doubt, now that I have 50 points, I will get nuttier letters still. The point is this: if you are not in the Army, you cannot possibly understand it; furthermore, if you are in the Army in the States, you cannot understand the function of the army overseas. So—what I want to bring out is this:—I don't have one d**?./// thing to say about it and I am not kidding. I didn't want to go to Germany and just lacked two points. I saw Colonels and Captains galore—but I went anyway when the time came. However, it worked out just as well because the kids back at Versailles and Paris will be getting out just as we, and vice versa.

Here is the deal:—When an order comes through from Washington that a certain number of WACs with certain critical scores are to be released, those names are posted on the bulletin board. As yet, mine is not on that board. You cannot do a thing until your name is on the board — unless you are over age. If your name appears on the bulletin board for release and you still want to remain in the Army, then you can sign something or other (which I am not even bothering to investigate). I have no intention of remaining overseas another winter, if I can get out. Of course, there is another angle for married WACs whose husbands have returned to the States; those girls can get out.

As far as being essential, the Stenos are no longer in that category — but if they want to, your office can hold you for thirty days extra. However, I am sure Col. H. would not do that as he knows when the time comes, I am most anxious to "scram." But don't get me wrong. As I have always said, I have never regretted being in the Army and coming overseas. It certainly has been the greatest experience I could have ever had.

I do hope I have made myself clear. Being overseas is really not such a "picnic" as one would think. Now that a lot of things are in the past, I can tell you this I sure had the best case of chilblains and so did many of us. November and December in Paris was sure hell with very little heat. However, things did improve to the point where life was quite enjoyable — but, Beck, I never did write complaining letters because in the first place they would make the family worry and secondly, you couldn't do anything about it so what was the use. Then, too, letters were censored.

Oh well — don't take this all too hard — am sending you a Kleenex to dry your tears!! The fellows in the office think the above is a real tear jerker.

Did I tell you that I shall be asking my Colonel for a pass to Paris the end of this month? Sure hope I do get it. By the way, things look pretty good at this moment — I probably will be home for Thanksgiving. Col. H. has put my name down as 1 November for release — but that is tentative.

…Now that I'm away from the Sarge and Bricker — seem to be interested in the California guy — Bricker.

As I said before — Kaye is just too darned undependable — haven't heard from that guy since July — don't know whether he went to the South Pacific. Or not — Oh well.

My love to Mom, Pop and Jackette. HAPPY NEW YEAR

FRANKFURT
13 Sept 1945

Dear Beck:

I didn't bother to mail the other two pages yesterday as I received your letter of 4 Sept just before I left the office last night, so I thought I'd add a few lines and mail it all out together.

By the way, you say something about my getting an outfit over here — presumably in Paris (I may get back there again) — well, anyhoo, guess this will have to be a bawling out letter, too (you can use the other Kleenex, s'il vous plait [if you please].) Even the prices in the regular dept. stores are more or less black market prices. You see France is just like that. You know if I wanted to I could sell my old clothes and get a pretty good price here — by old clothes — I mean even my underwear. Am sure that I could get at least $10.00 for a slip that I've worn for a year and paid two bucks for. How do you like that????? Furthermore, I know the G.I.s (soldiers) sell mattress covers (worth not more than $1.98) for 1500 francs ($30.00).

Furthermore — you know how we were gyped on our exchange of money.[12] Well — the French Govt. are now feeling sorry for us and *giving* the Americans 850 francs ($16.50) each month along with the regular pay that the troops get from the US Army. So you can see we were well gyped on our exchange *if* after a year their treasury can afford to pay that out. — The catch for me is that after my spending all my money there for one year, I don't get the benefit of it — instead some jerk that just came over has the opportunity. Oh well — that's the Army.

Have I made myself clear????????? But I guess it is difficult for you to understand what is going on over here — after perhaps by now I may even find it difficult to understand what is going on in the States. However, I think not. Am sure I can adjust myself to civilian life more readily than from civilian to army. But I have learned this, Beck, I can adapt myself very easily. I would have never found this out had I not been in service — of that I am sure....

Maisons Laffitte
15 Sept 45

Dear Mollie,

Nothing to do this afternoon so I am taking the time to write you this letter. When I came back from town last night, I found your New Year's card and letter dated 11 September waiting for me. The fact is, the fellows told me that I was the only one to receive any mail yesterday. The mail is very slow. I received two letters so far this week from home. Hope your score is better than that.

I will have to tell you about my afternoon yesterday. I wrote you that I was going to Butte Rouge for supper with Loddo. After the usual trip of the bus and hitch hiking I get to Butte Rouge about 3:00 P.M.. I sent someone upstairs to call Loddo for me. She came down and with a roguish look on her face said, "Bricker, I am going to ask you to do something but you don't have to if you don't want." You guessed it. I'll have to whisper I spent the afternoon in a WAC's room. Going up the stairs, I looked in every corner and behind every door, to make sure there wasn't a C.O. [Commanding Officer] hiding.

When I walked into the room, Lee and Marti were there. "The Character"[13] greeted me with that "old maid finding a man under her bed" look and exclamation. We spent the afternoon talking about various things, people and looking at Harper's Bazaar. Lee showed me the two pistols her brother gave her and even wanted to give me one of them. Say, you girls really had nice apartments. Oh well, the WACs get everything. Don't throw that book, I take it back. At this point I ought to interrupt and say all this makes for good material for the book I might write someday on "What I Learned about Women from WACs." Imagine being alone with 3 of them yet.

...Glad you like "Forever Amber." Pass it around to the girls because they'll call me all sorts of things if you send it back. If you want any more of the books let me know and I'll send you whatever you like. We have plenty of them around.

Loddo told me that Bats was getting an English award of some sorts. What's the story? Also told me about Smitty getting the T.D. to Frankfurt. Which brings up the point of your pass. Why can't you get T.D. and come back here? You can also put in for a three day pass. I hope you can get either one. Colonel Howard ought to be in a good mood since he received that Legion of Merit, so "tempt the lion in his den"....

---

16 Sept 45

Pardon the interruption. Last night about 4:45, while in the midst of your letter, the colonel phones me for something. I searched high and low until 5:30 P.M. and then gave up in a fit of anger. These brasshats will drive me nuts yet. I know darn well we didn't have what he wanted and when I prove my point, he isn't man enough to apologize.

...I also put in for a furlough to Switzerland. They can't do anything more than refuse it. I have no reasons other than to see Switzerland before I leave the ETO [European Theater of Operations]. My "buddy" Finklestein is the one to put the OK on it. Even as much as I hate him or rather dislike him, the boys tell me he will OK it. How's about you? Do you think you can rate another furlough? You might try and see if you can get one.

Well, Mollie, now comes your confession. When I opened your letter and read the cover, I had an idea of what was coming. Then as I read the letter nothing was forthcoming. Finally buried almost at the end was your confession. I was sitting down and it was no surprise to me. Believe me! I have always felt that you weren't telling me all about your feelings toward me, but was holding back. Why! Because to me there was every indication of your feelings for me in your face, yes and actions. I realized this just before we went to Nice. Do you know I went into this with my eyes wide open and just didn't do anything about it. What a heel I am! You should have hit me on the head long ago and brushed me off like a fly. I often think that I should have done something rash and that would have been the finish, but quick. The easy way out would be to say that I am sorry, but that's just the wrong thing. My mother brought me up to be respectful of another person's feelings and I am conscientious enough to put them before my own. Well, Mollie, I guess this puts us back to where we started from just before you left. Hope I can see you before either of us leaves.

That's all for now. Is there anything you need or want done? Say hello to the girls and fellows. Regards to your family.

Love,

Coleman

FRANKFURT, GERMANY

18 Sept 1945

Dear Beck:

I have your letter of 8th wishing me a HAPPY NEW YEAR. Thanks a lot. At least I am sure of spending the 1945-46 one at home…. It is a rather CONFIDENTIAL letter about my etc. situation.

There are a lot of details involved as far as the Sarge is concerned and all I would have to say is YES [to his proposal of marriage], but I guess Bricker is more of the type of fellow I could always depend on. I could write you a lot more but I have started this letter three times and it has gotten so involved that I know you wouldn't be able to make heads or tails out of it — so thought the briefer I make it the better it will be. Course you know that Bricker has a gal friend back home.

…I am trying to get to Paris on pass this weekend but somehow the Colonel won't say YES, that is, as yet. Smitty is leaving Friday and I want very much to go with her. Will let you know, of course, when and if I do go. Loddo (I understand) leaves tomorrow from Butte Rouge to go to Replacement Center on her way back to the States. Am sure she'll be back in the USA in October — just as I told her. Gosh I feel good about that!…

---

19 Sept.

Dear Beck:

Didn't bother to mail this as it was too late to go out in yesterday's mail.

By the way, I went to the affair last night and it was really grand. It was the Grand Opening of the Palmgarden Club and it was a set-up such that I have never seen. The ballroom is a huge room, sort of reminds me of the Palladium in Hollywood. The Club has a lot of accommodations—ping pong room, reading room, then, too it has a bar in the basement — huge — with an orchestra down there too. There is a beautiful Palmhouse (naturally, with palm trees) and it is called the "Garden Spot" of the Continent.

Am talking at this moment to one of the boys from another office and he said that he had never seen anything like the above — not even back in the States. So—you can imagine how wonderful it must be. And, it is about time that they had something nice for all these GI's because for the most part they do not fraternize [with German women] and so a nice place like the Palmgarden Club helps a lot. It isn't too far from our billets so more of the WACs will show up at the dances. I must say that the WACs are more popular than ever.

There is a beautiful rock garden with a waterfall in the Palmhouse and there is a string orchestra that plays on top of the hill where the rocks make up a most interesting formation. As you can tell from my mixed up description — it is most impressive.

…did meet a very nice fellow who is a chemical engineer with the Chemical Warfare Service — he even works in my building! He wanted to make a date with me for this week but I told him I was going to Paris—so he took my number and am sure I shall be hearing from him. I still don't know for certain whether I am leaving for Paris this Friday or not. Am still heckling my Colonel.

By the way, our WAC officers gave us a break and it acted as an incentive for more of the girls to show up at the dance. We had a 2 A.M. bedcheck but I came at 12:45 — which was late enough. We even had a company meeting cancelled last night so the girls could attend the opening of the Palmgarden Club…. See you sometime in the not too distant future.

Mollie sent a copy of the formal invitation to a dance at her friend's barracks as an example of the parties and dances that were held for the WACs. Although Frankfurt lacked the extensive civilian social life of Paris, the Army sponsored many dances and other events to help keep the troops entertained. This invitation demonstrated the great lengths that the soldiers stationed in Germany went to in order to plan and invite WACs to their parties.[14]

Frankfurt, Germany
20 Sept 1945

HI Jackette:
Received your letter of 12 Sept the other day and am glad to hear from you….

I just about had to twist my Colonel's arm yesterday but he finally gave in.

Yep, I am flying tomorrow noon to Paris. I'll have to give Beck more details. The Colonel wrote up temporary duty orders but frankly I don't expect to do any real work. Course I am all excited and wonder if I'll get airsick. Oh me, oh my. Will let you know the gory details later.

My pal Smitty was supposed to go back to Paris with me but somehow things got mixed up so instead I am going with two of the boys from her office and she will have to wait until one of the boys returns. I'm only going to be in Paris for four days.

Things are improving so much around here in every way that it looks like the Army of Occupation set up won't be too bad — that is for the girls — as far as I know. — but don't get excited I am not signing up for anything like that. For instance, now we have a new mess hall and, Jackie, it is really something out of this world. We have white tablecloths; tables set with flowers; tall glasses of water; and waitresses rush up to you with smiling faces (Polish gals) and are too happy to wait on us. They bring the food to us in large platters and we feel just like civilians. We have a nice orchestra.

The Army sure is putting on the dog for us at this late stage, eh what? Then, too whenever the fellows invite us to a dance at their Post, they even give the gals corsages.

Time out for tea — yep — the boys here are giving me a farewell party — oranges and cookies....

14. Saying Goodbye: Frankfurt
September–October 1945

During the last weeks that she spent in Germany, Mollie was eagerly anticipating her discharge from the Army and her return to the United States.
Although she was confident that she would be leaving soon, the uncertainties
surrounding the details — such as frequent changes to the date of departure —
were very frustrating. At the same time, Mollie was trying to decide which
path to take in her personal life. By this time Alex Korody was on his way to
the United States to be discharged from the Army, but he sent Mollie a postcard from France to encourage her to keep in touch with him once they were
both civilians again. He had made his feelings for Mollie clear, proposed to
her and was waiting for her to make a decision. The situation with Coleman
Bricker was more complicated. Although Coleman clearly cared deeply for
Mollie and wanted them to have a future together, both he and Mollie felt
constrained by his commitments to his family and his ties to his pre-war girlfriend back in California. Through frequent letters and phone conversations,
they tried to come to some conclusions about their feelings for each other and
what they should do next.

* * *

Calais Staging Area
25/9/45

Mollie, dear, I received your Rosh Hashanah card and it was a pleasure for
me to read about the Rededication. — We hope to leave Friday for a staging
area and in a day or two for U.S.A ... you'll be home very soon too, so see you
in America. Remember me to everybody.

Love,
Alex

FRANKFURT, GERMANY
28 Sept. 1945

Dear Beck:

Just a "quickie" to let you know that I went on my trip to Paris and have returned. Went by plane and it was quite a thrill. Had a little difficulty getting back on account of bad weather and priorities—Colonels, etc. having the opportunity to get ahead of enlisted personnel but I did make a connection and was able to fly back with not too much trouble. Wish I had time to give you all the details but don't—so will be very brief about it all.

Bricker has "beaucoup" problems....

Then, of course, too, Bricker has his girl friend back home ... something is bothering him. I guess another problem is he doesn't know what he will actually do getting back into civilian life. The whole affair is quite muddled up, Beck, and my going to Paris didn't really help much.

I would appreciate your not showing this letter around to anyone ... because I can't see much what you could do about it all. I wished I could have mentioned to Bricker about being able to go to school, etc., but you see he has his family to take care of. I don't know if he wants to see his reaction upon going home—with his old gal friend, or what.

Next day—29 Sept 1945

I didn't quite have the opportunity to complete this letter yesterday.

No doubt you wondered if I bought an outfit—well—I didn't buy a damn thing. I guess you probably read in the papers that the Duke of Windsor's wife is now in Paris and she had been asked if she were going to buy her winter clothes there—she answered that she would just look around and buy nothing as clothes were too expensive over here. Gosh—what can I say.

The latest rumor is that we leave Frankfurt on 21 October to go to Compiegne, France, as our Replacement Depot, prior to our going to a Port of Embarkation—which should be about 8 to 10 days after the 21st. However, that is strictly rumor at this point. I should, however, be home for sure sometime in November. Smitty is still here on T.D. [temporary duty] and should be going home at the same time as I do. However, expect she will be going back to Paris shortly.

Last night I sure felt like a civilian—remember my telling you about the Chemical Engineer—well his Colonel let him use the staff car and Smitty and her friend and the Chem. Eng. and myself went out to the G. I. Country Club near Oberursel,[1] Germany. It's about 10 miles from Frankfurt. Really is a gorgeous place—some sort of a chateau.

We had a little difficulty getting out there and got lost in Oberursel—

which was a bit weird to say the least. The sign that said "G. I. Country Club--
-------" was slightly misplaced so we got off on the wrong road and got lost in
the town. The streets were so narrow that Frank (my friend) could hardly drive
through and the German houses seem to stare back at us in the wildest manner. We felt as though we were living one of Grimm's fairy tales. There were a
few German people strolling about in the inkiness of a moonless night. It was
only 8 P.M. and complete darkness has descended on this town. Gosh — this
sounds like a mystery, doesn't it? Fortunately, we ran into a G. I. and were
given proper directions, which relieved us all.

There was supposed to be a dance out there but it was postponed and
Frank asked if I would go again with him tonight so I couldn't say NO — and
will be seeing him tonight. Smitty and her friend Lou are coming along with
us.

...By the way — the boys in my office are trying to get me to write a book.
I can just imagine — I'd probably not be able to get beyond the 1st paragraph
stage.

Maisons Laffitte
1 Oct 45

Dearest Mollie,

Received your letter of the 29th of Sept and was very happy to hear from
you.

You are right, Mollie. You can't make a situation easier by ignoring the
whole thing. In my ignorant way, I tried that. Please believe me when I say that
you have done nothing or said nothing to make me feel differently toward you.

I just couldn't get myself to say anything to you while you were here. I
know that you could have helped me. I confessed my love for you and chose to
remain silent thereafter. Why, I really don't know.

I knew that someday I would have to return home and merely shoved that
thought into the depths of my mind. I never intended any of this to come
about in the way it did. From the day I first met you, my feelings were of gratitude and friendship. As time went on I ignored or didn't believe that there
could have been any other feelings than friendship. The incident at Nice
opened my eyes somewhat. I realized then that there was more than friendship
between us. At least on my part. You said that you weren't very definite about
yourself. I think then and there you should have refused to see me anymore. I
guess I didn't realize the seriousness of our talks. I thought perhaps the talks
were over. You were moving to Versailles which meant a separation and it
would have been a little more out of sight and mind. Instead I guess it was,
absence makes the heart grow fonder.

I don't think it was the champagne that made me ask you if you loved me on the Metro. I can't find any earthly reason other than my egotistical mind and brand of stubbornness. No, you are not pointed or abrupt. I know what a position I have placed you in and what a wrong I have committed. First, you say your confession stands and then you say you never made such a confession. Yes, it does surprise me. Perhaps, I assumed too much or answered my own question. But the end of your letter tells me that you are hurt. God knows that isn't my wish. I don't want you to feel that I am trying to run away and ignore the situation. It hurt me too, to realize what a heel I find myself to be.

I don't think another person would have listened to my troubles so much and in my loneliness I sought your companionship and can't find words enough to express my appreciation for courage and advice. I might have really gone off on the wrong limb if it hadn't been for you.

No, Mollie, I don't think you rambled on in your letter. It had to be pointed. You say that in part you feel wholly selfish. Perhaps I have taken a lot for granted. Please answer me. Well, I guess that's all for now. I feel pretty low without making you feel that way, too, anymore that I have.

Love,

Coleman

As the arrangements for Mollie's demobilization and return to the United States became more certain, she began to include in her letters the details of the "itinerary" for her trip. In sharp contrast to the secrecy which surrounded every aspect of her arrival in Europe, Mollie was now able to keep her family much more fully informed about her travel plans. For example, she was able to tell her sister that she was expecting to go from Frankfurt to Le Havre in France, which was the location of U.S. Army camps used for the temporary accommodation of troops on their way home. These camps had originally been set up during the war for troops arriving from the United States on their way to their European assignments and were also known as the cigarette camps, as they were given the names of cigarette brands (such as Camp Lucky Strike, Camp Philip Morris) in order to conceal their geographical location from the enemy.[2]

> FRANKFURT, GERMANY
> 4 October 1945

Dear Beck:

...We are leaving Frankfurt on 21 Oct. to go to Le Havre, France. How long we lay around in the "Repple Depot" (Replacement Depot) I don't know. But with the cold weather coming on, I can't see the purpose of the Army keeping us there very long. Anyway, from there we'll be sent to England & ship out sometime — as I see it, in early November, I hope!

Bricker thinks he'll be leaving the latter part of Nov. if he is lucky. Received a wonderful letter from "Brick" today — but still confusing.

Am seeing my Chemical Engineer friend tonight. Very nice guy.

Hope everyone's well at home.

FRANKFURT, GERMANY

9 October 1945

Dear Beck:

I wrote to you a short time ago and told you not to write to me any more after a certain date as I probably wouldn't get the mail — so that still stands.... I shall be leaving Frankfurt 21 Oct. for Le Havre, France where we will "stage" (that's Army lingo for waiting for your ship to pull in and processing of clothing and so forth to get ready to go home) until goodness knows when and then we will cross the Atlantic on our way home. I really expect to be home around the 15th of November.

Am looking forward to those "kreplach" with a nice crisp salad — (do you still have those things back in the States?????) — So tell Mom to get out that old frying skillet.

You know I have forgotten what milk tastes like. In fact, I wonder if I shall be able to drink it. 'Member how I used to not be able to drink tea and coffee — just milk. Wonder what it will taste like. Can you beat that? How about bananas? Do you still get them? We had bananas (a banana) for breakfast about six weeks ago. However, we cannot kick though as our food is really very good and we do get plenty of meat.

Have been very busy socially — guess I told you about the Chem. Engineer. Have been seeing him just about every evening — however, yesterday he left for Switzerland for a 10 day furlough. He said that he didn't like to rush back from a furlough — but was going to from this one because he'll miss me if I am leaving on the 21st. He said he is coming to Detroit to look me up. Then he says — but what will your family say about a gentile fellow?

Sunday, he couldn't get the staff car so instead we used the "convertible" (open jeep). The weather was grand and just perfect for an open car. We saw a lot of the German country. We had an especially picturesque scene of quite an expanse of Germany at the top of an Observation Post. It had been marked *off limits* but we went up anyway. We went into the tower on top of the mountain. It was formerly a Nazi lookout post and the allied planes had found the spot without a doubt — most everything on that mountain top was in rubble. Although the tower still stood, it was easy to see all the facilities as a lookout post had been destroyed. The huge search light was completely smashed and we saw the fragments of glass strewn all over. This was about 25 miles from Frankfurt.

Then we went out to Oberursel, Germany (which is about 10 miles from Frankfurt) to the G.I. Country Club, for dinner. We had chicken and it was really good. We were quite fortunate getting into the place and being able to have a meal as one is supposed to have a 48 hour pass to go there, but with some fast talking and Frank knowing the Red Cross gal that runs the place, we made it all right.

***********   *********

This is really rather cute and I think you'd enjoy my telling you this story. I had told Frank that I was going out with the boys in my office on Friday so couldn't see him. Well — of all things he turned up where we were. It really was quite funny as I hadn't told him where we'd go.

***********   *********

I told you that Smitty was here on Temporary Duty for 4 days — well it stretched out to over a month. She was supposed to go back to Paris and get ready to leave on the 10th of Oct. shipment ... so they have decided to let Smitty remain here and go back with us on the 21st. She will break in someone on the job. Well — in the meantime I moved out of Smitty's room and in with Helen ... so — I am together with Helen now, although we all still live in the same apartment but just in different rooms. Helen just came back from Switzerland yesterday and was just bubbling over with enthusiasm. That was her first furlough. We were both tired last night (I had been out every night since Wednesday!) so we went to bed about 8:00 P.M. — but by the time we really went to sleep it was 9:45. We talked and talked — and of all things I forgot Helen wasn't going to work this morning, so she could rest some more.

Everyone is all excited about going home. Helen will be going with us too. Am so glad there will be a number of us that have been together for a long time — all going home on the same shipment.

We don't know where we will be discharged. All kinds of rumors are invading our billets — some say everyone has to go to Des Moines and others say — no. I am not worrying because whatever we decide will probably be changed anyhoooo by the time we get to the States.

****

Guess I had better get back to work.

By the way, did I tell you that my Colonel is away on a trip and the officers here want me to "volunteer" to remain two more weeks past the 21st as they don't want me to leave before the Colonel gets back. Phooey — I know the army I would probably get roped into staying three more months. Smitty said she'd break my arm if I'd sign anything. Can't recall whether I wrote to you

about all this. Well — anyway, I told the officers if they thought I was so important if they'd get me a plane ride back to the States, I might consider the
proposition. (But I wouldn't. You see I want to go back home with the kids I
know.)...

That's all for now — be seeing you. If you don't hear from me, don't be
worried....

The next letter is one that Mollie received from Frank, the Chemical
Engineer she had gone out with several times while they were both in Frankfurt. He was on furlough in Switzerland and was not sure that he would return
in time to see Mollie before she left Europe.

Tuesday Night: 9th
Mulhouse, France

Dear Mollie,

This is being written in case I do not return before your departure for
home. Yesterday I wanted to stop in & say Good-bye but my time was rather
limited. In fact, I missed the bus and had to hitchhike to the station. Went to
see the Col in the morning & have landed a job in the explosive branch but
with headquarters in Heidelberg. The latter not so good but one cannot have
everything. By the time I returned from Hoechst it was time to take off & I had
to fly low on my thumb.

With luck I may get back before you leave. I really hope so. If not, I want
you to know it was sure fun knowing you & my misfortune for not meeting
you before. I had fun & hope you did, too. And, don't be surprised if you
receive a phone call next spring. "No foolin'!"

Until then or in eight or nine days, be good & careful & don't forget the
heater.

Yours,
Franklin

Maisons Laffitte
9 Oct 45
Tues. morning

Dearest Mollie,

I received your letter dated 4 Oct, and was very happy to hear from you.
No, I haven't quite recovered from the contents of your letter. I feel pretty low
and disgusted with myself. I wanted to know how you feel, but you said to
skip it and I know once you make your mind up, you won't say anything

more. No, I don't agree with you that women are the most unpredictable people in the world. Well, I think I have learned a lesson and the hard way....

Your visit to Paris, more than answered those three letters. The only thing is that I didn't tell you in person what I tried to put on paper. Well, I can hear you, that Bricker all over. Am I right?

I am happy to hear you are seeing a little of Germany while you can. I imagine there is a lot of interesting things to be seen. I would have liked to have seen that castle.... Heidelberg is supposed to be a beautiful spot. I suppose you saw the university.

So you won't talk about the fraternization. I can see you really got riled up. I'll bet you felt like giving them hell....

Love,

Coleman

FRANKFURT, GERMANY

10 Oct 1945

Dear Beck:

I received your letter of 2 Oct. yesterday and was glad to hear from you. Guess I haven't been receiving so much mail of late but it doesn't make as much difference as—hold on to your hat—we are leaving on 15th of Oct. for Le Havre, France. It was moved up from the 21st to the 16th & now, it is the 15th.

I'm still at the office but will quit on Friday, 12 Oct. Guess I won't see my Col. again as he is still on his trip to Stockholm. Before he left on his trip, I had a feeling that I would not see him again overseas & so when I wished him "good luck" on his trip, I said "good bye" sort of final-like. The Colonel insisted he'd be back to see me—but I said—"No, I don't think so." He will probably think I should be telling fortunes. But I guess I understand the uncertainty of the Army better than he does.

When I bade my Chem. Engr. Friend "good bye" when he left for his furlough to Switzerland, I said "In case I don't see you again overseas, blah, blah" and he said—"oh no, I shall see you before you leave. I hate to return ahead of time on my furlough but I'll be back on the 19th."—but I'm leaving on the 15th. But that's the Army.

Smitty is off to Paris to pick up her clothes. She is "laboring" under the thought that we leave on the 21st. I sure hope she gets back in time to leave with us. We are going to wire her tonight....

Beck, I am so d—excited. I can't think straight. I'm just a little frightened, too. Now I know how the boys feel about returning home.

You probably wonder about the "etc. situation." Well, I don't know what to say. Yes, I still hear from Bricker. In fact, I have a letter today in which he tells me that he is trying to phone me. But if I know the Army, he won't be able to on account of priority. I might add things are a bit mixed up — I think.

Been thinking — sort of like to have a nice little party at the Statler, Book Cadillac,[3] — or somewhere — just a few couples — but who??...

I fortunately invited the boys from the office down to dinner tomorrow night. We are allowed only one guest each but 3 other gals let me use their names. I didn't realize it was going to be a "farewell party."

Maisons Laffitte
14 Oct 45

Dearest Mollie,

I guess I didn't say very much on the phone this evening. I'm still low and mixed up, but Mollie, please don't say it's you. Your letter cleared up a few things I was too thick-headed to understand by myself. Your saying that you never made a confession of love to anyone else, but me, makes me feel all the more of a heel. I don't think I can ever make amends for the way I acted. The crux of the matter is that I have a heck of a conscience. I am always afraid of doing the wrong thing. I did it this time and its left me pretty low. Made you and I run around in circles as you wrote. I suppose you are right about taking too much for granted. I did impose myself on your time and good nature. I never realized it until after you left and that's partly what I meant by taking too much for granted. You supplied the rest of the answer in your letter. Do we call this another understanding? I don't like to put it at that, because your feelings mean more to me than just plain words. Mollie, I don't think I'll ever be able to really put all my thoughts into words on paper. I want to value and cherish your friendship and not feel that I have hurt you in the manner that I have. I hope this makes a square of the circle.

...The army really takes the excitement out of going home the way they handle you. You get ready and then the date is postponed. "Hurry up and wait," should be the Army's motto. Won't it be swell not to be regimented to queues and you must be this or that? I feel the same way, Mollie. I want to go home, but I wonder how am I going to act when I do get home. I hope I haven't lost any desirable habits and replaced them by the ones the Army forces upon you. I guess I'll have a time trying not to get excited and mad at irritating people and questions.

Well, I'll know soon enough about the future.

I would like to hear from you. If you still would care to write me, please do so. Remember, I still have the greatest respect for you. You have my address and if you ever visit California, I want you to look me up.

...Darn it, I hate goodbyes. Why can't they all be, "I'll be seeing you" ...
What do you think?

Love,

Coleman

Dear Beck:

Well — today was the day for us to leave — but wouldn't you know the
Army — now we are supposed to leave on the 19th. First, it was the 21st, then
the 15th and now the 19th. They sure drive us nuts.... I expect to be home (if
everything runs smoothly) by the 10th of November. That is, if they don't
change our date again for leaving Frankfurt.

Well — last night I decided to stay in. One of the girls wasn't feeling well
and I had been out a number of times during the week and besides Bricker was
calling me long distance. Finally Bricker's call came through and it was a wonderfully clear line. Sounded as though he were in Frankfurt. You know our letters had been rather bawled up of late and I think we got a few things
straightened out. He is going to call me again on Thursday evening. Things
sure are mixed up. In my last letter to him I told him if he wanted to quit corresponding to let me know. In our talk on the phone he said he wanted to continue writing and was writing me that night. I really don't know what to say.
Am just letting things ride.

That's not all. While I was talking to Bricker, two good-looking guys walk
in to the Orderly Room in our billet and I hear one of the boys ask for a
WEINSTEIN. Of all things— it was Sidney Pakula — the fellow that Mrs. Korman [Mollie's cousin in New York] wanted me to meet. You know I finally did
drop him a line some time ago. Anyway, I sure wasn't dressed in my best — in
fact, I had just washed my hair and had it up under that red scarf and with my
crazy glasses sure must have been a sight. Besides I had been taking care of my
sick pal all day long. Anyhoo, Bricker heard me talk to the other guy and it
sure was funny.

Sidney and I didn't hit it off too well. It seems that he doesn't like WACs.
Here's the story he told me.... "Not exactly, once my buddy and I were in their
Day Room and hung around trying to meet some girls but no dice." ... I tried
to explain that most of the girls don't bother to go around trying to meet fellows because they go out with the boys in their own offices— go on picnics and
out in crowds where they know everyone. Not only that — but most of the girls
have been over quite a while and have already made contacts and like to go out
with the same boys.

I guess he was a bit peeved when I didn't want to go out with him to the show right away. But I did have to stay in with the gal that wasn't well and besides I washed my hair. I asked him if he would like to come over for dinner before I left. But we just didn't hit it off.

Sounds very much like the story about Ted Kaminsky — remember my telling you that I suggested "beaucoup" places to go to and he just wasn't interested. Then he finally came around the last evening. He had such a wonderful time that he has been writing me about it ever since, telling me how sorry he was that he didn't take those suggestions I had offered. It seemed that he didn't like WACs either.

Oh well — it's just too bad about those guys. I really don't care. Probably won't ever run into him. (He was a good looking guy, too.)

Yesterday, a couple of the boys from the office invited me to go to the football game with them. Just wasn't interested. Now they tell me that General Eisenhower and General Patton were there. I really am not too impressed as I've seen them before. In fact, I saw Eisenhower drive by the I. G. Farben Bldg and there were a group of us standing on the corner — darned if we didn't have to salute him, riding along in that great big car....

Guess that's all for now. I really think we will be leaving on the 19th to go to Le Havre.

The next letter was the last one that Mollie wrote to her family before she returned to the United States and to the loved ones that she had left behind in Detroit after two years in the Army. She felt that she had accomplished all that she had set out to do during her military service and that all of her assignments, including the one to Germany which she had not wanted, proved to be meaningful and important. She also knew that she had serious decisions to make about her personal life.

FRANKFURT, GERMANY
16 Oct 45

Dear Beck:

Well here I am back at the office today with another package for one of the boys to wrap up for me. I am so afraid that you might open up one of the packages and throw something out that you had better just not open any of them....

Anyhoo, you better just not unpack anything because I know in the other boxes you would throw something out. (You know Norman's wife threw out quite by mistake a bracelet like the one I sent you. She never did get another like it.)

I probably will be home by the time the boxes arrive.

I was talking to Dottie Dicks today. She isn't so sure we will get home by the 10th or 15th because of the strikes or whatever is going on.[4] However, we are sure to make it by Thanksgiving. Anyway, don't count on any particular date because THIS IS THE ARMY!

It's about 5:30 and I want to catch our weapon's carrier to go back to the billets. Nope, I haven't been working for a week. It's wonderful just loafing around.

I'll write you whenever I have the opportunity, but don't be surprised if you don't hear from me because I might not be in the mood to write and might be just rushing around and on the move.

PART FIVE : GOING HOME

15. The Journey Home
October–November 1945

In October 1945 Mollie began the long journey from military service in Europe back to civilian life, home and family in Detroit. It was not possible for her to send letters along the way, so instead she kept a little black diary which she entitled "A WAC Returns from Overseas, T4[1] Mollie Weinstein," in which she kept notes of the events of each day. The trip was long, cold, uncomfortable and filled with delays at every stage. The scheduled 32-hour train ride from Frankfurt to Le Havre lasted more than twice that long. In spite of all the problems she encountered, however, Mollie remained patient and philosophical and kept her sense of humor, remembering that she was on her way home at last. Her greatest regret was that she had to say goodbye to the close friends she had made during her military service.

* * *

Friday, 19 Oct 1945
(2 yrs ago today I enlisted)

Awoke at 6 A.M. Smitty helped me roll my blankets into a blanket roll. Dropped duffel bag in front of Co. A barracks. Off to breakfast at 7:15. Smitty & I said good bye very briefly. She hopes to catch up with us.

Went to South Station in Frankfurt at 8 A.M. Our train left at 9:30 A.M. We have German train, camouflaged brown, red, yellow stripes. There are 3 car loads of WACs.

There are 6 of us in the compartment — Helen Lushok, Helen Fister, Dottie Peters, Ruby Maurer, Jean Tataru.

We are supposed to make this trip in 32 hrs.

It was cold, dank & dirty when we started out. 3 of us sat on one side of compartment & 3 on the other. We each looked at one another & began laughing. We surely looked like 6 sad sacks. We all decided to make the best of it —

239

began eating candy, chewing gum & acting happy. Helen decided to make up her berth—which was the top one & consisted only of *hard* wood, which was each of our lot.

I took the opposite one & threw my blankets over the wood & thanked Smitty again for making me take the little pillow she had made for me.

On the way we traded cigarettes, candy & gum for apples, tomatoes, & pickles.

We ate K-rations for dinner & supper.

There were no lights so we got ready for bed at 6:30 when darkness begun to fall. We note that we are having very poor train movement & feel sure we will not make our destination in 32 hrs....

We all tossed & turned.

Saturday, 20 Oct.

At 3:30 A.M. one of the WACs Sgts. came thru & awakened everyone. We were stopping at THIONVILLE, France for a hot meal. 3:30 A.M.—just like the Army. We were told to be ready in 10 minutes. Helen L. had gotten undressed & had to get into her clothes.—We got off at 5 A.M.!

Breakfast was powdered eggs, sweet coffee, bread & watery thin cream of wheat. Was very cold. We ate out of doors on tables with no benches.

Our train has not moved since 5 A.M. & here it is 1:00 P.M.

Finally, got an engine & we are on our way again.

Passed through Longuyon, Montmedy, traveled 30 miles since 5 A.M. & it's 5 P.M. now.

At 8:30 P.M. we stopped at Mezieres (Charlotteville) & had a nice hot meal. We were told we were 5 hrs from Paris.... Had a hard night on our "shelves."

We were not going to Paris—but our course was changed & we are on our way.

Sunday, 21 Oct

9 A.M. we hit Paris at Gare de l'est. Ate breakfast at transient mess. At 9:30 I telephoned Bricker's office & talked with Saul Martell. Missed Norman [Mollie's cousin stationed in Paris]. Thought we were going to leave immediately. Instead everything snafued.[2] At 4 P.M. we ate supper. Then were taken to Gare St. Lazars. Girls had baggage detail....

We left at 9:30.

We all sat up & struggled thru the night.

Finally Mollie and her fellow WACs arrived in Le Havre, France. Le Havre was the location of a "cigarette camp" known as Philip Morris, where American soldiers were processed before their return to the United States. It was rainy and miserable, living in very basic conditions with no real duties and a lot of waiting around — very different from the exciting life that Mollie experienced in Paris during the war.

Monday, 22 Oct

Arrived at Le Havre at 6 A.M. Trucks met us (Cattle trucks).

Processed us immediately. Helen L. & Helen F. & I will be sent to Fort Dix [in New Jersey, which was used by the Army as a demobilization center after the war].

We live in tents with cement floor — 4 girls to a tent. Helen L., Helen F., & Ruby M & I are together.

Filled out cards today for baggage and certification — no pistols, etc. Teeth examined; flu shot.

Food not too good here. No duties at all. Washed hair & took shower after Helen L. & Ruby found the secret for hot water. PW's [prisoners of war] were out to lunch!

Ran into Alice Shienhut. Went to see Betty Landsman. Not in.

8 P.M. ready for bed.

The two Helens made grilled cheese (K ration) & toast on little tent stove.

Went to bed at 10 P.M. but couldn't relax. Our shots (Helen L. & Ruby & mine) bothered us.

Tuesday, 23 Oct

Awoke at 7:30 A.M. Ruby, 2 Helens & I ate breakfast.

...Recd 850 francs.

Went to gift shop in our fatigues. Everyone watched us (2 Helens & I). We sure looked rugged.

PW shined our shoes.

PW swept our tent.

...Had snack of hot dogs, bouillon at 9 P.M. Went to bed at 10 P.M.

Rain all day.

Wednesday, 24 Oct

Awoke at 8 A.M. for breakfast. (Rain awakened us.) Turned in our francs and marks for American currency.

Mollie and her fellow WACs in front of the tent they shared at Camp Philip Morris, Le Havre, October 1945. Left to right: Ruby Maurer, Helen Fister, Mollie and Helen Lushok.

2250 francs =   45.00
536 marks =   53.60
          $ 98.60

Physicals but brief at 3 P.M.
Had our baggage tickets signed — also certification slips signed.
Rain all day long....
We went to bed at 10 P.M.

Thursday, 25 Oct

Awoke at 8:30. I made breakfast on stove. Tres bon [very good]. Toast, ham & eggs (K ration), coffee for Ruby & 2 Helens.

...Had dry run at 1:30. I am in the 2nd platoon, 6th row & 8th place.

...Someone lost records on our money turned in. At 5:30 P.M. announcement was made that we were restricted to leave at 7 A.M. tomorrow for England. We began packing. We took showers—

We ate. Then announcement was made that we were no longer restricted. (Ship didn't come in, it was rumored & weather too bad.)

Rained today.

Friday, 26 Oct.

Wind & rain today. Awoke at 8:30. No breakfast — just K ration cheese & oranges.

Ate lunch — Ice cream (2 dishes) at 2 P.M.....

Had trouble with tent stove. G.I.'s came in at 8 P.M. to repair stove.

Am going to bed at 9 P.M. Stove not repaired as yet so cannot cook.

...Boys returned to repair stove.

We cooked. K ration cheese sandwiches (Helen F.)

Saturday, 27 Oct.

During the night stove fell apart & pipe broke. Missed breakfast.

Physicals (looked at our throats on the double).

Went to PX. Had 2 dishes of ice cream with last francs. Borrowed 2 francs from G.I.'s.

Ruby & 2 Helens cutting up with G.I.'s— saw Betty Landsman & walked with her to her barracks. We said "good bye".... Everyone at dry run at 4:45 — I almost missed it. Ran into my place just in time to answer to my name....

Then slept between nest of blankets.

Packed during day.
Went to bed at 10 P.M.

From Le Havre, Mollie crossed the Channel on the *Excelsior* to get to England for the transfer to the *Queen Mary*[3] which would take her across the Atlantic and back to the United States. She found the conditions for WACs leaving France to be no better than they had been for leaving Germany.

Sunday, 28 Oct

Awakened at 4 A.M. Breakfast at 4:30 A.M.
Mustered for ride to P.O.E. (Port of Embarkment). Went in cattle trucks. Had donuts & coffee served by Red Cross before we left to cross Channel.
Went on *Excelsior* 8:30 A.M. Ruby, 2 Helens & I got together again.
Rained on board ship.
Helen & I got seasick (just a little but enough).
Arrived at 5:30 P.M.
Got off at 6:30 P.M. & we were in first group of 280 to go to Tidworth [a British Army garrison town in southern England]. Went in trains (6 of us in compartment). Red X furnished donuts & coffee.
Arrived at Tidworth at 8 P.M.
Barracks for 40 double decker — with sheets.
Tried to get supper from PW's who seemed to run mess hall but no dice. We had difficulty with PW's who were very arrogant — spoke perfect English & laughed at us.
Took shower, washed hair. To bed at 11:30.

Monday, 29 Oct.

Awoke at 7:45 A.M. Had breakfast.
Went back to bed.
Went to Tidworth to Red X; met beaucoup jerks, played cards, had one hamburger a piece. Went back at 11:30 P.M.

When she finally reached England, Mollie was able to get a pass to visit London and show her friends some of the places she had seen when she was stationed there.

Tuesday, 30 Oct.

Didn't get up for breakfast — just Ruby did.

Went to Salisbury & got passes for London, too.

Went back to Red X.

Met Jerry who stuck to me — really was a jerk with beaucoup dough. The other gals met jerks — but Helen ran into a nice boy from her home town. He gave Helen 2 pounds.

Went to dinner at Red X. Jerry was there.

Went home at 10 P.M.

Wednesday, 31 Oct.

Awoke at 7:25 A.M.

We all got ready for London.

Had to queue up for Andover [the nearest town with a railway station]. 3 buses passed us. Finally one picked us up. 2 Helens & Ruby.

Arrived in London 3:20 P.M. at Waterloo station. Had some difficulty in finding WAC Red Cross but finally arrived there. Cleaned up & ate supper at Red X. Went to Piccadilly Circus to show the 2 Helens. Went to Rainbow Corner Red X. Met 3 boys — 2 G.I.'s & Canadian (Irish Regt). Went into one pub on Piccadilly Circus....

Went to Court House Café. Then to Lyons Corner House [a chain of popular restaurants in London]. Had sausages, potatoes, tea, toast. Then home at 1:30 A.M.

Thurs., 1 Nov

Made the 9 A.M. train to Tidworth. Arrived at Andover 10:45 & stood in queue & then just made a truck going into Tidworth & arrived.

Went to PX & then returned.

Washed hair. To bed at 10:30.

Coleman Bricker continued to correspond with Mollie as he was about to start his own journey back to the United States.

Maisons Laffitte
1 Nov 45

Dearest Mollie,

I am really walking on air this week. First of all, I returned from a swell trip to Switzerland. Secondly, I spoke to my Dad, mother and brother on the telephone. Thirdly, I start my journey home on Monday, the 5th of November.... I wish you could have gone to Switzerland or better still been on the one I just finished.... Here we were on a furlough and what do we hear but reveille. We looked out the window and saw a French bugler waking up German POWs [prisoners of war]. The building we were billeted in was in the grounds of the Maginot Line.[4]

...After the tour we went on a buying spree. We had to use up the francs we had left.... I bought my folks some handkerchiefs, Dena's [his girlfriend in California] father a pipe and some more scarves....

Up until this point, I hadn't heard anything about my phone call. When I got to the hotel in Olter, I decided to check with the long distance operator. She said she would let me know.... She said to stand by for the call. I went to bed and I'll bet I didn't sleep a wink. I was on pins and needles. The call didn't come through by 9:30 A.M. and I had to be at the station by 10:26. I called the operator again and she said calls from the states were coming after 10:00 A.M. and that my call would be in at 10:15. Exactly on the dot, the call came in and my Dad said hello. Then my mother spoke to me and my kid brother.... They didn't break down and cry which I was happy about. The call ended and I had to run all the way to the station. The train pulled out exactly 10:26 on the dot and I just made it. I had a grin, a mile long on my face, the rest of the day.

Love,
Coleman

Friday, 2 Nov.

Dry run at 9 A.M. Then took it easy.

At 1 P.M. physical but brief. Nurse walked in & asked if anyone had sore throat.

At 2 P.M. Dentist came thru & asked if anyone had toothache....

Wrote to Bricker at 8 P.M.

Maisons Laffitte
2 Nov 45

Dearest Mollie,

If you can stand it, here goes another letter. I have three of your letters before me, so I thought I would answer everything while I had a chance. I am really "sweating" it out now. On Monday, we leave for our 2d Reinf [Reinforcement] Depot at Namur, Belgium. From there we go to Antwerp for staging. I was told that the troops move faster out of Antwerp than from Le Havre....

I read about your trip from Frankfurt to Paris while in Switzerland. When

I checked the dates, I said to myself, "Poor Mollie, she must be on that train." How could the Army do things like that? It's OK to pull that stuff on fellows, but it's different with the gals. They give you a chance to gripe until the very end. I knew you would pass through Paris (you said you wouldn't). The fellow that answered the phone was Sal Mentil. I wished that I could have been here at the time to get to see you at the station. Do you know that all along the route to Strasbourg, I kept watching the trains just in case I might have seen you. Our trains probably passed each other in the night....

Did you take any pictures in your new "glamour" costumes while at Philip Morris? Would like to have one of it.

...There were PW's at Mulhouse and do everything for you, there also. I often wonder how long those men will be kept prisoners.

...Regards to your family. I'll bet they are still excited about your being home. Well, why shouldn't they? Can't wait to be a civilian, myself.... And I'll drink a toast to Mollie and say "Here's mud in your eye, Weinstein."

With all my love,
Coleman

After several days in England, Mollie boarded the *Queen Mary* for the final stage of her journey back to the United States and the civilian life that she had left more than two years ago. Once she was on the ship, Mollie marked each occasion when they passed through another time zone by turning her watch back one hour. In total they passed through five time zones so that by the time they arrived in New York, they were on East Coast time.

Sat., 3 Nov.

Awoke at 6 A.M. Ready to leave at 7:45 A.M. Went to Tidworth in cattle trucks. Took train from Tidworth to Southampton. Arrived there at 11 A.M.

Boarded Queen Mary at 11:30 A.M. I'm in state room 77A....

Ate meal at 6:30 P.M. on board ship. Still at Southampton. We are to leave tomorrow am at 10.

I pulled MP [military police] guard on Sundeck at 7 to 9. Enjoyed same. To bed at 11 P.M.

Sunday, 4 Nov

Sailed at 10 A.M. while we had breakfast. Long chow line.

Boat drill at 11 A.M. Met Jerry while returning from boat drill.

Went out on deck for 3 hrs....

Took sponge bath at 7:30 P.M. Read rest of evening. Moved watch back one hour.

Monday, 5 Nov.

Awakened at 2nd sitting. Ate breakfast with the kids at same table. Very nice K.P's [kitchen police].

Boat drill.

Played cards.

...Ate supper. Sea began to get rough. We all didn't feel too well.

Sat around Red Area Hdqtrs. Then went to bed early.

Sea extremely rough. Almost tossed "my cookies."

Turned watch back one hour.

Tuesday, 6 Nov.

Sea much calmer today.

We all ate breakfast. KP's all there....

Washed hair.

Ate supper.

Met the boys from Piccadilly Circus [the soldiers Mollie and her friends had met in London just a few days ago]. Talked a while. Then attended Variety show in Mess Hall.

Very pleasant evening.

Turned back watch one hour.

Wednesday, 7 Nov.

We are running into storm today.

Awoke at 3rd seating. Helen couldn't make breakfast.

All of our KP's there but everyone "green"....

Boat drill out on deck. Began to rain.

Jumped back to bed.

Make supper but almost had to leave. Gave us apples.

I thought Helen F. would bring some food to Helen L. so I didn't bother to go over — was too sick but didn't "toss my cookies." Fell into bed with clothes on. Didn't even wash my face. Got undressed & to sleep at 8 P.M.

Turned watch back one hour.

Thursday, 8 Nov.

Thank goodness. Calm day.

Awakened early & was washed at 6 A.M.

Everyone looked much better. Sea very calm.

Ate breakfast with the kids— KP's met us at boat drill.

Ate supper.

Helen L. & I met Red & O'Connor. Very nice evening.

Packed duffel bag. Took salt water bath.

Turned watch back one hour.

On the final day of the voyage, Mollie and her friends got up in the early hours of the morning to witness their arrival in New York and watch as the Statue of Liberty came into view; at last they all knew they were home. As a troop ship carrying soldiers returning from the war, the *Queen Mary* was met by bands playing and the servicemen and women were offered refreshments by the Red Cross.

Friday, 9 Nov.

Bustle around room. Everyone wakes up early— 2:30 A.M. I finally arose at 3 A.M. & dressed. Met Ruby & 2 Helens. Went out on starboard side & saw the lights— NY. Band in boat met us. We kept watching in the distance the twinkling lights. We all wanted to see the Statue of Liberty. The greatest sight— her looming figure in the midst of darkness.

The boys picked me up so I could see the Statue — 5:45 A.M.

We had breakfast at 6 A.M.

Then back to rooms to watch our ship dock.

We heard the band on dock.

We docked & came off at 8:30 A.M.

Red X gave us milk & donuts.

Walked to train ... Camp Shanks [an Army processing camp in Orangeburg, New York] at 11:30 A.M. Had orientation class at Victory Hall.

Then to dinner — steak, onions, French fries, lettuce, mayonnaise, peas, corn, milk, hot rolls, butter, cake, ice cream.

Grabbed shower. Rested.

Ate supper.

Went to PX.

Drank beer to celebrate Helen F.'s birthday. To bed at 8:30 P.M.

Saturday, 10 Nov.

Couldn't sleep well — Awakened at 5:30. Helen L. couldn't sleep either. Finally we all arose at 6 A.M. & ate breakfast at 6:30....

Went off with 2 Helens & phoned home. Said good bye to Ruby.

Formation at 11:30. Train at 12. Left Shanks at 12:15. Ate box lunch 12:30. Arrived at Fort Dix around 3:30 P.M.

Made us take our duffel bags off train & herded us into station. Everyone browned off.[5]

Major gave us a little speech.

...Fell into company with Bats, Peg, Mary J, Schad, Lil, Woody, Lulu — all in same barracks. I am 162 on roster, 36 in barracks — black & white. Temp. set up they tell us. We ate supper & I went off to Orderly Room & had the 2 Helens paged. They are in the barracks next to mine (8). They did not make the first roster.

We went into PX & bought ice cream, etc.

I had already separated my clothes [separating Army-issued clothing from her own civilian clothes].

Sunday, 11 Nov.

Awakened at 6 A.M.

Breakfast 7 A.M.

8 A.M. we moved to separation area.

Said good bye to 2 Helens but we expect to meet again at Fort Dix.

Turned in [Army-issued] clothes.

Ate dinner.

Telephoned home, Mrs. Korman [Mollie's cousin in New York], Alex [Korody].

Met Betty Landsman. Had supper.

Ironed everything.

To bed at 10:30.

As the diary entry above indicates, Mollie began to contact family and friends in New York, including Alex Korody, to let them know she would soon be passing through that city on her way back to Detroit. At this time Mollie also received another letter from Coleman Bricker, who was still waiting to return to the United States.

Namur, Belgium
12 Nov 45

Dearest Mollie,

Hi ya, "civilian." You ought to be in Mufti [civilian clothes] by the time you receive this letter. Hope the Army didn't make you sweat out your last days in khaki.

Well, here I am sitting on my imagination.... It shouldn't happen to a dog, what's happening to me. Yes, I am in the 2d Reinforcement Depot in Namur, Belgium. I left Paris last Monday and after a long dirty truck ride arrived at 9:00 P.M....

Here is where the rub comes in. We were supposed to be included in the shipment set up by the office in Paris. It was to leave today. Instead the depot snafued and we were left off. We called back to Paris, but it didn't do any good. I think we will leave this Thursday however. Well, that's the Army. I had hopes of being home for Thanksgiving, but I know it's out of the question now.

I didn't have a chance to see Norman [Mollie's cousin in Paris] before I left.... Say hello for me to him when you all get together. He should be on his way home soon also. Also Sammy [Mollie's cousin who had been wounded in action and was back in the U.S. by this time] and your folks.

...Well, that's all for tonight, Mollie. Hope you found everything the way you left Detroit. Regards to your family. Also the kids of Room 220 [the room in the hotel in Paris that Mollie shared with her WAC friends], if you should write....

Love,
Coleman

The entry below from Mollie's diary shows the discharge schedule:

Monday, 12 Nov.

Awakened early for breakfast
2 Helens walked in & will be assigned to my area — in the P.M.
Monday — 3 P.M.
My name & 2 Helens all on roster for discharge 14th (14 A)
13 Nov — Physical 8 A.M.
— Counseling 10 A.M.
14 Nov — Signing papers 8 A.M.
— Showdown & Emblems 9 A.M.
— pay 10 A.M.

—Transportation 11 A.M.
To bed at 10 P.M.

Tuesday, 13 Nov.

Physicals at 8 A.M. so awoke early (6 A.M.) for shower — water hot for once.

2 Helens now in our area.

Met the kids in mess hall.

Physical rapid. I gained 14 lbs [during the two years she was in the WAC].

Counseling — the usual drool about insurance, previous jobs form 100. I was a bit tongue-tied & don't think I gave enough information….

We ran over to Finance Office (wearing scarves on our heads). Helen wanted to find out about her ration money during Swiss trip. We were bawled out by 2nd Lt (WAC) for running around in scarves, etc.

Really didn't care much as we were leaving Wednesday A.M.

Went to bed early.

On November 14, 1945, Mollie was formally discharged from the Army. Mollie and the other WACs marked the occasion by immediately beginning to call each other "Miss" since they were now civilians. Although Mollie could have gone directly to Detroit after her discharge, she decided to spend a few days in New York first, to enjoy her new freedom as a civilian and also to take the opportunity to spend more time with Alex Korody to help her decide whether or not to accept his proposal of marriage.

Wednesday, 14 Nov.

Awakened early & took shower.

Had breakfast with the kids.

All packed & ready to leave at 7:30 A.M.

Rained.

Met the 2 Helens & went to meeting room.

Taken in trucks to WAC supply where we left our suitcases & gave our jackets in to have discharge emblem sewn on same.

Walked to "Discharge Room" where everyone was seated. Names called out alphabetically & we signed our discharge papers — original & one carbon with indelible pencil.

We returned to our seats & we are rearranged to sit alphabetically. Went up to be paid.

Went back to supply room — picked up jacket with emblem. Showdown of clothing.

Returned & sat alphabetically.

Chaplain gave us a benediction.

Major handed us individually our discharge papers. We saluted first & shook hands.

We were then free.

The girls all began calling each other "Miss."

Returned to supply room & picked up our suitcases. Got into bus paid our first transportation in the USA — 30 cents.

Was taken to RR [railroad] station. Purchased RT [return ticket] Trenton & one way Detroit.

The 2 Helens & I ate at a joint but enjoyed it immensely.

Returned to station & took 1 P.M. train to NY.

Arrived in NY & went to Service Women's Club on 50th immediately. They were all filled up so they sent us to the Annex on 39th St. We were all separated. However, we really didn't mind it as the rooms were beautiful.

We all took baths & put up our hair. I called Korody but he wasn't there. Helen phoned Ed Stoner — not there. I called Korody about 6. Very glad to hear from me — but he was tied up with some South American deal. Made date to see him Thursday.

The 2 Helens & I got dressed & one of the Canadian girls asked if we wanted to share her taxi with her which we did.

She got off & then the taxi driver asked where we wanted to go. We asked him for name of a restaurant that had excellent steaks. Took us to McCarthy's. As soon as we walked in, a man bought us a drink. Had a wonderful dinner.

Then we went to Roxy's [movie theater] & saw "Dolly Sisters."

To bed at 1:30 A.M.

Thursday, 15 Nov.

Awakened at 10. Dressed & we all went out for breakfast at an automat joint.

Helen L. had to leave us to meet Ed Stoner at our billet. Helen F. & I walked around a bit, then met Ed & Helen at 1 P.M. at Lindy's [restaurant] on 50th. Had lunch.

Helen & I left Helen L. & Ed & went back to billet....

Then took bath, washed hair & rested.

...I met Korody. He looked very different in civilian clothes.... I met 2 of his friends. Went to show & saw Sinatra. Telephoned the Kormans [Mollie's cousins] to let them know I was in NY & would see them the next day. Then Korody & I went to Latin Quarter.

Home at 2:30.

…

Went to bed at 3.

Friday, 16 Nov

Awakened at 9:30. Dressed & packed….

Went down to station (Penn), checked our bags & then went out to eat. Had wonderful steak dinner. Bought the Helens a little box of candy.

Said au revoir [good bye] at the station.

I then went on by subway to the Kormans (Leona).

There was a message for me. Alex had called & said he could not make a plane reservation for me [to fly to Detroit].

Alex phoned me at 2. We made a date for Sat.

I lay down to rest.

Then had dinner with Frances & Sam Korman. Went to show with Leona & Fran. Saw Mildred Pierce [a movie]. Then to Starks [restaurant] for wonderful dessert.

To bed at 12:30.

Saturday, 17 Nov

Awakened at 9 A.M.

Breakfast

Dinner

Shower

Ate early supper. Alex came.

Went to his Aunt & Uncle (Washington Hts). Had wonderful Turkey Dinner. They had Alex & my picture on desk.

Ben R.[6] phoned & we made appointment to meet Sunday or Monday….

Alex & I went downtown. Went to Golden Fiddle [nightclub]. Had several drinks—a bit tipsy.

Home at 2:30 A.M.

Sunday, 18 Nov.

Awakened early.

Ben phoned me at 11.

Went out to lunch at Gaby's [restaurant] with Ben.

Made date for Monday evening with Ben.
He had to go to work.
...Stayed in.
To bed at 12.

Monday, 19 Nov

Routine day.
Ben came at 6 P.M. & rained cats & dogs.
Kormans asked us to dinner.
We stayed as it was a continuous rain.
Went for walk at 10 P.M. — practically downtown — stopped somewhere for wonderful whipped cream pie & coffee. Returned by subway.
To bed at 12.

Tuesday, 20 Nov

Routine day.
Expected Alex to phone. He no doubt thought I had left.
I tried to reach Alex by phone but no luck.
8 P.M. Beck & Pop called.
11 P.M. bed.

This is the last entry in Mollie's diary and marks the end of her wartime adventure which took her across the United States and throughout Europe. When she spoke to her father and sister on the phone that night, they told her: "You must come home NOW!" The next day she used the one-way ticket to Detroit which she had purchased on the day of her discharge from the Army. After two years of doing her part to fight a war, Mollie listened to her father and returned home to Detroit tout de suite.

Epilogue

And the story continues....

Mollie returned home safely as did all of her close friends. They had all changed and matured during their years of military service and the world had changed as well as a result of the war. Although she had just finished one important stage of her life, Mollie felt that she was on the brink of another, equally life-changing experience. She knew that she had some serious decisions to make about her future and in particular whether she wanted her wartime romances with Coleman Bricker or Alex Korody to lead to marriage.

Not long after Mollie's return to Detroit, however, her life took an unexpected twist with the intervention of Ruth Schaffer. Ruth, a friend from Chicago, had corresponded with Mollie throughout the war and was frequently mentioned in Mollie's letters to her family. Ruth's older brother Jack was a captain in the Army who had been stationed in the CBI (China-Burma-India) Theater leading convoys of supply trucks from India to China across the Himalayan Mountains and now he, too, was coming home. However, instead of returning directly home to Chicago, he traveled to Detroit first to visit his mother, who was staying with one of his other sisters who lived in Detroit. Ruth felt that Jack and Mollie would be perfect for each other and arranged for them to go on a blind date on New Year's Eve 1945. Ruth was right! After their second date, Mollie said to Jack, "For two cents, I'd marry you." Jack promptly gave Mollie two cents and within three weeks of their first meeting they were married in Chicago. So, after all of her indecision about her boyfriends in Army, she knew immediately that Jack was the one for her. Chicago became her home and Mollie never lived in Detroit again.

After the excitement of serving her country in Europe, Mollie settled into the traditional role of wife and, soon, mother. Her first daughter Roberta was born 11 months after the wedding, followed by another daughter, Cyndee, and then a son, Joel. Mollie was a stay-at-home mother for a few years but then she resumed her prewar career as a hospital medical records stenographer. Jack and Mollie were married for 54 years until his death in 2000 at the age of 92. During their long marriage neither traveled overseas again.

Jack Schaffer and Mollie in Detroit on their first date, December 31, 1945.

This is how life continued for some of Mollie's family and friends:

Rebecca (Beck) Winston. Mollie's sister completed her law degree and had a career as an attorney in Detroit for many years, eventually becoming a partner in the firm with John McNeil Burns. She was president of her local chapter of B'nai B'rith. Becky never married and passed away in 1999.

Jack Weinstein. Mollie's brother worked in a bank in Detroit. He also never married and remained in Detroit until his sister Becky passed away. He subsequently moved to the suburbs of Chicago to be near Mollie and her family.

Sarah Weinstein (Nash) Kaminsky and Ted Kaminsky. Mollie's friend and wartime correspondent Sarah married Ted Kaminsky when he returned home from the war. They lived in the Detroit area, where Ted owned and operated an auto parts store. Sarah is still living in the Detroit area, although Ted passed away in the 1990s.

Ella Marcus. Ella, who also joined the WAC and served in Italy and North Africa during the war, returned home to Detroit before the war ended. She worked for an attorney until her retirement. Ella never married and still lives in the Detroit area.

Mary Grace Loddo Kirby. Before the war, Loddo met her future husband, Gene Kirby, in Indian Town Gap, Pennsylvania, while she was processing his Army enlistment medical records. They corresponded throughout her service in the WAC in Europe and his service in the South Pacific, marrying after they were both demobilized and had returned to the United States. Gene found that he missed life in the military and soon re-enlisted. With their daughter Cathy and son Paul, they lived in duty stations around the world, including Salzburg (Austria) and Copenhagen (Denmark). After Gene's retirement, Loddo and Gene lived in Oregon for many years, where she pursued her love of art and produced impressive oil, pastel and china paintings. After Gene's death, Mary Grace spent her final years in Honolulu near her daughter Cathy. Mollie and Loddo corresponded regularly and never missed an anniversary, birthday or Christmas greeting until Loddo's death in 2007.

Smitty (Faye Lyne). Smitty corresponded with Mollie throughout the 1950s and 1960s and always drew a picture of her family on her Christmas greetings cards.

Samuel Weinstein. Mollie's cousin served in combat during the war and returned home after being wounded in action. He married twice and had four children, two girls and two boys. Sam lived in Detroit and was a sheet metal worker until he retired. After his wife passed away in the 1980s, he moved to Las Vegas where he still lives.

Norman Weinstein. Mollie's cousin and Sammy's brother, Norman married his girlfriend in Kansas City, Missouri before he was sent overseas. He had met his wife while he was at basic training. They had two daughters and owned and operated a grocery store for 30 years. Norman passed away in 1998 at the age of 80.

Sidney Cohen. Sidney, Mollie's friend from Third Street in Detroit, returned home after many months of being held as a prisoner of war. After the war he became an accountant, married and had two daughters and a son. Sidney passed away in 2000 at the age of 88.

Coleman Bricker. Coleman returned home to California to his family and girlfriend, Dena, whom he married on his birthday in February 1946, just a few weeks after Mollie and Jack were married. Coleman went back to work in the same grocery store where he had been employed before joining the Army and remained there for almost 40 years until he retired and started a new career as a travel agent. The perks of Coleman's second career allowed him and Dena to travel throughout the world. They have been married for over 60 years, have three sons and two grandchildren and continue to live in California.

Alex Korody. Alex remained in New York, where he married and had one daughter. He and Mollie kept in touch through the 1970s, exchanging holiday greetings and occasionally seeing each other when Alex was in Chicago on business.

Danny Raskin. Danny Raskin continues to write for the *Detroit Jewish News*. To date, he has written a weekly column for 67 consecutive years.

Chapter Notes

Preface

1. The Army would only enlist those men and women who were at least 5 feet tall, weighed over 105 pounds and had at least 12 teeth. *Armchair Reader World War II* (Lincolnwood, IL.: Westside, 2007), p. 88. Also, Judith Bellafaire, *A Commemoration of World War II Service* (CMH 72-15) p. 15. Available at http://www.history.army.mil/brochures/wac/wac.htm. Accessed October 2009.

2. Throughout the commentary in this book, WAC will be used to refer to the organization the Women's Army Corps, and to a woman serving in that organization.

3. The Army's Surgeon General established the Medical Intelligence Division to collect and provide information about local diseases, disease-spreading insects, sanitation, sewage disposal, water supply and buildings which could serve as hospitals in preparation for sending troops into specific locations. J. D. Ratcliff, *The Army's Health Spies* (Pleasantville, NY: Reader's Digest, 1943), pp. 119–120.

Introduction

1. Leisa D. Meyer, *Creating G.I. Jane: Sexuality and Power in the Women's Army Corps During World War II* (New York: Columbia University Press, 1996), p. 71. Historian Susan Hartmann argues that "20th century transformations in warfare produced a military establishment capable of utilizing women and feminization of areas in the civilian economy created an occupational structure which provided women with the skills required by the military." Susan Hartmann, *The Homefront and Beyond: American Women in the 1940s* (New York: Twayne, 1982), p. 47.

2. Meyer, pp. 11–12.

3. *Ibid.*, pp. 82–83.

4. *Ibid.*, pp. 86–90.

5. *Ibid.*, pp. 86–90.

6. Mattie Treadwell, *The United States Army in World War II: The Women's Army Corps* (Washington, D.C.: Chief of Military History, Department of the Army, 1954), pp. 380–387.

7. Meyer, pp. 83–84.

8. *Ibid.*, pp. 86–88.

9. *Ibid.*, pp. 87–88.

10. *Ibid.*, pp. 128–129.

11. *Ibid.*, pp. 86–90. The first unit, the 1st WAAC Separate Battalion, arrived in England on 16 July 1943. Treadwell, p. 384.

12. "Housing," p. 7, File: June 1944–August 1945, European Division ATC Historical Record Report, WACs in the European Division ATC June 1944-August 1945, Box 308.04-1

(31 January 1945)— 308.072 (June 1944–August 1945), Air Force Center for Historical Research, Maxwell AFB, Montgomery, Alabama. See also Edith Davis, WAAC and ETO Experiences, Oral History #1, 16 May 1986, 5th WAC Reunion, Fort McClellan WAC Museum Oral Histories, Fort McClellan, Alabama. "We Also Can Serve," June 1943–June 1945, Yearbook from the 6070th Post Headquarters Company, Box 11, Oveta Culp Hobby Papers, Library of Congress.

13. File: WDWAC 314.7 Military Histories, Historical Data and Notes on SWPA WACs, Box 55, Series 54, RG 165, NA. See also Treadwell, pp. 418–50.

14. Miriam Cooke, *Women and the War Story* (Berkeley: University of California Press, 1996).

Chapter 1

1. Jeanne Holm, *Women in the Military: An Unfinished Revolution*, rev. ed. (Novato, CA: Presidio, 1992), pp. 21–27.

2. To increase recruiting and enlistment of WACs, the War Department and the WAC leadership devised the "All States Campaign" and the "Job-Station Campaign" to attract women to service in the Army. The "All States Campaign" encouraged state governors to work with well known citizens to recruit women who would represent their state while in basic training, while the "Job Station Campaign" promised women the choice of assignment after completion of basic training. These efforts helped to increase enlistment among women. Judith Bellafaire, *A Commemoration of World War II Service* (CMH 72-15), p. 13. Available at http://www.history.army.mil/brochures/wac/wac.htm. Accessed October 2009.

3. Deborah Dash Moore, *GI Jews How World War II Changed a Generation* (Cambridge, MA: The Belknap Press of Harvard University, 2004), pp. 55–57.

4. All comments within brackets in Mollie's letters are explanatory notes added during editing and were not in the original letters.

5. A casual battalion is comprised of personnel awaiting orders or duty assignments. See Timothy Zurick, *Army Dictionary and Desk Reference* (Harrisburg, PA: Stackpole, 2004), p. 37.

Chapter 2

1. The movie *It's Your War, Too*, narrated by George C. Marshall, was part of a "Women in War" united recruiting drive which was aimed at encouraging women to contribute to the war effort in some type of full time capacity. Stars and producers from the motion picture industry lent their expertise in making short bulletins to be attached to newsreels and 16 millimeter short films for distribution to churches, schools and war plants. Mattie E. Treadwell, *The Women's Army Corps* (Washington, D.C.: Office of the Chief of Military History, Department of the Army, 1954), pp. 254–255.

2. Perce Westmore was a very famous make-up artist who worked on many early Hollywood motion pictures.

3. Howard Fleck was a well-known hairdresser.

4. The Sky Room is the name of a restaurant and night club on the top floor of the Breakers Hotel in Long Beach. It was famous as a nightspot for Hollywood stars and during the war it opened its doors to servicemen and women. See http://www.theskyroom.com/new/theskyroom/content.asp?contentID=2016793800. Accessed October 2009.

5. An amusement park in Detroit.

6. The Zenda Ball Room was the largest "dance café" in Los Angeles at the time. See http://www.latimemachines.com/new_page_43.htm. Accessed October 2009.

7. Sergeant Charles Knotts was a soldier with whom Mollie corresponded throughout the war and whom she met again when they were both stationed overseas.

8. The Brown Derby was a restaurant in Los Angeles, famous for being frequented by Hollywood stars. See http://www.laokay.com/Extinct.htm. Accessed October 2009.

9. The Hollywood Canteen opened during the war as a restaurant and club for servicemen and women. Any man in uniform was admitted and given free food, served by the stars and staff of the entertainment industry. See http://www.hollywoodcanteenla.com/history. Accessed October 2009.

10. The U.S. military justice system was governed by the Articles of War which were established by the Second Continental Congress in 1775 to manage the conduct of the Continental Army. Although some revisions were made subsequently, the American military justice system continued to operate under the Articles of War until 1951 when the Uniform Code of Military Justice was established. The Library of Congress, Especially for Researchers, Research Centers. Military Legal Resources. *Articles of War (1912–1920)*. http://www.loc.gov/rr/frd/Military_Law/AW-1912-1920.html. Accessed May 2009.

11. Bond rallies, which often featured famous entertainers, were held around the country as a way of encouraging people to invest in bonds to help the U.S. government pay for the war effort.

12. *The Drunkard* is a play written in the nineteenth century about the evils of alcohol. It was revived in 1933 at a theater in Los Angeles and continued to be performed at the same location until 1959. During the Second World War, special performances were staged for servicemen and women. See http://latimesblogs.latimes.com/thedailymirror/2008/07/the-drunkard.html. Accessed February 2010.

13. D'Ann Campbell, *Women at War with America: Private Lives in a Patriotic Era* (Cambridge, MA: Harvard University Press, 1984), pp. 179–180.

Chapter 3

1. Olga Gruhzit-Hoyt, *They Also Served: American Women in World War II* (New York: Birch Lane, 1995), pp. 70–82.

2. Since before the Second World War, the U.S. military has operated a system of numbered post offices which handle mail to service personnel. Family and friends who write to a member of the armed forces are asked to address the envelope to their Army/Air Post Office (APO) or Fleet Post Office (FPO) number to ensure that the items are processed through the military mail system and arrive at their correct destinations. See http://www.postalhistory.com/Military/APO/index.htm. Accessed February 2010.

3. Shopping during wartime was made more complicated by the system of rationing which was introduced in the United States in 1942, in which food and other things such as clothing could only be purchased in limited quantities and the purchase marked against the allowance of the person or family identified in their ration book. It was possible to buy items which were subject to rationing without a ration book, however, if they were for U.S. service personnel overseas. Mollie frequently points out in her letters where she is making a request for certain things so that the letter could be shown in the shop as proof that the items were intended for someone in the armed forces.

4. Goldie was the sister of Sarah Weinstein (Nash), one of Mollie's closest friends from Detroit.

5. C. Kay Larson, *'Til I Come Marching Home, A Brief History of American Women in World War II* (Pasadena, MD: the Minerva center, 1995), p. 43.

6. Doris Weatherford, *American Women and World War II* (New York: Facts on File, 1990), p. 74.

7. Deborah Dash Moore, *GI Jews How World War II Changed a Generation* (Cambridge, MA: The Belknap Press of Harvard University, 2004), p. 53.

8. Gruhzit-Hoyt, p. 78.

Chapter 4

1. C. Kay Larson, *'Til I Come Marching Home: A Brief History of American Women in World War II* (Pasadena, MD: the Minerva center, 1995), p. 43.

2. For more information about the SS *Île de France*, see http://www.oceanlinermuseum. co.uk/Ile%20de%20France.html.

3. Many of the letters that Mollic wrote and received while overseas were sent using Victory mail or V-mail, which involved the use of special, one-page forms for writing letters. The letters written on these forms were photographed and the film containing the photos of many thousands of letters could be shipped in small canisters in just a fraction of the space that would be required to ship the same number of paper letters, thus saving valuable cargo space for the transport of war materials. When the canisters of V-mail film arrived at their destinations, they would be developed and printed as $4 \times 5\frac{1}{2}$ inch photographs and delivered to their intended recipients. See Judy Barnett Litoff and David C. Smith, *We're in This War, Too* (New York: Oxford University Press, 1994), p. 120.

4. D. M Giangreco, *Eyewitness D-Day* (New York: Union Square, 2005), p. 43.

5. Sanders was (and is) a well-known cake shop in Detroit also serving ice cream and other desserts. Several of Mollie's letters home refer to Sanders.

6. George Korson, *At His Side: The Story of the American Red Cross Overseas in World War II* (New York: Coward-McCann, 1945), p. 261.

7. Mollie frequently asked her family to send her items that she was unable to buy during her postings overseas, such as: typewriting erasers; stationery; soap; chewing gum; Life Savers candy; chocolate bars; caramel candies; candy from Sanders cake shop in Detroit; canned tuna; canned sardines; olives; nuts; hand cream; and sandwich spreads.

8. Brenda Ralph Lewis, *Reader's Digest Women at War* (Pleasantville, NY: Amber, 2002), p. 56.

9. Emily Yellin, *Our Mothers' War: American Women at Home and at the Front During World War II* (New York: Free Press, 2004), p. 9.

10. *The Stars and Stripes, World War II Front Pages* (New York: Hugh Lauter Levin, 1985).

11. Files of Jewish Interest, The National Archives http://www.nationalarchives.gov.uk/releases/2005/highlights_march/march1/jewish.htm accessed May 2009.

12. Nigel West, et al., *The Crown Jewels* (New Haven: Yale University Press, 1999).

13. www.madame-tussauds.co.uk/history.htm. Accessed May 2009.

14. The "Hobby" hat, named after the first director of the Women's Army Corps, Oveta Culp Hobby, was a hat with a visor and chin strap. Women Veterans Historical Collection, Jackson Library, University of North Carolina at Greensboro. http://library.uncg.edu/dp/wv/results28.aspx?i=1094&s=8. Accessed June 2009.

15. Jeremy Brecher, *Strike* (Cambridge, MA: South End, 1988).

16. *Pins and Needles* was a 1939 trade union production that was popular in Detroit. Deborah Dash Moore, *GI Jews: How World War II Changed a Generation* (Cambridge, MA: The Belknap Press of Harvard University, 2004), p. 3.

17. Robert Clive (1725–1774) started out as a clerk in the East India Company but joined the military arm of the company where he led a number of successful battles which helped consolidate England's control over India. He eventually became a member of Parliament and a baron. The biography of his life was made into a 1935 Hollywood film, *Clive of India*, which was very popular.

18. A local historical society in the Detroit area.

Chapter 5

1. Ben Rosen was a friend from Detroit who was also serving in the U.S. armed forces in England at this time, working as a map reader.

2. C. Kay Larson, *'Til I Come Marching Home: A Brief History of American Women in World War II* (Pasadena, MD: the Minerva center, 1995), p. 82.

3. Korjeclach were a special, hard sugar cookie that Mollie's mother baked and which represented the Jewish home cooking that she missed while in the Army.

4. Martin Blumenson, *Liberation* (Alexandria, VA: Time-Life, 1978), p. 26.

5. Norman Longmate, *The Doodlebugs: The Story of the Flying-Bombs* (London: Hutchinson, 1981), pp. 92–95, 103, 331–332.

6. Although the British newspapers reported the bombings, it was not until Winston Churchill's speech of July 6, 1944, when he spoke to England and the rest of the world about the German unmanned flying missiles that Mollie was able to mention them in her letters. See Longmate, pp. 331–332.

7. George Korson, *At His Side: The Story of the American Red Cross Overseas in World War II* (New York: Coward-McCann, 1945), pp. 265–266.

8. Paula Nassen Poulos, *A Women's War Too: U.S. Women in the Military in World War II* (Washington, D.C.: National Archives and Records Administration, 1996), pp. 48–49.

9. In fact, during 1943 there were so many rumors circulating about the immoral behavior of Army women that the U.S. government launched an official investigation to discover the source, fearing that enemy agents were behind the campaign. In the event the investigators determined that the slander was being created and spread not by Nazi propaganda but by male American soldiers, who resented the presence of women in their midst. Jeanne Holm, *Women in the Military: An Unfinished Revolution*, revised edition (Novato, CA: Presidio, 1992), pp. 51–53.

Chapter 6

1. D. M Giangreco, *Eyewitness D-Day* (New York: Union Square, 2005), p. 21.

2. Martin Blumenson, *Liberation* (Alexandria, VA: Time-Life, 1978), pp. 76–85.

3. Mattie E. Treadwell, *The Women's Army Corps* (Washington, D.C.: Office of the Chief of Military History, Department of the Army, 1954), pp. 387–388.

4. A bath in a helmet meant that Mollie and her fellow WACs would fill up their helmets with water and go to an enclosed area which was designated as the bathing area. There they would hang their water-filled helmet on a hook and proceed to wash themselves. Emily Yellin, *Our Mothers' War: American Women at Home and at the Front During World War II* (New York: Free, 2004), p. 177.

5. Kathy Peiss, *Hope in a Jar* (New York: Metropolitan, 1988), pp. 240–244.

6. All French translation is by Roberta Schaffer. Mollie often wrote several sentences in French in her letters to her sister, Beck.

7. The C-ration was one of three types of combat rations used during the war. It was designed for use where no mess hall facilities were available and to provide rations that could be carried by the individual soldier while providing three full, satisfying meals a day. The original K-ration was developed for paratroopers to provide a lightweight ration because the C-ration included heavy cans.

8. A busman's holiday is a vacation in which the person does the same things that they do at work. *American Heritage Dictionary of the English Language*, 4th ed., 2000.

9. Olga Gruhzit-Hoyt, *They Also Served: American Women in World War II* (New York: Birch Lane, 1995), p. 72.

10. Thousands of French civilians would gather up whatever possessions they could carry and travel on foot in an attempt to find safety from the fighting, often without knowing where their next meal would come from. See Blumenson, p. 62.

Chapter 7

1. Mollie lived in the Hotel Reynolds, which was located near L'Etoile and the Arc de Triomphe.

2. David Pryce-Jones, *Paris in the Third Reich: A History of the German Occupation, 1940–1944* (New York: Holt, Rinehart and Winston, 1981), pp. 197–198.

3. Willis Thornton, *The Liberation of Paris* (New York, New York: Harcourt, Brace & World, 1962), pp. 13, 28, 119, 133. Anthony Beevor and Artemis Cooper, *Paris After the Liberation 1944–1949* (New York: Doubleday, 1994), p. 53.

4. Beevor and Cooper, pp. 114–117.

5. Here Mollie is referring to Suzanna (or Zuzanna) Rot (or Roth), a young woman she befriended while in England and continued to correspond with throughout the war. Mollie mentions the Rot family in her letters home from time to time, usually in relation to a request to send packages of things that might make Suzanna's life and the lives of her husband and son a little more comfortable.

6. For more on the Allied bombing of France, see Ronald Schaffer, *Wings of Judgment: American Bombing in World War II* (Oxford and New York: Oxford University Press, 1985), pp. 35–43, and Williamson Murray and Allan R. Millett, *A War to Be Won: Fighting the Second World War* (Cambridge, MA: The Belknap Press of Harvard University Press, 2000), pp. 411–434.

7. Archbishop of New York, Archbishop of the U.S. Armed Forces and later Cardinal, Francis Spellman also acted as a representative for President Roosevelt during the Second World War, traveling to many locations in Europe and Asia. http://www.catholic-hierarchy.org/bishop/bspellman.html. Accessed July 2009.

8. Deborah Dash Moore, *GI Jews: How World War II Changed a Generation* (Cambridge, MA: The Belknap Press of Harvard University, 2004), pp. 128–131.

9. Pat Zacharias, "Conquering the Dreaded Crippler, Polio," *The Detroit News*, 9 May 1999. Available at http://apps.detnews.com/apps/history/index.php?id=179. Accessed October 2009.

10. The Statler Hotel in Detroit was one of a number of large, luxurious hotels built by E.M. Statler in major cities around the United States. The Detroit Statler opened in 1915, was acquired by the Hilton hotel chain in the 1960s and closed in 1975. See http://www.forgotten detroit.com/statler/index.html. Accessed June 2009.

11. Jeanne Holm, *Women in the Military: An Unfinished Revolution*, revised edition (Novato, CA: Presidio, 1992), pp. 56–57.

12. This letter was written on German Red Cross stationery.

13. Ella Marcus, a friend from Detroit who joined the Army before Mollie and was stationed in Africa and Italy during the war.

14. K rations were introduced during World War II as a way of providing soldiers in the field with meals which contained the necessary calories and vitamins and were also easy to carry. Most K ration packs contained a package of ersatz lemon powder which was intended to be added to water to make a lemon-flavored drink, but the taste was widely disliked and women soldiers often used it instead to make a rinse for their hair.

15. Thomas Rodney Christofferson and Michael Scott Christofferson, *France During World War II: From Defeat to Liberation* (New York: Fordam University Press, 2006), p. 110.

16. Jean Arthur was a popular American film actress in the 1930s and 1940s who starred in many comedies.

Chapter 8

1. J. D. Ratcliff, *The Army's Health Spies* (Pleasantville, NY: Reader's Digest, 1943), pp. 119–120.

2. Erich von Stroheim was an Austrian-born actor who initially made his reputation as a star of silent films.

3. At this time Paris was not a very safe city after dark, as the French authorities struggled to ensure law and order, both in the capital and throughout the country. See Anthony Beevor

and Artemis Cooper, *Paris After the Liberation 1944–1949* (New York: Doubleday, 1994), pp. 105–107.

4. Also known as the Feast of All Saints, celebrated on November 1.

5. Martin Blumenson, *Liberation* (Alexandria, VA: Time-Life, 1978), pp. 13–14.

6. This is a reference to the Rot or Roth family of Yugoslav refugees, who were friends of the Sarge (Alex Korody) and whom Mollie met in England and continued to correspond with throughout the war.

7. JM Heslop, "U.S. Army Signal Corp: Focus on Liberation," available at USHMM.org.

8. Maurice Kaye, a soldier Mollie met in California and corresponded with throughout the war.

9. Here Mollie is referring to the package which she asked Beck in her letter of 16 October 1944 to put together for the Sarge to take back to his family home in Yugoslavia, which was in an area that had recently been liberated from Axis control.

10. Kreplach is a type of Jewish small dumpling usually filled with meat.

11. During this period the official exchange rate for American service personnel was very unfavorable for changing U.S. dollars into French francs but it was only amended after Mollie had left France so she was unable to benefit from the new rate.

12. Charles Whiting, *Ardennes: The Secret War* (Conshohocken, PA: Combined, 2001), pp. 6–8.

13. French Forces of the Interior, formerly the fighters of the French Resistance.

14. B'nai B'rith or Children of the Covenant, was founded in New York in 1843 and is an international Jewish organization which works for human rights, humanitarian aid and against anti–Semitism. http://www.bnaibrith.org/. Accessed July 2009.

15. The Allied Club was a gathering place for servicemen and women from all the Allied forces stationed in Paris.

16. Judy Barnett Litoff and David C. Smith, *We're in This War, Too* (New York: Oxford University Press, 1994), p. 30.

17. This refers to Little Nell, one of the central characters in *The Old Curiosity Shop* by Charles Dickens.

Chapter 9

1. Brenda Ralph Lewis, *Reader's Digest Women at War* (New York: Amber, 2002), p. 54, and Emily Yellin, *Our Mothers' War: American Women at Home and at the Front During World War II* (New York: Free Press, 2004), p. 79.

2. The bombing was reported in *Stars and Stripes* on December 28, 1944.

3. In order to keep up with her correspondence, Mollie would sometimes write one letter which she would copy using carbon paper and send to several people.

4. Miss Grace Ross had been Mollie's supervisor at work in Detroit and joined the WAC after Mollie did.

5. Mollie means that if she had written about the Sarge in her letters home while he was working in the same office, others she was working with, perhaps including the Sarge himself, might have gotten to know about it because soldiers' letters were censored by officers in the same unit.

6. Helen Morgan, Libby Holman and the Boswell sisters were all popular American singers.

7. This refers to Dottie Dicks, another WAC from Detroit. Mollie and Dottie traveled together from Detroit to Fort Oglethorpe in March 1944 and then from there to their first overseas postings in England. Although they were subsequently stationed in different locations, they did manage to meet up in France and Germany.

8. On 18 November 1944 there was a drawing on the cover of the *New Yorker* magazine of a woman in uniform putting a small bunch of flowers on a male soldier's desk. This made Mollie's colonel and others who worked in the office think of Mollie and the Sarge.

9. Susan B. Hartmann, *American Women in the 1940s: The Home Front and Beyond* (Boston: Twayne, 1982), p. 41.

10. Jeanne Le Monnier was a French fashion designer who became very famous in the 1920s, when her hats were worn by some of the most glamorous French actresses of the time. http://www.costumegallery.com/Designers/main/monnierl.htm. Accessed October 2009.

Chapter 10

1. The Allied Club was a place where service personnel from all the Allied forces could go for entertainment.

2. The V-2 was a German rocket which was used extensively against Allied forces and civilian targets during 1944–45.

3. Sir Cedric Hardwicke was one of the great character actors who appeared on stage and in films between the 1920s and his death in 1964.

4. Jack Winokur was Mollie's cousin, whose death in a flying accident was one of the factors which motivated her to join the WAC.

5. D'Ann Campbell, *Women at War with America: Private Lives in a Patriotic Era* (Cambridge, MA: Harvard University Press, 1984), p. 41.

6. This refers to the fact that Mollie was a Corporal and therefore one rank higher than Ted, who was a Private First Class.

7. Sarah Nash was the married name of Mollie's friend Sarah Weinstein. Her marriage was very short as her husband was killed in the service during the war.

8. For an example of the experiences of combat soldiers on leave in Paris at this time, see Lone Sentry.com, The Thunderbolt Across Europe (83rd Infantry Division), available at http://www.geocities.com/searchlight352/thunderbolt2.html. Accessed October 2009.

9. The Montmartre district of Paris is an area where many artists live and work. It is known for its bohemian atmosphere and its lively nightclubs.

10. Pigalle is a part of Paris known for its nightclubs and its rather risqué entertainment.

11. All of the places that Mollie refers to in this passage — Bel Tabarin, Chantilly and Moulin Rouge — are famous nightclubs.

12. More religious Jews may conduct Seders on the last two days as well.

13. Lily Pons was a French-born opera singer who became a naturalized U.S. citizen. She was married to conductor Andre Kostelanetz and together they performed a series of concert tours during and after the war.

14. It was common for WACs to volunteer at military hospitals. Doris Weatherford, *American Women and World War II* (New York: Facts on File, 1990), p. 76.

15. Sarah Weinstein (Nash).

16. In the U.S. military ranks, a G-2 is an officer with responsibility for intelligence, so Mollie is making a joke that her friend Lenore, who is able to look up soldiers' files and find out information about them, is providing her with intelligence.

17. President Franklin Roosevelt died on April 12, 1945.

18. Elna Hilliard Grahn, *In the Company of Wacs* (Manhattan, KS: Sunflower University Press, 1993), pp. xv–xvi.

19. Emil Ludwig was a well-known writer, biographer and journalist. Originally from Germany, he emigrated to the United States in 1940.

20. The 30th General Hospital, where Charles had been treated, was located on the Cherbourg Peninsula in Normandy.

Chapter 11

1. For more information about the assignment of points, see Earl F. Ziemke, *The U.S. Army in the Occupation of Germany 1944–1946* (Washington, DC: Center of Military History,

United States Army, 1990), p. 328. A detailed discussion of the application of the points system to members of the Women's Army Corps can be found in Mattie E. Treadwell, *The Women's Army Corps* (Washington, D.C.: Center of Military History, United States Army, 1991), pp. 727–735.

2. A famous park created in the second half of the nineteenth century which is located on the western edge of Paris.

3. The Roth (or Rot) family were the Yugoslav refugees whom Mollie met in London and continued to correspond with throughout the war.

4. The parade to mark the anniversary of the founding of the Women's Army Corps.

5. John Burns' son, who was also serving in the armed forces.

6. John Burns' son-in-law and daughter.

7. Betty was another of John Burns' daughters.

8. The father-in-law of John Burns' daughter.

9. A French singer, actor and film star.

10. June 6, 1945, was a declared a holiday in France to mark the first anniversary of the D-Day landings which began France's liberation from Nazi occupation.

11. In other words, anyone who would be able to read what was written in a V-mail and Mollie did not want her co-workers, who of course also worked with the Sarge, to see her correspondence with her sister about her relationship with him and with Coleman Bricker.

12. Jascha Heifetz was a Russian-born violinist who was a child prodigy. His family left Russia during the turmoil surrounding the 1917 revolution and he later became an American citizen.

13. Alec Templeton was a pianist who played a mixture of popular and classical music and who hosted a radio show in the United States in the 1940s.

14. Dwight Eisenhower, commander of the Allied forces in Europe at the end of the war and later president of the United States.

15. Charles de Gaulle was the leader of the Free French forces during the war and afterwards became president of the provisional government created to restore order to postwar France.

16. In the summer of 1945, the U.S. Army in Europe suspended the demobilization of all WACs performing clerical duties until acceptable replacements could be found, citing "military necessity" and declaring that stenographers were indispensable. See Jeanne Holm, *Women in the Military: An Unfinished Revolution, revised edition* (Novato, CA: Presidio, 1992), p. 99.

17. Laurence Olivier was a British stage and film actor.

18. Eagles and stars are insignia worn by senior commissioned officers, who are at the top of the military hierarchy and far above Mollie's rank of sergeant.

Chapter 12

1. Earl F. Ziemke, *The U.S. Army in the Occupation of Germany 1944–1946* (Washington, D.C.: Army Historical Series Center of Military History, United States Army, 1990), p. 295.

2. Mollie is pointing out the change in title from ETOUSA (European Theater of Operations U.S. Army) to USFET (U.S. Forces European Theater), which came into effect in July 1945 and marked the shift from wartime operations to post war duties by the U.S. Army.

3. Coleman is referring to his attempt to become an officer when he first joined the Army. His application to Field Artillery Officer Candidate School was unsuccessful and he was sent overseas as an enlisted man.

4. Earl F. Ziemke, *The U.S. Army in the Occupation of Germany 1944–1946* (Washington, D.C.: Center of Military History, United States Army, 1990), pp. 320, 328, 329.

5. Anthony Beevor and Artemis Cooper, *Paris After the Liberation, 1944–1949* (London: Penguin, 1994), pp. 182–191.

6. Berchtesgarten is a village in the mountains of Bavaria which is the location of Hitler's country house, the "Eagle's Nest."

Chapter 13

1. Earl F. Ziemke, *The U.S. Army in the Occupation of Germany 1944–1946* (Washington, D.C.: Army Historical Series Center of Military History, United States Army, 1990), p. 320.

2. Judy Barnett Litoff and David C. Smith, *We're in This War, Too* (New York: Oxford University Press, 1995), p. 235.

3. Ziemke, pp. 269–275.

4. Mattie E. Treadwell, *The Women's Army Corps* (Washington, D.C.: Center of Military History, United States Army, 1954), p. 390.

5. Ziemke, pp. 328–330.

6. Fraternization, which was the Army's term for American soldiers dating German women, was initially strictly forbidden although the Army later relaxed its ban. Mollie felt very strongly that American soldiers should not fraternize with German women, who had so recently been part of an enemy nation, and she became upset when she saw evidence of it. For more on fraternization, see Ziemke, pp. 321–327.

7. This refers to Dottie Dicks, another WAC from Detroit. Mollie and Dottie traveled together from Detroit to Fort Oglethorpe in March 1944 and then from there to their first overseas postings in England. Although they were subsequently stationed in different locations, their paths did cross briefly in Paris (see Chapter 9) and again in Frankfurt.

8. The Battle of the Bulge began on December 16, 1944, with a surprise attack by German forces on Allied troops in the Belgian Ardennes. Approximately 77,000 U.S. servicemen were killed, wounded, reported missing in action or taken prisoner as a result of that battle. See Charles Whiting, *Ardennes: The Secret War* (Conshohocken, PA: Combined, 2001), pp. 6–8.

9. David Marsh, *The Germans: The Pivotal Nation* (New York: St. Martin's, 1990), pp. 15–17.

10. See http://www.jewishvirtuallibrary.org/jsource/vjw/frankfurt.html#holo. Accessed February 2010.

11. Chilblains are red, itchy swellings on the fingers, toes and ears caused by poor circulation in areas that are exposed to the cold and damp. See Treadwell, p. 388.

12. While Mollie was stationed in France, American service personnel had to exchange their U.S. dollars into French francs at a very unfavorable rate, but unfortunately for Mollie, the French government did not begin compensating American soldiers for the unfavorable rate until after she had left France.

13. This refers to a bust of Josephine which was in the room Mollie shared with her friends in Paris (see Mollie's letter to her brother Jack dated 29 September 1944 in Chapter Seven) and was taken with them to their new accommodation in Versailles.

14. Doris Weatherford, *American Women and World War II* (New York: Facts on File, 1990), p. 89.

Chapter 14

1. Oberursel was the location of a camp where Allied pilots who were shot down over Germany were taken for interrogation before they were sent on to prisoner of war camps. When the U.S. Army took control of the site at the end of World War II, it became an intelligence post. http://www.campking.net/. Accessed November 2009.

2. The Cigarette Camps: U.S. Army in Le Havre, France. http://www.skylighters.org/special/cigcamps/cigintro.html. Accessed October 2009.

3. Both the Statler and the Book Cadillac were luxury hotels in Detroit with elegant restaurants and were popular locations for celebratory dinners.

4. At this time the United States was experiencing a wave of strikes affecting almost every industry and every part of the country. Detroit, as the center of the American automobile indus-

try, was particularly affected. http://www.detroit.lib.mi.us/GoldenJubileeExhibit/GJ%20WEB/
III_Politics_and_Pressures.htm. Accessed November 2009.

Chapter 15

1. T4 stands for Technician Fourth Grade or Sergeant, which was Mollie's rank at the time she was discharged from the Army.

2. Snafu is an expression that originated in the U.S. military during World War II, meaning Situation Normal, All Fouled Up.

3. The *Queen Mary*, which transported many soldiers back from Europe to the United States after the war, made its last voyage from Southampton, England, to Long Beach, California, in 1967. Since 1993, it has operated as a luxury hotel in Long Beach, California. http://www.queenmary.com.

4. The Maginot Line was a series of concrete and steel fortifications erected by France in the 1930s. It was intended to prevent an invasion by German forces but proved ineffective when German troops chose a route through Belgium and the mountainous and wooded Ardennes region of France which avoided the Maginot Line.

5. Browned off is an expression that originated in the British Royal Air Force, meaning disgusted, annoyed or out of patience.

6. This refers to Ben Rosen, who grew up with Mollie in Detroit and whom she met in Oxford when they were both stationed in England during the war.

Bibliography

American Heritage Dictionary of the English Language. 2000. Fourth Edition. New York: Houghton Mifflin Harcourt.

Armchair Reader World War II. Lincolnwood, IL: Westside, 2007.

Army/Air Post Office (A.P.O.). http://www.postalhistory.com/Military/APO/index.htm.

Articles of War (1912–1920). The Library of Congress, Especially for Researchers, Research Centers. Military Legal Resources. http://www.loc.gov/rr/frd/Military_Law/AW 1912-1920.html.

Beevor, Anthony, and Artemis Cooper. *Paris After the Liberation, 1944–1949.* New York: Doubleday, 1994.

Bellafaire, Judith. *A Commemoration of World War II Service* (CMH 72–15). http://www.his tory.army.mil/brochures/wac/wac.htm.

Bishop Francis Spellman. http://www.catholic-hierarchy.org/bishop/bspellman.html.

Blumenson, Martin. *Liberation.* Alexandria, VA: Time-Life, 1978.

B'nai B'rith. http://www.bnaibrith.org/.

Brecher, Jeremy. *Strike.* Cambridge, MA: South End, 1988.

Brown Derby restaurant. http://www.laokay.com/Extinct.htm.

Campbell, D'Ann. *Women at War with America: Private Lives in a Patriotic Era.* Cambridge, MA: Harvard University Press, 1984.

Christofferson, Thomas Rodney, and Michael Scott Christofferson. *France During World War II: From Defeat to Liberation.* New York: Fordam University Press, 2006.

Cigarette Camps: The U.S. Army in Le Havre, France. http://www.skylighters.org/special/cigcamps/cigintro.html.

Cooke, Miriam. *Women and the War Story.* Berkeley: University of California Press, 1996.

Davis, Edith. WAAC and ETO Experiences. Oral History #1. May 16. 5th WAC Reunion. Fort McClellan WAC Museum Oral Histories. Fort McClellan, Alabama, 1986.

Dickens, Charles. *The Old Curiosity Shop.* Penguin Classics, 2003.

The Drunkard. http://latimesblogs.latimes.com/thedailymirror/2008/07/the-drunkard.html.

Files of Jewish Interest. The National Archives. Richmond, England. http://www.national archives.gov.uk/releases/2005/highlights_march/march1/jewish.htm.

Giangreco, D.M. *Eyewitness D-Day.* New York: Union Square, 2005.

Grahn, Elna Hilliard. *In the Company of Wacs.* Manhattan, KA: Sunflower University Press, 1993.

Gruhzit-Hoyt, Olga. *They Also Served: American Women in World War II.* New York: Birch Lane/Carol, 1995.

Hartmann, Susan B. *The Home Front and Beyond: American Women in the 1940s.* Boston: Twayne, 1982.

Heslop, JM. U.S. Army Signal Corps: Focus on Liberation. USHMM.org.

Historical Data and Notes on South West Pacific Area Wacs. Military Histories. Box 55, Series 54, Record Group 165, File WDWAC 314.7. National Archives and Records Administration. Washington, D.C.

Hobby Hat. http://library.uncg.edu/dp/wv/results28.aspx?i=1094&s=8.

Hollywood Canteen. http://www.hollywoodcanteenla.com/history.

Holm, Jeanne. *Women in the Military: An Unfinished Revolution*. Revised Edition. Novato, CA: Presidio, 1992.

Hotel Statler. http://www.forgottendetroit.com/statler/index.html.

Jeanne Le Monnier. http://www.costumegallery.com/Designers/main/monnier1.htm.

Korson, George. *At His Side: The Story of the American Red Cross Overseas in World War II*. New York: Coward-McCann, 1945.

Larson, C. Kay. *'Til I Come Marching Home: A Brief History of American Women in World War II*. Pasadena, MD: the Minerva center, 1995.

Lewis, Brenda Ralph. *Reader's Digest Women at War*. Pleasantville, NY: Amber, 2002.

Litoff, Judy Barnett, and David C. Smith. *We're in This War, Too*. New York: Oxford University Press, 1994.

Longmate, Norman. *The Doodlebugs: The Story of the Flying Bombs*. London: Hutchinson, 1981.

Madame Tussauds. www.madame-tussauds.co.uk/history.htm.

Marsh, David. *The Germans: A People at the Crossroads.*. New York: St. Martin's, 1990.

Meyer, Leisa D. *Creating G.I. Jane: Sexuality and Power in the Women's Army Corps During World War II*. New York: Columbia University Press, 1996.

Moore, Deborah Dash. *GI Jews: How World War II Changed a Generation*. Cambridge, MA: The Belknap Press of Harvard University, 2004.

Murray, Williamson, and Allan R. Millett. *A War to Be Won: Fighting the Second World War*. Cambridge, MA, and London: The Belknap Press of Harvard University Press, 2000.

New Yorker. November 18, 1944.

Oberursel. http://www.campking.net/.

Peiss, Kathy. *Hope in a Jar*. New York: Metropolitan/Henry Holt, 1988.

Poulos, Paula Nassen. *A Women's War Too: U.S. Women in the Military in World War II*. Washington, D.C.: National Archives and Records Administration, 1996.

Pryce-Jones, David. *Paris in the Third Reich: A History of the German Occupation, 1940–1944*. New York: Holt, Rinehart and Winston, 1981.

The Queen Mary. http://www.queenmary.com.

Ratcliff, J.D. *The Army's Health Spies*. Pleasantville, NY: Reader's Digest, 1943.

Schaffer, Ronald. *Wings of Judgment: American Bombing in World War II*. Oxford and New York: Oxford University Press, 1985.

Sky Room. http://www.theskyroom.com/new/theskyroom/content.asp?contentID=2016793800.

SS *Île de France*. http://www.oceanlinermuseum.co.uk/Ile%20de%20France.html.

Stars and Stripes. December 28, 1944.

The Stars and Stripes: World War II Front Pages. New York: Hugh Lauter Levin Associates, 1985.

Strikes in Detroit. http://www.detroit.lib.mi.us/GoldenJubileeExhibit/GJ%20WEB/III_Politics_and_Pressures.htm.

The Thunderbolt Across Europe (83rd Infantry Division). Lone Sentry.com, http://www.geocities.com/searchlight352/thunderbolt2.html.

Thornton, Willis. *The Liberation of Paris*. New York: Harcourt, Brace & World, 1962.

Treadwell, Mattie E. *The Women's Army Corps*. Washington, D.C.: Office of the Chief of Military History, Department of the Army, 1954.

WACs in the European Division. June 1944–August 1945. European Division ATC Historical Record Report. Box 308.04-1 (31 January 1945)— 308.072 (June 1944–August 1945). Housing, p. 7. Air Force Center for Historical Research. Maxwell Air Force Base. Montgomery, Alabama.

We Also Can Serve. June 1943–June 1945. Yearbook from the 6070th Post Headquarters Company. Box 11. Oveta Culp Hobby Papers. Library of Congress. Washington, D.C.

Weatherford, Doris. *American Women and World War II.* New York: Facts on File, 1990.

West, Nigel, et al. *The Crown Jewels.* New Haven: Yale University Press, 1999.

Westend Synagogue, Frankfurt. http://www.jewishvirtuallibrary.org/jsource/vjw/frank furt.html#holo.

Whiting, Charles. *Ardennes: The Secret War.* Conshohocken, PA: Combined, 2001.

Yellin, Emily. *Our Mothers' War: American Women at Home and at the Front During World War II.* New York: Free Press, 2004.

Zacharias, Pat. "Conquering the Dreaded Crippler, Polio." *The Detroit News.* May 9. http://apps.detnews.com/apps/history/index.php?id=179. 1999.

Zenda Ball Room. http://www.latimemachines.com/new_page_43.htm.

Ziemke, Earl F. *The U.S. Army in the Occupation of Germany 1944–1946.* Washington, D.C.: Army Historical Series Center of Military History, United States Army, 1990.

Zurick, Timothy. *Army Dictionary and Desk Reference.* Mechanicsburg, PA: Stackpole, 2004.

Index

Numbers in **bold italics** indicate pages with illustrations.